China's Energy Geopolitics

China's need for energy has become an important factor in contemporary world politics and a precondition for sustaining China's continuing high economic growth. Accordingly, Chinese energy policy has been a political and strategic rather than a purely market-driven policy. This book examines China's energy geopolitics, focusing in particular on the need for a stable and secure investment environment which is necessary for the provision of energy to China from the Central Asian states.

The author argues that the institutionalization of the Shanghai Cooperation Organization (SCO), the Friendship and Cooperation Treaty between Russia and China and Chinese bilateral agreements with individual Central Asian states present an avenue and a framework of stability in which pipeline construction can commence. However, in order to stabilize the region for Chinese investment in energy resources, the author argues that the United States needs to be present in the region and that a strategic framework of cooperation between Russia, China and the United States has to be developed.

The book will be of interest to academics working in the field of International Security, International Relations and Central Asian and Chinese politics.

Thrassy N. Marketos is lecturer at the Athens, Greece, branch of the 'Centre d'Etudes Diplomatiques et Strategiques' (CEDS), Paris, France.

Routledge Contemporary China Series

China's Energy Geopolitics

The Shanghai Cooperation Organization
and Central Asia

Thrassy N. Marketos

Routledge
Taylor & Francis Group

LONDON AND NEW YORK

First published 2009
by Routledge
2 Park Square, Milton Park, Abingdon, Oxon OX14 4RN

Simultaneously published in the USA and Canada
by Routledge
270 Madison Ave, New York, NY 10016

Routledge is an imprint of the Taylor & Francis Group, an informa business

Transferred to Digital Printing 2010

© 2009 Thrassy N. Marketos

Typeset in Times New Roman by
Taylor & Francis Books

British Library Cataloguing in Publication Data
A catalogue record for this book is available from the British Library

Library of Congress Cataloging in Publication Data
  Marketos, Thrassy N.
  China's energy geopolitics : the Shanghai Cooperation Organization and
Central Asia / Thrassy N. Marketos.
     p. cm. – (Routledge contemporary China series ; 30)
  Includes bibliographical references and index.
  1. Energy policy–China. 2. Geopolitics–China. 3. China–Foreign
relations–Asia, Central. 4. Asia, Central–Foreign relations–China. 5.
Shanghai Cooperation Organisation. I. Title.
  HD9502.C62M37 2008
  333.790951–dc22

                                                         2008001506

ISBN13: 978-0-415-45690-6 (hbk)
ISBN13: 978-0-415-58617-7 (pbk)
ISBN13: 978-0-203-89428-6 (ebk)

ISBN10: 0-415-45690-8 (hbk)
ISBN10: 0-415-58617-8 (pbk)
ISBN10: 0-203-89428-6 (ebk)

Contents

Maps

Acknowledgements

The publisher and author would like to thank the copyright holders for granting permission to use the following maps:

Map 1.2 Petroleum and gas transferring projects in Asia
Source: Philippe Rekacewicz, le Monde diplomatique, Paris, May 2005

Map 2.2 Russia: main natural gas export pipelines
© Center for Security Studies, ETH Zurich, reproduced with permission. Map first published in: Russian Analytical Digest, no. 18, 3 April 2007, p. 13

Map 2.3 Russia: main natural oil export pipelines
© Center for Security Studies, ETH Zurich, reproduced with permission. Map first published in: Russian Analytical Digest, no. 18, 3 April 2007, p. 12

Map 2.4 Map of selected oil and gas pipeline infrastructure in the former Soviet Union
Source: Philippe Rekacewicz, le Monde diplomatique, Paris, June 2007

Every effort has been made to contact copyright holders for their permission to reprint material in this book. The publishers would be grateful to hear from any copyright holder who is not here acknowledged and will undertake to rectify any errors or omissions in future editions of this book.

Abbreviations

ADB	Asian Development Bank
CACO	Central Asian Cooperation Organization
CAU	Central Asian Union
CEA	Central Eurasia
CENTRASBAT	Central Asian Peacekeeping Battalion
CFE	Conventional Forces in Europe Treaty
CICA	Conference on Interaction and Confidence-Building Measures in Asia
CNPC	China National Petroleum Corporation
CSBMs	Confidence and Security-Building Measures
CSTO	Collective Security Treaty Organization
ECSC	European Coal and Steel Community
EEC	Eurasian Economic Commonwealth
EEZ	Exclusive Economic Zone
ELN	Ejercito de Liberacion Nacional
ETIM	East Turkistan Islamic Movement
EU	European Union
EURASEC or EAEC	Eurasian Economic Community
GUAM	Georgia–Ukraine–Azerbaijan–Moldova Coalition
IMU	Islamic Movement of Uzbekistan
NATO	North Atlantic Treaty Organization
OPEC	Organization of Petroleum Exporting Countries
OSCE	Organization for Security and Cooperation in Europe
PfP	Partnership for Peace Program
PLA	People's Liberation Army
PRC	People's Republic of China
RATS	Regional Anti-Terrorism Structure
SCO	Shanghai Cooperation Organization
SLOCs	Sea Lanes of Communications
TRASECA	Transport Corridor Europe–Caucasus–Asia
UNCLOS	United Nations Convention on the Law of the Sea

Introduction

Since the beginning of the twenty-first century, competition among the great powers over energy resources and pathways have become remarkably intense, promoting rapid growth in energy prices and geopolitical considerations involving energy security. Central Eurasia (CEA), forming the heart of the crescent Eurasian space, has been of particular interest to the great powers because of its vast energy resources and strategic location. Geographically, Central Asia is here defined to include Kazakhstan, Kyrgyzstan, Tajikistan, Turkmenistan and Uzbekistan, whereas CEA consists of the five Central Asian countries plus the three south Caucasus countries of Armenia, Azerbaijan and Georgia. The CEA states are located to the east and west of the oil-rich and natural gas-rich Caspian Sea. Kazakhstan and Azerbaijan have the biggest oil reserves and are the largest exporting countries, although Turkmenistan's oil and gas exports have been growing rapidly in recent years as well.

Indeed, CEA is a region where the effects of geopolitics and great power competition have perhaps been more clearly seen than elsewhere. Ethnic and religious conflicts, domestic political turmoil, energy competition among big oil and natural gas companies, and strategic positioning have been a recurrent feature of great-power competition in the region. This, in turn, has made CEA a pivot in the new world order, and especially so when seen in the context of its rich energy reserves and the growing world demand for energy.

As such, any study on energy can no longer be limited solely to a discussion of supply and demand in the energy world market, but must also seek to examine international energy security from geopolitical and geoeconomic perspectives. Here, major powers have invested a lot of time, money and effort together with diplomatic and military muscle to win control over major foreign stockpiles and transits of energy. In this context, major oil and gas importers such as the United States, Europe, China and India are paying close attention to the CEA region, particularly Kazakhstan, Turkmenistan, Iran and Azerbaijan, whereas other regional powers such as Russia are striving to retain influence over these strategic resources.

According to the BP Statistical Review of World Energy (2004), proven oil reserves of the five Caspian littoral states total 216.4 billion barrels, and total gas reserves are estimated at 2819.2 trillion cubic feet. In terms of percentages, the five Caspian littoral states have about 18.8 per cent of the world's total proven oil reserves and 45 per cent of the world's total proven gas reserves.[1] Officials and analysts from the US Energy Information Agency stated in 2004 that the world's unproven oil reserves are expected to double in the next two decades, and states located in former Soviet territory will account for a projected fourfold increase.[2] As such, there should be no doubt that the total Caspian oil and gas reserves are set to be adjusted upwards in the coming years, and the major share of this increase will flow from Kazakhstan, Turkmenistan and Azerbaijan. Meanwhile, the proportion of the Caspian region's energy exports as a share of total world energy supply has increased. In 2001, the five Caspian littoral states exported a total of about 9.2 trillion barrels of oil and 12.05 trillion cubic feet of natural gas to the international market, but exports are estimated to increase to 31.5 trillion barrels of oil and 41.5 trillion cubic feet of natural gas by 2010.

Geopolitically, the CEA region belongs to what Mackinder designated as the 'heartland' and is the centre of Zbigniew Brzezinski's 'black hole' of power, equating to 'the Eurasian Balkans', implying a major risk of ethnic conflicts and great-power regional rivalry. Yet despite this strategic significance, the US geopolitical assessment of the CEA region in the late 1990s has been left basically unchanged since George W. Bush took office in early 2001, although it has lately undergone major revisions, especially after September 11.[3] As argued by Svante E. Cornell:

> With strategic access crucial to the prosecution of the war [on terror], the republics of Central Asia took centre stage in the most important conflict to confront the United States in decades. Although less prominently covered in the media, the states of the South Caucasus were equally vital; situated between Iran and Russia, they were the only practical corridor connecting NATO territory with Central Asia and Afghanistan.[4]

However, the emerging strategic landscape of the region has not only affected the interests of the United States, but also the national interests of neighbouring countries, such as Afghanistan, China, Iran, Pakistan, Turkey and even Ukraine, as well as outsiders such as the European Union, India and Japan. All of these contest for influence in one way or another, although some are more successful and have more leverage over the CEA states than others.

This great-power rivalry which has primarily manifested itself in the early twenty-first century has penetrated CEA affairs politically, economically and militarily to the extent that it has been described in terms of a 'new great game'. This game was intensified by the precarious situation that the CEA states found themselves in as the Soviet Union disintegrated. All CEA states faced major problems in achieving domestic social stability and economic growth. This, in turn, created a power vacuum in CEA igniting geopolitical turmoil over the vast energy resources found in the post-Soviet successor states. As Mehdi Parvizi Amineh, an expert on CEA energy security notes:

> With the end of Soviet control over CEA and Caspian region natural and human resources, there emerged a New Great Game amongst the many players interested in access to the region's oil and gas reserves (...) This mixture of changing world politics suggest that the post-Soviet New Great Game for the influence and control of CEA and the Caspian resources is far more complex than the 19th century competitive colonization of the region by the Anglo-Russian Powers.[5]

This has sparked interest from Beijing to Washington, New Delhi to Moscow and Tokyo to Brussels. National leaders and corporate executives have today stepped up their efforts to gain control over major sources of oil and natural gas in CEA. Events such as the 1973 oil crisis, a rapidly growing world demand, increasing dependency on the Middle East and the collapse of the Soviet Union have intensified this race to secure alternative and diversified supplies.[6]

Eurasia and in particular its central part, Central Asia, increasingly seems to be either the stage for a revised version of the 'great game', where the main actors today are China and the United States rather than the nineteenth-century actors Russia and Great Britain (even though Russia still holds a failing grip over the region) or the object of an attempt by China to re-create a classical vassal relationship between China and the Central Asian states.[7] The importance of Central Asia in China is greater than it has been since the region west of today's China became an integrated part of the Chinese tributary system. Chinese expansion in the region has only been slowed by the current Russian influence, however decreasing, and the competing US attempts to exert influence over the region. Beijing has developed a prioritized policy orientation towards Central Asia, in contrast to the American policy, which seems to have a much more reluctant *ad hoc* presence based on the war against terrorism. From a Chinese perspective, the most important reason for a Chinese presence in the region appears to be an effort to dominate Central Asia in order to secure China's growing need for oil and natural gas. Moreover, there seem to be important security reasons for China's attempt to create a traditional 'vassal' relationship between China and the Central Asian states through investments, trade and military cooperation. It is clear that both the security on China's western border and the internal security in Xinjiang depend upon peaceful development in its Central Asian neighbouring states and China's relations with them.[8]

Central Asia is situated at the crossroads between the East and the West and has historically been in contact with a variety of cultures and economies. This interaction made the Central Asian kingdoms and khanates the most powerful and culturally advanced regions historically.[9] Central Asia's centrality in world affairs was reduced to relative insignificance during the

Soviet occupation and today the region is plagued by many problems. In addition to terrain that stretches from burning deserts to ice-cold mountains, the lack of infrastructure and an almost endemic problem with drugs and militarized conflicts, especially ethnic conflicts, hinders development. However, Central Asia, as a consequence of its increasingly important position in world affairs through its oil and gas findings and its strategic location, has been called China's 'Dingwei' (*Lebensraum*), the beginning of the new great game as Peter Hopkirk has defined it, the emergence of a Grand Chessboard as Zbigniew Brzezinski has formulated it, or the start of the final clash of civilizations as Samuel Huntington has described it.[10]

China has increased its attention towards the region militarily, politically and financially since 1991, when the Central Asian states became independent. As an example, the most efficient regional organization today in Central Asia is the Shanghai Cooperation Organization (SCO), which was founded in Shanghai in 1995 as the Shanghai Five by China, Russia, Kazakhstan, Tajikistan and Kyrgyzstan. The Chinese President Hu Jintao has declared that the Central Asian region is central to Chinese development. This cannot only be seen in the increased number of military exercises and the amount of political cooperation between China and the Central Asian states but also in the rapidly increasing trade and investments from China. The question remains: what determines Chinese interaction with the Central Asian states? Trade and economic integration between China and the Central Asian states are promising when considering deepened cooperation and there are no serious interstate security risks.

China has traditionally viewed Central Asia as its personal trading area and a region heavily influenced by Chinese culture. Many of history's most impressive trading centres were positioned in Xinjiang or west of China's current borders, such as Jarkand, Samarkand, Urumuqi and Kokand. The trade between China and Central Asia has always been crucial and favoured by both sides, as it is today.[11]

The situation in Central Asia seems to be developing into a new version of the 'great game' that was played out between Great Britain and Russia in the nineteenth century in Central Asia, but this is only one aspect of the newly developed relationship. The Chinese attempts to dominate the region look like a new version of classical vassal relations and China has worked hard to bring Central Asia once more under its economic and political influence. The principal actors today are China and the United States, especially following the US intervention in Afghanistan. Neither China nor America is concerned over Russian pressure in the long term, for they know Russia has severe economic and social problems of its own to deal with. This became apparent during the US intervention in Afghanistan, where Russia followed the US lead and hoped to gain financially from the intervention, but also earlier when Russia agreed to share its influence over Central Asia with China through the SCO. Beijing initially thought that time and the economy were on its side, in the case of Russia, but time is not what China can afford today as the United States is positioning itself in Central Asia. It is apparent that Beijing has begun to use financial means to make the Central Asian states more dependent on China, a dependence that builds on gas and oil as well as political–military cooperation. This dependence would make it possible for China to build a political and economic base in Central Asia.[12]

It is, however, clear that neither China nor the United States can exclusively dominate the region. Russia, Europe, Iran, India, Pakistan and Turkey are other actors of varied importance that also attempt to influence the region, and this will prove to be to the advantage of the Central Asian states as they will benefit from the competition.[13] Russia and India realized early on that they would not be able to dominate the region and their focus has been to minimize the negative effects of Chinese and American influence over Central Asia.

It is also important to point out that Russia has been the most important military power in the region, and could arguably be so for years to come if the 201st Motorized Rifle Division is kept in place in Tajikistan. However, the war against the Taliban and bin Laden has put US forces on the same ground as Russian troops. This has shifted the military balance in the region and it is likely that America will try to stabilize (change) the regional states in order to suit its own purposes, and one of the possible ways to do this is to arm pro-American states.[14]

China, on its side, has signed several military agreements with Kazakhstan, Kyrgyzstan and the other Central Asian states. It is evident that China has begun to move into the Russian sphere of interest, and with increased US involvement it has boosted its military engagement, as has been seen in the increased number of military exercises and money to the security sector. This could be the beginning of the end for Russian military dominance in the region as the Russians have neither the political will nor the resources to meet the Chinese challenge, despite the fact that many Russians fear Chinese expansion.[15] China's hope is that the US troops will soon move out of the region and that this would work in their favour as they could move into the power vacuum without any significant challenge from Russia. There are, however, no indications that the United States will move out in the coming years; on the contrary, it seems that the United States is strengthening its position in Central Asia. One can perceive the same tendency also in Afghanistan, where the US is sending more NATO troops for securing the fragile Kabul government and the secure future passage of hydrocarbon products from Central Asia, targeting the markets of India and possibly China.

Both India and Russia have indicated interest in a strategic alliance with China to consolidate some control over the region, but China did initially reject any propositions on this matter. The situation has changed in the light of the US intervention in the region, and China is now much more interested in cooperation with Russia, especially considering the relatively good relations between the United States and India. This has been most apparent in the close cooperation between China and Russia in the SCO, the strategic alliance against hegemony and that China would like to increase its cooperation with Russia concerning the oil and gas industry.[16]

Since several of the Central Asian states could potentially have fallen into a dependency relationship with China in regard to military development, the US involvement in the region has been viewed positively by the Central Asian governments.[17] They have received some military aid from America and can probably expect more attention in return for cooperation with America in the war against terrorism. The earlier Chinese strategy to limit US involvement in the region has suffered a severe setback and the only possibility for China to succeed is to make it politically impossible for the United States to stay in the region after the terrorist threat is under control (which is a matter of perception) or use the SCO to manoeuvre the United States out of the region.[18]

Beijing has been actively seeking to exert military, political and financial influence in Central Asia ever since the USSR was dissolved in 1991. China's realpolitik philosophy is that the international system is characterized by a constant struggle for domination, and that China must engage in that battle, its main adversary being the United States. China is, at present, a regional power with global aspirations, and if it continues on the path of economic growth and projection of influence, its aspirations may be realized.

Chinese President Hu Jintao has even touted Central Asia's centrality to Chinese development, a sentiment which probably accounts for the recent joint military exercises, increased political cooperation and increase in trade. Some compare recent Chinese involvement there to modern vassal relations through investment, trade and military cooperation, in which China uses Central Asia as a buffer zone and an economically integrated entity which will help to advance the Chinese global agenda.[19]

In the last decade, China has taken a more active role in the international system, marking a transformation in its foreign policy.[20] It has expanded bilateral relations, joined regional and economic organizations and intensified its participation in multilateral organizations. China attaches great importance to the SCO partnership with its neighbours in Central Asia. As a co-founder, China anticipated this organization to be a platform where broad cooperation among all countries and regional organizations can be sought. It originally started with functional issues, including the demilitarization of the Sino–Russian borders, tackling drug trafficking and boosting intraregional trade. It is absolutely true that the creation of the SCO reflects the Russian and Chinese shared security interests in Central Asia, but has not for the time being focused on the issue of energy security, an indispensable element of Beijing's global geostrategy. What are the prospects of this problematic? First we should look at the way China views Central Asia.

1 Chinese strategic interests in Eurasia

Eurasia, herein defined as Northeast and Central Asia, has been ravaged by historical and current conflicts of both a military and a political nature, such as Japan or Russia's occupation of their neighbours, border disputes, etc. This has created an environment where there is a chronic lack of trust among the regional actors and relations are often seen as a zero-sum game, or in relative gains. From an international perspective, it is symptomatic that there is very little cooperation in the military and political fields. For instance, Northeast Asia has no institutionalized regional organization that deals with political and military conflicts whereas transregional organizations that include cooperation between Northeast Asian and Central Asian states are limited to only exercises against terrorism.[1] There have been several organizations initiated in Central Asia working on cooperation but their viability is limited. This is due to limited political support from the respective Central Asia governments and also because of the intraregional rivalry between the five Central Asian states.[2] Thus, these organizations remain relatively weak and their future prospects uncertain. In order to have conflict management and resolution frameworks in place, and to establish greater trust between the different actors, these organizations would need to integrate deeper into the region, politically and economically.

Since the end of the Cold War, Central Asia has emerged as a newly defined, separate geopolitical space. Its abundant raw materials, particularly oil and gas, and its unique geographic location give the region its importance. Nevertheless, the region was until recently as much geographically as strategically distant and indifferent to the United States and Europe. The events of 9/11 have catapulted the region into the world's spotlight and it has grown in strategic importance.

Since then, the United States has been activated as a major geopolitical player in Central Asia, in addition to Russia and China. Europe is deeply concerned and involved in the region and has the potential to become a fourth power. Turkey and Iran, having particular interests and influence thanks to historical vantages, should be seen as lesser powers in the region. As can India and Japan, who are quietly penetrating Central Asia in the economic sphere.

The special statuses of China, Russia and the United States in Central Asia are mainly attributed to their involvement and influence in the region on the one hand, and on the other, to the framework of the special relations that the three powers have forged in separate relations with one another. In the aftermath of the establishment of a US military presence in Central Asia, dealing with the bilateral and trilateral relations among the three powers *vis-à-vis* their relations with Central Asia has become a significant strategic issue for China, Russia and the United States.

Once the Soviet Union collapsed and Central Asia had become an independent geopolitical space, China's entry into the region thawed a frozen relationship stretching back to the days of the Great Silk Road. Beijing's geographical closeness to Central Asia and its long common border with Kazakhstan, Kyrgyzstan and Tajikistan (over 3000 kilometre) has allowed the growing of a robust trade, but also the rise of potentially serious threats to China's security and development.

China's positioning in post-Cold War Eurasia

Since the start of the twenty-first century, the People's Republic of China (PRC) has entered a new phase of economic development and in the evolution of the country's role as a fast-rising world power. China's economic engine is now so large that it requires vast and expanding volumes of energy, minerals and agricultural raw materials to keep it going. In other words, China's economic needs have expanded far more rapidly than the country's strategic reach. For the moment, the PRC lacks the military capabilities that would provide it with reasonable assurance of continued access to resources, regardless of circumstance. Thus, for now, the country is entering a period in which its ability to maintain domestic growth and social stability will be hostage to external events and, perhaps, to the forbearance of those it regards as political foes.

Because Chinese strategic thought and strategic-planning process, contrary to that of the West, are rooted less on planning a specific sequence of moves towards a precisely specified goal and more on assessing, shaping and exploiting the overall 'propensity of things' in order to move in a generally favourable direction,[3] the PRC's post-Cold War grand strategy is organized around four notional axioms.

Avoid conflict

The collapse of the Soviet Union removed a long-standing potential threat to the PRC's security and allowed Beijing to pursue new possibilities for expanding its influence into Central Asia, while simultaneously shifting resources from frontier defence to the projection of air and sea power off China's coasts. At the same time, there was a greater risk that the tacit anti-Soviet alliance that had held the United States and China together for almost two decades would begin to fray and might fall apart. With the Tiananmen Square revolt (June 1989) still fresh in people's minds, the fear that Washington might try to promote a 'peaceful evolution' by overthrowing Communist Party rule – just as in Russia – was uppermost in the thoughts of the Chinese Communist Party (CCP) leader Deng Xiaoping when he penned the directive outlining the principles of the strategy for securing China's place in the post-Cold War protracted era of unipolarity, or a US-dominated world (1991).

US leaders, knowing that they must block and derail the rise of China if the US is to retain its own position of dominance, have implemented a twofold strategy towards China since the early 1990s: on the one hand, they promote economic and social engagement, whereas on the other they practise military and diplomatic containment. In this way, they envision strengthening the US ability to project power throughout Asia under the guise of 'transformation', encouraging Japan to increase its own capabilities, and seeking new, quasi-alliance partners (India) to contain the PRC's rise, resulting in slowing in the growth of Chinese power, keeping the expansion of China's influence in check, weakening and dividing the country domestically, and ultimately overthrowing the CCP. Given China's present condition of relative weakness, Beijing is obliged to maintain the best possible relationship with Washington.

The events of 9/11 may have resulted in the deployment of US forces to Central Asia and in the acceleration of Japanese rearmament, but the net impact for China has been positive. After a decade-long focus on East Asia, US strategy has shifted to the Middle East. The asymmetrical threats of terrorism and nuclear proliferation have forced Washington to consider cooperation from other countries, including China, and this has given the ancient 'Middle Kingdom' additional leverage for influencing America's policy. This has increased the likelihood that confrontation can be avoided, at least in the near to medium term.[4]

Build comprehensive national power

The PRC needs time to 'build' a combined measure of economic, military and technological capabilities so as to improve significantly its overall national strength.

Advance incrementally

Continuing relative weakness and potential vulnerability will have to mobilize Chinese policy-makers to take full advantage of the post 9/11 'period of strategic opportunity to help dissuade, deflect, and delay what Beijing senses as US efforts at containment and subversion. In fact, China has capitalized on the recent cooling of relations between Russia and the United States and is working hard to draw Moscow closer through arms purchases, energy deals and military exercises, both at the bilateral and at the multilateral level, in the framework of pursuing the Shanghai Cooperation Organization's (SCO) regional strategic aims.

Maintain stability, defend sovereignty, achieve pre-eminence, pursue parity

Given that China continues as a one-party autocracy, the CCP has staked its legitimacy in large measure on the promise that the party will pursue stability and reclaim the territory taken from China during its century of weakness and humiliation. The CCP is committed to preventing Taipei from making a formal declaration of independence, or letting external enemies or domestic 'separatists' from weakening Beijing's control over Tibet or the western province of Xinjiang. The rightful ownership of large swaths of what is now the Russian Far East may have to wait for a suitable moment.

The countries in China's immediate neighbourhood, its 'surrounding environment' to which Chinese strategic thinkers assign top priority, need to realize that the PRC's goal is to become 'East Asia's major power', or the 'pre-eminent' or 'dominant' power in Asia.[5] To this end, China's neighbours would support the PRC's position both in international institutions and in any disputes between China and non-Asian powers. Beyond this, China might press the nations of Asia to 'adopt trade and investment policies compatible with Chinese interests ... be generally open to immigration from China; prohibit or suppress anti-China and anti-Chinese movements within their societies; respect the rights of Chinese within their societies ... (and) promote the use of Mandarin as a supplement to and eventually a replacement for English'.[6] Thus, the goal of Chinese strategists is to achieve a position in Asia roughly equivalent to that enjoyed by the United States in the Western Hemisphere since the early part of the twentieth century.

To claim success in its grand strategy, Beijing needs to scramble for resources in sending the PRC off in many different directions at once, into three concentric geographic zones. The first is made up of China's immediate neighbourhood, or 'surrounding environment', the 360 degrees around China's coasts and borders, including the long interior frontier from Siberia, through Central, South and continental Southeast Asia, as well as the maritime portions of Northeast and Southeast Asia, and the islands of Oceania. Here the PRC is seeking both energy and raw materials. The Middle East and Persian Gulf are contained in a second zone, from where China imports energy, and from the third, that is Africa and the Western Hemisphere, including both South and North America, it seeks energy and raw materials. Truly, ever since the late 1990s Beijing has intensified efforts to secure access to oil and natural gas in Russia and Central Asia.

In the implications of China's fast-growing, truly global pursuit of resources, noteworthy is the vulnerability emerging from its dependency on critical imports to sustain the country's rapid growth, and thus potentially to cause disruptions or sharp price increases. The security of oil and natural gas supplies will, if not already, be a prominent concern, since a sharp economic downturn would have profoundly unsettling effects inside China and might even threaten the continued rule of the CCP.

China's desperate need for 'resource security' makes energy diplomacy one of the most important considerations of the country's diplomatic strategy. Given the PRC's heavy reliance on maritime transport and the prevailing balance of power at sea, the primary danger to supplies in transit now comes from the US navy. Among the possible methods China's military planners and strategic thinkers are considering for reducing the country's exposure to naval blockade is a shift towards a greater reliance on contiguous sources and overland transport, already pursued through variable energy deals with the energy-rich neighbouring Russia and Central Asian states. It is noteworthy that, both bilaterally and within the scheme of the SCO, Beijing seeks to acquire the capabilities necessary to project military power in order to defend friendly foreign governments in Eurasia and their national economic interests, such as the authoritarian regimes of the Central Asian states.

In this context, Beijing's effort to hold Russia close by the lure of its large market for energy and materials and positive consideration of President Putin's proposal (Shanghai SCO summit, June 2006) to give the SCO an energy dimension by creating the 'Asia energy club' or 'Gas OPEC' is indicative of China's energy policy goals. It is also natural that the SCO member states of Central Asia, a key resource-exporting region to both Beijing and Washington, may converge US and Chinese interests in maintaining stability and regional security.

PRC interests in Central Asia

In particular, Chinese aims in Central Asia are the following: first, to constrain the separatist forces of 'East Turkestan'; second, to keep Central Asia as China's stable strategic rear area; and third, to make Central Asia one of China's diversified sources of energy resources and a regional economic partner.

The term 'East Turkestan' was initially used by Russians and Europeans in the eighteenth century to designate the south part of Xingjian province in western China. In 1933 and 1944 two 'East Turkestan Republics' were established but were both short-lived. A contemporary 'East Turkestan' movement in Xingjian aimed to set up an independent 'East Turkestan' state. Sometimes its followers engaged in terrorism and violence.[7] The Chinese state considers all organizations engaged in creating such a state as terrorist, adopting political separatism and religious extremism, and treats them in accordance with its traditional Han Dynasty policy, which considers striking out separatism and maintaining national unity as the mission and agenda for the Chinese government. It is, in a sense, a continuation of China's ongoing struggle to unite all its territory as one nation.

The 'East Turkestan' forces have historic, ethnic, cultural, linguistic and religious ties with Central Asia. In addition, two-thirds of all Uyghurs, the main Turkic population in Xingjian, live in Central Asian states (about 350,000) and many Kazakhs, Tajiks and Kyrgyz live in Xingjian. As a background to the Sino–Soviet confrontation, a number of different 'East Turkestan' organizations were encouraged by the Soviet Union: the independence of the five Central Asian states boosted these organizations' activities and they made Central Asia one of their bases. They obtain spiritual and material support, as well as military training, from international terrorist organizations, including those in Central Asia, such as the Taliban, Hizb-ut-Tahrir, the Islamic Movement of Uzbekistan and the Turkestan Islamic Party. Central Asia is a safe haven for separatists fleeing China and serves as the major channel by which international terrorism penetrates China.

Since Central Asia now significantly affects the security of northwest China, China's Central Asian policy requires that Central Asian governments restrict and prohibit 'East Turkestan' forces conducting activities in their territories and prevent terrorist and extremist forces from sneaking into China through their territories. Considering that the security of Central Asia is closely associated to China's Xingjian security, it is obvious that Beijing is willing to join Central Asia and Russia in establishing regional collective security mechanisms, nowadays a central function of the SCO (see Map 1.1).

A brief look at a map of the region and its bordering states will immediately reveal the strategic location of the region and the clear source of its problems. Since the dissolution of the former USSR in 1991, Xinjiang has become the only province in China bordered by eight countries, five of which are mostly Muslim. There is a ferocious nationalist movement, the East Turkistan Islamic Movement (ETIM) – recognized by the United States as an international terrorist organization –which has been struggling openly since 1997 for Xinjinan independence. After denying the problem for decades and stressing instead China's 'national unity', official reports and the state-run media began in early 2001 to detail terrorist activities in the province officially known as the Xinjiang Uyghur Autonomous Region.[8]

The SCO can to be seen to have its origins in China's 'Xinjiang problem' with its inception as the 'Shanghai 5' in 1996, the same year that China launched its 'Strike Hard' campaign against 'splittests' in Xinjiang. International campaigns for Uyghur rights and possible independence have become increasingly vocal and well organized, especially on the internet. Following 9/11, the vast majority of these organizations disclaimed any support for violence or terrorism, pressing for a peaceful resolution of the ongoing conflicts in the region. Nevertheless, the growing influence of 'cyber-separatism' is of increasing concern to the Chinese authorities, who are seeking to convince the world that the Uyghurs do pose a real domestic and international terrorist threat.

History has not been kind to the Uyghurs over the last two millennia. Like the Kurds and Chechens, their legacies of earlier empire and kingdom never produced viable nations or states. After initially welcoming the PRC as 'liberators' in the 1950s, the region gradually lost any real autonomy as

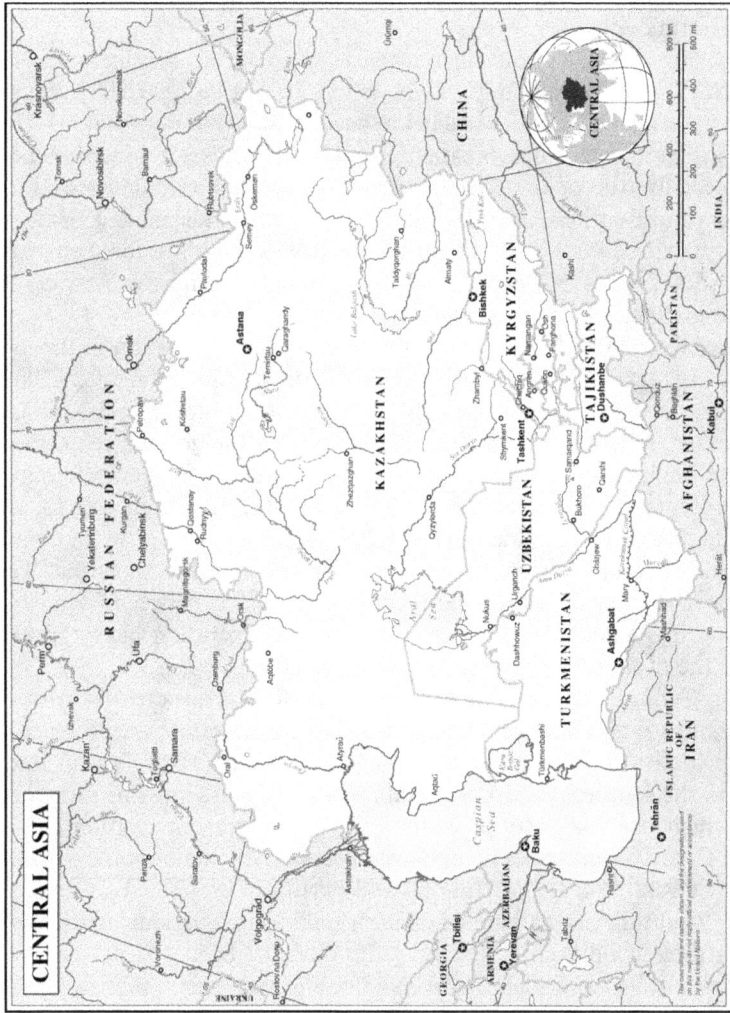

Map 1.1 Central Asia

Source: UN Department of Peacekeeping Operations, Cartographic Section

Beijing tightened its control. In the late 1980s and mid-1990s, the Uyghur's loyalty to the state gave way to increasing expressions of dissent, not only among Uyghurs but also among a wide cross-section of local residents that felt the northwest was not keeping pace with the rapid development of the rest of the country. The government has consistently rounded up any Uyghur suspected of being 'too' religious, especially those identified as Sufis or the so-called Wahabbis (an euphemism in the region for strict Muslims, not an organized Islamic school).

It is also important to note, that whereas the Uyghur Muslims are less than half of China's 21 million Muslims, as reported in the year 2000 census, the majority of China's other Muslims, especially the Chinese-speaking Hui Muslims, are completely unsympathetic to Uyghur calls for independence. This is especially true of the Kazakh, Kyrgyz and Tajik populations, all of whom live almost entirely in Xinjiang. Many fear an independent 'Eastern Turkistan' would be for Uyghurs primarily and have no place for them, just as we see ethnic states in Central Asia being oriented almost exclusively to serving the main ethnic group's interests.

The shift of the SCO from mainly trade and border resolution in the late 1990s into an anti-terrorist security cooperation organization after 2001, has met with mixed success. Although the incidents of violence in Xinjiang have decreased, most visitors to the region report that anger and resentment continue to simmer, even as the government continues to report frequent arrests. In Central Asia, groups like the Hizbut-Tahrir, which call for an independent Islamic Caliphate, continue to proliferate and grow in popularity despite concerted efforts by each government to stamp them out. The SCO has been responsible for greater security cooperation between China and its neighbouring states, yet it is not clear if this cooperation has produced more than the occasional repatriation of suspected separatists.

Securing Central Asia as China's stable strategic rear area is part of China's grand-strategy geopolitics, since Beijing's primary strategic mission and foreign policy priority is to avoid possible US support of Taiwan independence in the southeast and US containment of China's growing influence, both of which are likely to precipitate Sino–US strategic confrontation. Therefore, China concentrates its main resources on the major strategic front and keeps Central Asia stable, tranquil and part of its strategic rear area.

Securing Central Asia as part of China's stable strategic rear area is predicated on three conditions: (a) solving the disputed border issues between Central Asian states and China and maintaining peace and security in the border areas (both tasks have been fulfilled); (b) conducting bilateral relations between Central Asian states and China in goodwill; and (c) preventing Central Asia from falling into the control of any major power or group of major powers that have complicated geopolitical and strategic relations with China or threaten its interests in the region. If China can meet these conditions, then it can focus attention on other strategic priorities and feel secure that it can manage any contingency that arises in Central Asia.

Since China's energy import has doubled in the last five years[9] and the country is bound to depend heavily on the international market, the Chinese government should guarantee the energy supplies demanded by China's sustainable economic development and diversify a stable energy supply (see Map 1.2).

In an effort to diversify energy supplies, in 1997 China agreed with Kazakhstan to the construction of the Atyrau (west Kazakhstan) to Alashankou (Xingjian) oil pipeline, in operation since 2006. The pipeline is connected with the existing Kenjiyak–Atyrau pipeline. China imports at least 10–20 million tons of oil from Kazakhstan every year, which is more than 10 per cent of China's oil imports. Even though the volume of energy the country imports from Central Asia has not reached the level of strategic significance, prospects for the next several years are more than optimistic since oil production in Kazakhstan has been growing rapidly. As an example, we mention the unprecedented deal China has struck with Kazakhstan, under which oil is to be pumped directly across China's borders for the first time via the Alataw Pass in Xinjiang.

China has further solidified its relations with Central Asia through massive economic investments in Kazakhstan, Kyrgyzstan, Tajikistan and Uzbekistan. A major irritant, however, have been border disputes between China and its resource-rich neighbours. China has since moved fast to remove that irritant in order to begin burgeoning relations with its neighbours. Kazakhstan, which is the largest economy in the region with a gross domestic product (GDP) of around US$43 billion in 2005, was the first to have its territorial claims settled, largely to its satisfaction.[10] The border settlement was an important part of a hefty oil deal that was signed between Astana and Beijing.[11]

Similarly, China and Tajikistan have reached a negotiated settlement of their territorial conflict, apart from the still contested Babakhshon region.[12] China and Kyrgyzstan, with the latter sharing a border with Xinjiang, have also settled their border claims. Having mended its frontiers with its neighbours, China has earned a great deal of their goodwill, which has helped raise its profile in the region. Some observers, however, believe that a Chinese presence in the region appears to be an attempt to dominate Central Asia in order to secure China's energy needs.[13] Given its immense energy resources and strategic location, Central Asia has come to be known as China's Dingwei (*Lebensraum*). In the 1990s, China increased its military presence in Xinjiang to 200,000 troops.[14] Xinjiang is 'Beijing's giant oilfield'.

In terms of investment, however, China largely concentrates on Kazakhstan, followed by Kyrgyzstan, Tajikistan and Uzbekistan. Besides being the largest economy of Central Asia, Kazakhstan also has proven oil reserves of 2.7 billion barrels.[15] In 1997, China pledged US$10 billion in investment for oil exploration and construction of infrastructure.[16] In December 2005, it bought Kazakhstan's flagship oil company, PetroKazakhstan, for US$4.18 billion.[17] In addition, it invested US$700 million in building a pipeline that will connect Kazakhstan to China through Kyrgyzstan. The last 240 kilometres of the 3,000-kilometre Kazakhstan–China pipeline will run through Xinjiang, where crude oil will be refined and sent eastwards. Similarly, China is

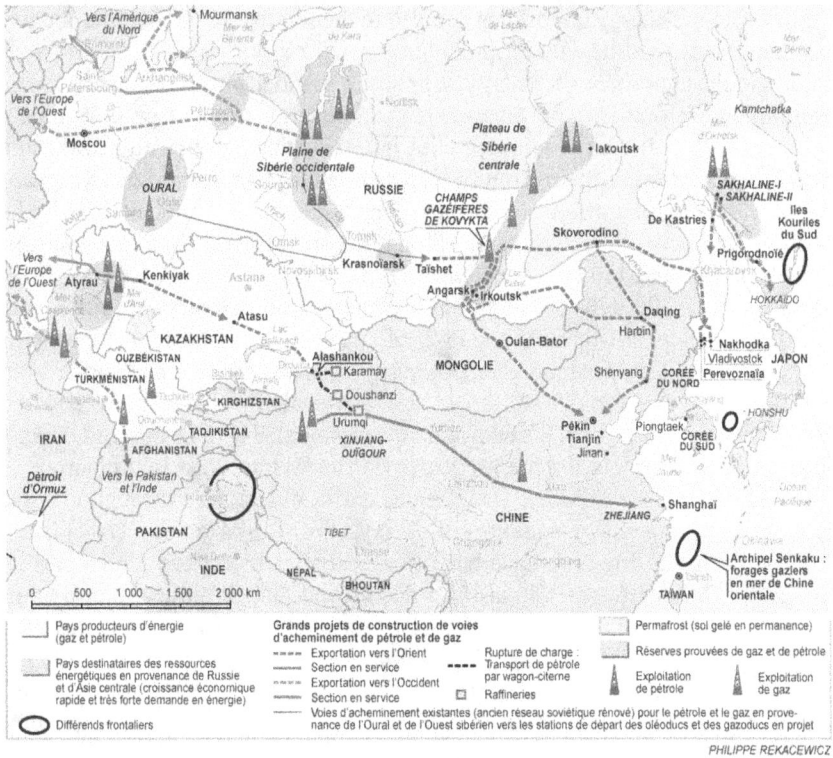

Map 1.2 Petroleum and gas transferring projects in Asia
Source: Philippe Rekacewicz, le Monde diplomatique, Paris, mai 2005

building a vast network of rail and road links in Kyrgyzstan, which is a transit state, to connect China with Uzbekistan. For this communication network, Beijing pledged in 2005 an investment of US$900 million in Kyrgyzstan, which is almost half of its US$2 billion GDP.[18] In all, China has committed US$9 billion to building a region-wide network of overland pipelines to ship Kazakh oil.[19] In addition, the China Petroleum Corporation has invested US$4 billion in Kazakhstan's oil industry.[20] Earlier in August 2002, China gave Kyrgyzstan US$970 million in military aid.[21]

Beijing is also helping Uzbekistan to develop its modest oil fields in the Fergana Valley. In May 2006, the Uzbek President Islam Karimov visited China, a visit which yielded Beijing's first serious pledge of investment to the Uzbek energy sector.[22] Although Uzbekistan is not so well endowed in oil resources, it sits on vast reserves of uranium, which make it attractive to power-lacking nations such as India and China, and even power-exporting Russia. With annual production of 2,900 tons of uranium, Russia has recently seen its uranium reserves decline. It has since brought Uzbekistan into a framework of nuclear partnership.

Mindful of Tashkent's potential for supplying key natural resources, especially natural gas, Beijing also signed a framework agreement with Tashkent on investments worth US$1.5 billion in July 2005.[23] In addition, China and Uzbekistan signed an agreement for a US$950 million long-term loan, as well as for an additional US$350 million soft loan. China has since invested nearly US$600 million in Uzbekistan's energy sector. Uzbekistan boasts 1.2 per cent of the world's natural gas reserves,[24] which make it the region's second-largest gas-rich nation. Uzbek gas riches make it attractive to a China that is quickly moving away from oil consumption, which is currently 6.3 million barrels per day and is projected to grow to 10 million barrels per day in the next two decades.[25] Although China's current gas consumption accounts for only 3 per cent of its total energy intake, it is growing at an annual rate of 7.8 per cent.[26]

The region's ultimate site of gas reserves, nevertheless, is Turkmenistan. In April 2006, Beijing signed a 30-year deal with Ashgabat, under which Turkmenistan will provide China with 30 billion cubic meters (BCM) of gas from 2009 to 2039.[27] The major challenge, however, is the shipment of gas, which is receiving the urgent attention of both countries. During Turkmen President Sapirmurad Niyazov's visit to China on 2–7 April, 2006, the two countries agreed to take swift measures to complete the Turkmenistan–China gas pipeline project. The proposed gas pipeline will run through Kazakhstan. Both governments will jointly explore and develop gas deposits and conclude comprehensive purchase agreements.[28] Recently, it also became clear that China intends to pipe Turkmen gas through Tajikistan in a pipeline scheduled to be completed in 2009–10.[29] Earlier, China announced its plans to connect a natural gas pipeline from Kazakhstan to China that would run parallel to its Atasu–Alashankou oil pipeline.[30]

Although China started to pay more attention to Central Asia after the September 11 attacks on the United States, increased energy engagement only appeared on the agenda after Japan emerged in 2003 as a competitor for an extension of the Siberian oil pipeline. Fearing a likely Chinese monopoly of the oil supply from Russia, Japan tried to persuade Moscow in late 2002 to extend the pipeline to the Pacific coast instead. Japanese Prime Minister Junichiro Koizumi reaffirmed these intentions on his first official visit to Russia in January 2003 when the two parties signed a six-point 'action plan' calling for cooperation in economics, energy and international diplomacy. The offer Japan provided was a financial package worth US$7 billion, including a US$5 billion investment for pipeline construction and US$2 billion in loans for the development of the Siberian oilfields.

Other factors that spurred Beijing's entry into Central Asia included a wish to reduce the dependency on the sea lines of communication for oil transport. In the event of conflict or a terrorist attack, these could easily be disrupted, choking Beijing's energy supply, especially at the vulnerable Malacca Straits. The discovery of Kazakhstan's giant Kashagan oil field was another factor that made the Chinese leadership look to Central Asia and the Caspian.[31] Considering Beijing's growing energy needs and continuous economic growth, with oil imports reaching 91 million tons in 2003 of which 75 per cent originated in the Middle East and Africa, diversification of energy supplies became urgent.[32] Lacking a 'blue water navy' to protect the sea lines of communication, Central Asia and Russia's energy reserves appeared as favourable options. The discovery of the Kashagan oil field also made Beijing reconsider its position regarding the feasibility of a Kazakhstan–China pipeline.

Accordingly, the Chinese state-owned company CNPC and Kazakhstan's state oil company, KazMunaiGaz (KMG), jointly constructed the western-most section of the cross-border oil pipeline, running 448 kilometres from Atyrau to Kenkiyak in Kazakhstan, a project that was finally completed in March 2003. The easternmost part of the pipeline, running 988 kilometres from Atasu in Kazakhstan to Alashankou at the Chinese border, was completed at the end of 2005 and became operative in May 2006 with a total investment of US$700 million.

The launch of the oil pipeline also marked a turning point for China's energy security in other aspects. With the completion of the pipeline, China secured an energy resource that for the first time was beyond the striking capabilities of US aircraft carrier battle groups, which have the ability to target Chinese supplies in the Middle East and Sudan. In addition, once the middle section between Kenkiyak and Kumkol is complete, China's oil imports from Kazakhstan will increase substantially from the current 1 per cent to 15 per cent of its total crude oil needs.[33] The pipeline also helped Kazakhstan realize its ambitions to become a major oil exporter as well as Kazakh President Nursultan Nazarbayev's plan to make China Kazakhstan's closest partner.

Another victory China scored in Central Asia was the successful takeover of PetroKazakhstan (Petrokaz) in 2005, an international petroleum company registered in Canada but with all of its assets in Kazakhstan. What was particularly interesting for China with this deal was the full ownership of the oil field Kumkol South, and joint ownership of Kumkol North with Russia's Lukoil. Since the Kumkol oil fields were located at the midpoint of the China–Kazakhstan oil pipeline, obtaining Petrokaz's assets over these oilfields not only enhanced CNPC's oil reserves in Kazakhstan, but also helped improve the efficiency of the pipeline. China also saw its increasing role in energy cooperation with Kazakhstan in line with the long-term strategic interests of the two countries, especially when faced with a greater US military presence in Central Asia after 9/11.

China's energy search in Uzbekistan went smoothly as well. In June 2004, the CNPC signed contracts with Uzbekneftegaz on oil and gas cooperation. In 2006, the CNPC signed two more agreements with Uzbekneftegaz to explore and develop prospective petroleum deposits in five onshore blocks of the Aral Sea, together with Russia's Lukoil, Malaysia's Petronas and South Korea's National Oil Corporation. Kyrgyzstan also received assistance from Chinese companies engaged in petroleum activities, but on a smaller scale.

Prospects are also optimistic for regional economic cooperation. Xingjian's trade with Central Asia (about US$4 billion in 2003, over 60 per cent of the volume of its foreign trade) plays a significant role in this Chinese province's economic development. As this international trade, promoted by the Chinese government 'Go West' campaign, is an important channel for China's re-entry into Central Asia, Beijing plans to turn Central Asia into a free trade zone in the framework of the SCO.

Five factors drive Chinese engagement in Central Asia: the economic development of Xinjiang; domestic political stability; regional stability; energy security; and the creation of an alternative transport corridor to Europe.

Through its 'develop the west' programme, launched by Chinese President Jiang Zemin in 1999, China has sought to integrate the western region of China into the booming Chinese economy, and make it more competitive. Although the western development programme includes Tibet, Qinghai, Gansu, Sichuan, Yunnan, Shaanxi and Guizhou provinces in addition to Xinjiang, Xinjiang has been the main area of focus. Sharing a 3,500 kilometre long border with the Central Asian republics, Xinjiang's economic integration is of crucial importance for its development.

A precondition for this development, however, has been a massive resource transfer from Beijing for the development of infrastructure, including road and rail ties, between China's east and west.

By deepening economic cooperation between China (especially Xinjiang) and Central Asia, China seeks to diminish the influence of those groups that promote ethno-religious extremism and separatism.[34] China fears that these influences will spill over into Xinjiang because of the historical trans-border interactions between these peoples. China's policy is fairly straightforward: to increase incentives to Central Asian governments that assist in repressing 'East Turkestan' secessionist forces, and not to let Central Asia become a base from which secessionists can operate.[35] This promotion of China's territorial integrity has been promoted both on a bilateral and multilateral level through the SCO.

Second, as repeatedly demonstrated in the past, drastic shifts in Central Asia tend to create problems for China. From the Manchu's establishment of the northwest province of Xinjiang in the 1860s to the Republic Revolution in 1911, this region has seen several major revolts, most of which are believed to have been instigated and supported by those with an anti-Chinese agenda. Mass ethnic upheavals in the 1940s and emigration to the Soviet territory in the 1960s were unwelcomed external influences from Soviet Central Asia.[36]

China's present concern over possible turmoil in this region is clearly demonstrated in its very nervous reaction to the March 2005 Tulip Revolution in Kyrgyzstan. In addition to fear of a domino effect and growing regional instability, China's support of the Uzbek government following the Andijan events of 2005 further confirmed its dedication to the status quo.[37]

Third, China hopes for a relatively secure energy supply from Central Asia and especially Kazakhstan. Such energy links would benefit the cooperative political structures that have been initiated in the region, but which have encountered problems. Economically it would benefit the states in the region by decreasing costs and securing long-term energy security. China needs to diversify its energy supplies. By relying on oil transported by sea lanes through the Malacca Straits, China places itself in an insecure position since those straits are often closed to Chinese transport.[38] Currently, there is also a premium of US$1–2 per barrel on the oil that is imported to Northeast Asia due to world demand on Middle Eastern oil and to the simple reality of distance.

To reduce dependence on the Malacca Straits, China has shown a keen interest in the alternative route via the port of Gwadar in Pakistan, in which China has invested over US$200 million.[39] To transport energy supplies from the Gwadar port, China has made efforts in rehabilitating the 616 kilometre Karakorum highway linking Pakistan with Xinjiang, although this is unlikely to carry more than a little oil. Plans are also under way to build a highway linking Gwadar with Kandahar and Islamabad, as well as the east–west trunk railroad from Urumchi to Kashgar.[40]

Fourth, the construction of the second Eurasian land bridge via Central Asia and Xinjiang will reduce the overload at Chinese ports on the east coast. Development of the corridor will also increase access by China's underdeveloped western regions to world markets and balance the wealth gaps within China. Large oil deposits in Kazakhstan and Azerbaijan and gas deposits in Turkmenistan are already drawing Chinese attention, leading to expanded political interaction. In the case of Azerbaijan alone, this has led to the Chinese showing interest in developing the Baku–Tbilisi–Kars railway corridor, as well as to further multiple production-sharing agreements with the Azerbaijan State Oil Company following a 2004 grant by China's Shengli Oil Company to develop the Garachukhur oil field.[41]

The security dimension of China's involvement in Central Asian affairs.

Security impediments to China's deeper engagement in Greater Central Asia and continental trade have two dimensions: first, the direct threats to Chinese citizens, entrepreneurs and construction workers in Pakistan and Greater Central Asia; and, second, the more overarching security threats of drug-trafficking, terrorism and cross-border criminality. Although both of these may impede the expansion of regional and continental trade, they do not impede trade to the extent often claimed, nor do they put any significant brakes on Beijing's expansion into the region. In fact, the causation may be reversed, as increased economic interaction inadvertently gives rise to a safer and more stable security environment. Nonetheless, Chinese concern over separatism and over unstable socio-political climate in Central Asia have moderated Beijing's determination to boost trans-border trade and investment initiatives.[42]

One of the foremost concerns for Beijing is the fear that the weak Central Asian states could provide safe-havens for various kinds of criminal groups. The Chinese point in particular to the Semirechye region in Kazakhstan, the Ferghana Valley in Uzbekistan, Osh in Kyrgyzstan and Khojent in Tajikistan. Worse, China believes that these areas are home to groups affiliated with Xinjiang's separatist movements.[43] The almost unchecked drug economy in Afghanistan and Tajikistan also affects China's willingness to decrease border controls and increase cross-border trade.[44]

All in all, security concerns serve as a cautionary note as Beijing expands trade with Greater Central Asia and Pakistan.[45] Yet of the impediments affecting trade, security should not be overestimated as a factor determining trade policies, for Beijing realizes that increased trade with its neighbours will alleviate the security situation in the long term.

However, border disputes can interrupt water flows and energy supplies, sowing uncertainty among farmers and villagers who need predictable supplies of both.[46] The failure to meet these challenges is partly rooted in the lack of effective region-wide cooperative structures in Greater Central Asia. This is due in part to fears that Uzbekistan aspires to become a potential regional hegemon.[47]

These various impediments will have adverse long-term effects on Central Asia's development in other sectors. If the present trend continues, with Central Asia serving mainly as a natural resource base for China and Russia, it will erode the region's processing industries and drain capital. China will supply cheap manufactured goods to the detriment of Central Asia's long-term human resource and capacity development. This suggests that China will eventually have to actively promote the development of Central Asia's human resources if it truly seeks stability and prosperity for the region. This is not needed only in Central Asia, but also in Xinjiang, where massive amounts of investment have been devoted to infrastructure, but almost none to human capital, health or education.[48]

Regional energy cooperation

In the energy sector, substantial complementarities promise a lot for the region if energy cooperation is to be promoted. There have been several attempts at bilateral and trilateral energy cooperation, and even some cases of multilateral energy cooperation such as ASEAN+3, the SCO, and the Northeast Asian Economic Forum. A serious problem with these programmes to date is that they do not take into account the interests of all actors, including the national sources of natural resources, the refining points, and the transit countries for oil and gas. Successful integration needs to include all available actors in a truly multilateral forum. There have been several suggestions on how best to accomplish regional cooperation on energy issues.[49] But as yet there are very few actual mechanisms in the region to make such cooperation real. The geostrategic aspect of energy greatly complicate matters, with Moscow, for example, keeping Beijing's proposals for a true 'strategic partnership' in energy at arm's length.[50]

There are no organizations in Eurasia today that have the credibility needed to bring about such cooperation. Most states acknowledge the need for further cooperation. For example, China developed a strategy for energy security in the 1990s called the 'Pan-Asian Continental Oil Bridge' that would link Japan with the Middle East by means of structures that would have been under Chinese control.[51] From a Chinese perspective this was seen as positive, since the regional economies would become tied with one another. Others in the region viewed this as a bold attempt by China to dominate regional markets. Doubtless, any state that controls the energy transit routes would have significant power in the region.

The picture is further complicated by the fact that major external actors would view strengthened energy cooperation on the Eurasian continent with suspicion since it would, over time, integrate participating states both economically and politically. Such a Eurasian energy bloc might decrease the political and economic influence of the European Union, Middle East states, and, most important, the United States.[52] If such a grand project is to succeed, it needs strong external support similar to that which was received during the formative period of the European Coal and Steel Community (ECSC) project. This will also further the interest of the Euro-Atlantic community.

It all boils down to giving both consumers and producers as many options as possible. Energy cooperation and diversified export routes could increase confidence at all levels and reduce Russia's leverage over its former dependants. The construction of the Baku–Tbilisi–Ceyhan pipeline was a landmark in this regard. The trans-Afghan pipeline (Turkmenistan–Afghanistan–Pakistan–India) could open up similar vistas: as a confidence-building measure between India and Pakistan, a symbol of normalization in Afghanistan and a window to the south for Turkmenistan – a state now strongly subject to control from Russia. Just as the Baku–Tbilisi–Ceyhan pipeline would have been financially impossible without Western backing, most of the planned pipelines on the Eurasian continent have similar conditions for realization, often requiring the involvement of China, Russia or both. Although all may not be fully cost-effective, they could all have huge political pay-offs in terms of strengthened sovereignties and better mutual relations.

Russian and US interests in Central Asia: China's role

In order to better measure Beijing's interests in Central Asian states and estimate the SCO's security role, we should also briefly refer to the other two major powers' interests, that is Russia and the United States. Russia, has been making significant inputs in the region since President Putin came to power in the Kremlin in 2000, although the events of 9/11 were no doubt a shock to Russia's presence in Central Asia. The US presence was a major encroachment into Russia's sphere of influence and a rift to the Russian geopolitical posture, as it undermined the concept that Russia was the only power entitled to deploy troops and have military presence in Central Asia. It is noteworthy that, although the United States has not made any explicit commitments to Central Asia security, its military presence *per se* offered a security alternative to the Central Asian states, which had further eclipsed Russia's role in Central Asian security and especially that of the Russian-led Collective Security Treaty Organization (CSTO). It is noteworthy that the Kremlin is fearful for the country's territorial integrity since many Russians explain the presence of American forces in Central Asia as a conspiracy targeting Russia itself. As a prominent scholar of the West has said: 'A loosely confederated Russia – composed of a European Russia, a Siberian Republic, and a Far Eastern Republic – would also find it easier to cultivate closer economic relations with its neighbours'.[53] Notwithstanding, the declining Russia's strategic presence and influence in Central Asia in the wake of Soviet disintegration, as well as the events of 9/11, Russia is still the most deep-rooted power in Central Asia.

Moscow is acutely sensitive to the security situation in Central Asia: this region is adjacent to Russia, the regimes of the five newly independent Commonwealth of Independent States (CIS) are weak, their economies are difficult, and their societies are severely fragmented, which is the soil in which terrorism and extremism grows. No doubt, Russia is interested that Central Asia remains part of its 'backyard' and is prevented from being controlled by another major power. After 9/11, US military deployment in Central Asia to attack Taliban and Al Qaeda forces in Afghanistan was allowed, which eliminated a security threat to Central Asian states but also a significant threat to Russia itself. Much of Russia's post-9/11 activity there, such as the establishment of the Kant airbase, has been interpreted as political balancing again the United States.

In addition to Russia's strong commercial interests in Central Asia, its main economic goal rests in controlling energy outlets taking advantage of its geographic privileges and infrastructure. In this way, the Kremlin maintains its political influence on Central Asia and gains economic benefits from the transportation of the Central Asian energy export. Also, given that ethnic Russians in Central Asia are estimated to be about 6 million, or about 12 per cent of the total population, one of Russia's main policies in Central Asia has been the protection of the rights of the Russian minority and the promotion of equality.

Russia and China are indeed natural partners on energy, which arguably makes up the most important aspect of their relationship. All the major East Asian economic players, China, Japan, South Korea and Taiwan, among others, lack significant oil and gas fields, making the region highly dependent on outside sources for its energy needs. Russia is ideally placed to supply both oil and gas from its huge reserves in the Far East and Siberia. Moreover, Russia is keen to diversify its energy exports following its spat with Ukraine over gas prices in early 2006 and the disorientation, uncertainty and anger that the disruption of supplies provoked among Russia's European customers. Russia and China might not be Western-style democracies, but both are moving towards consumer-oriented societies at a rapid rate. China's recent emphasis on industrial development indicates that the country's energy requirements will increase sharply in the future.

However, East Asia not only lacks oil and gas fields, but also the distribution infrastructure to transport energy to and around the region. This is a difficulty Russia cannot easily overcome, since it lacks transport infrastructure, particularly from deposits in the Far East and Siberia. The total investment needed to develop this infrastructure will run to hundreds of billions of dollars.

During Putin's recent visit in Beijing (March 2006), several major agreements were signed to help alleviate these difficulties. The China National Petroleum Corporation (CNPC) will provide a loan of up to US$400 million to build an oil pipeline from Skovorodino to China, with oil expected to start flowing by the end of 2008, and Russia's pipeline monopoly, Transneft, is partnering with CNPC in conducting a feasibility study on the construction of a branch oil pipeline. The construction of both oil and gas pipelines will be easier now that Russia and China have formally agreed on a demarcation of their 4,300 kilometre (2,500 mile) long common border, settling their long-running border disputes. These developments, however, do not change the fact that Russia has long vacillated on whether to build a pipeline to Japan or China or both, partially because it fears that 'the rise of China' could pose problems to Russia in the future. While these problems are being resolved, all of Russia's oil exports to China will continue to go by rail. In 2004, China imported 12 million tons of crude oil from Russia (10 per cent of its total imports) and expected to import 15 million tons in 2008. Rosneft provides around 70 per cent of Russia's exports to China and is expected to export 8.8 million tons of crude to the country in 2006, almost doubling the 4.5 million tons it exported in 2005.

CNPC and Rosneft have agreed to build a refinery in China, and Gazprom's Sibneft unit plans to sign a deal with China's Sinopec to refine oil in China. CNPC and Rosneft also agreed to undertake joint exploration for new oil deposits in Russia. There has been little geological research since the collapse of the Soviet Union, and geologists suspect that the Russian Far East and Siberia may hold the world's largest undiscovered deposits.

Additionally, Gazprom agreed to a memorandum of understanding with CNPC to build pipelines that will supply China with 60–80 billion cubic metres of gas a year within five years. Gazprom was expected to sign a commercial agreement on the pipeline deal in 2008. Cooperation may also mean swapping pipeline supplies for Chinese cargoes of liquefied natural gas (LNG).

The spring and summer of 2006 saw important developments in the implementation of the agreements signed in March. In April, construction began on the East Siberia–Pacific Ocean oil pipeline, which will pump up to 1.6 million barrels per day from Siberia to Russia's Far East for export to the Asia-Pacific region, particularly China. The first stage of the project will connect Taishet in the Irkutsk region to Skovorodino in the Amur region, scheduled for completion in the second half of 2008.

In a clear sign of the two countries' interpenetration of each other's energy sectors, CNPC bought $500 million worth of Rosneft shares during the Russian firm's July IPO on the London Stock Exchange. In early August, the Chinese Xinhua News Agency quoted a Rosneft official as saying that the company would establish a joint venture with CNPC by the end of the year to produce and market oil products. The joint venture could also take part in bidding for licences to explore and produce oil and natural gas in Eastern Siberia and the Russian Far East. In early August, Rosneft and a subsidiary of Sinopec began drilling an exploratory well on the Sakhalin-3 project under an earlier agreement signed in July 2005 during Chinese president Hu Jintao's Moscow visit.

Another major development in August was the announcement by Russian–British joint venture TNK-BP that it was joining Rosneft in a plan to send Russian oil to China via Kazakhstan. The company had drafted a project to build a special rail reloading facility near Barabinsk rail station in the Novosibirsk region. After arriving at Barabinsk by rail, the crude would be loaded into a special pipeline linked to the larger trunk line running from Omsk in West Siberia to Pavlodar in Kazakhstan. The crude could then be shipped using the export line from Atasu in central Kazakhstan to Alashankou in China's Xinjiang region.

According to Kazakh officials, this pipeline, which is half owned by CNPC, has already been filled with Russian oil. Russia's Lukoil also wants to send oil to China through the new pipeline. China is keen to develop alternative supplies to avoid heavy dependence on Russia, and has also signed an agreement with Turkmenistan to take delivery of natural gas.

In August 2006, China's Deputy Minister of Commerce, Yu Guangzhou, underlined that energy resources were key to bilateral trade and economic cooperation between China and Russia, and stated that China had invested in 700 programmes in Russia up to the end of July with a contracted capital of US$1.34 billion dollars, whereas Russia had started 1,912 companies in China with a contract value of US$1.52 billion and actual investment totalling $570 million. He also said that China would achieve its goal of investing US$12 billion in Russia by 2020.

On the economic and energy front, the two countries are thus recording significant progress, but while bilateral cooperation is eminently natural and sensible, both countries face major strategic problems in their future geopolitical relations with each other.

Energy security in Eurasia

Today, China, Japan and Russia are competing for influence and market shares internationally, and such rivalry is most intense in Central and Northeast Asia. The competition we are presently witnessing has been accentuated by a lack of trust between the different actors due to their age-old military and political conflicts with one another. Meanwhile, the smaller actors in Eurasia, especially in Central Asia, have their own agenda aimed at diluting the influence of the major actors in the region and preventing domination by specific actors, such as Russia, in Central Asia. This potentially explosive situation is compounded by the fact that the states in Northeast Asia are increasingly facing a perceived energy crisis due to increased competition over energy resources and high energy costs. A growing number of policy-makers are beginning to believe that an energy crisis or an intense struggle over resources is imminent. This sense of emergency is created by the lack of cooperative structures in the field of energy and because of the intense competitive behaviour between the states seeking energy security, especially China and Japan.

Within Eurasia, Russia and Central Asia have significant amounts of oil and gas they would like to export but they have been using their resources as political leverage, which in turn contributes to zero-sum thinking among energy-hungry China and Japan. For Northeast Asia, the failure to integrate and cooperate on energy issues has thus resulted in higher energy prices, reliance on Middle Eastern oil and dependence on sea lines of communications (SLOCs) for transportation of oil to Northeast Asia, not to mention greater rivalry.[54]

Meanwhile, the Russians, while being heavily courted by both China and Japan for its Far Eastern energy resources have been wary of both. Russia is concerned that the demographically and economically rising China would overwhelm the Russian Far East, which is suffering from a huge population decline. During the late 1990s, a weakened Russia needed China to maintain international relevance while China considered Russia as a potential junior ally. By 2004, the reverse has happened with Russia seeing China as a potential threat to its Far Eastern interest while China sees Russia as its route to energy security.[55]

Russia's relationship with Japan is also not without hitches. There is also a leftover sense of historical distrust over the Japanese occupation of Siberia in the early twentieth century. Furthermore, territorial disputes between Russia and Japan over the Kuril Islands north of Japan, which the Soviets seized at the end of the Second World War, remain a prickly issue between both sides.[56]

South Korea is also entering into the energy competition arena. In 2004, South Korean and Russian firms signed US$4 billion worth of energy contracts, most of them focused on oil.

Overall, in Northeast Asia the segregation of the region is making the quest for energy security a zero-sum game played out mainly among Japan,

China and Russia on a bilateral basis. It is important to note that these three countries have all been at war with each other at some point in history.

The 'rise of China' is no less worrying to Russia than it is to the United States, Japan and China's other Asian neighbours, but this is hardly a new problem. Despite the howls of protest from the Russian media and politicians about the North Atlantic Treaty Organization's (NATO) eastward expansion in the early 1990s, the Russian Ministry of Foreign Affairs was, at the time, even more concerned about China because of the influx of Chinese shuttle traders into the sparsely populated Far East region, whose population of some 6 million stands in stark contrast to the 110 million Chinese just across the border. Since then, however, the problem has become more acute. China's economy is now twice as large as Russia's, and it is growing at 8–10 per cent per annum compared with Russia's more modest rate of 6–7 per cent, differences that, over the long term, will increase the current economic disparity even further and thus reduce Russia's relative political power.

Moscow is therefore concerned about exporting energy and arms as well to a country that is likely to become a global power in the future and could potentially pose a major challenge to Russia's own position internationally.

In order to balance this challenge, Russia hopes to become a more powerful Pacific player by developing its energy resources in the Far East and increasing its energy exports to the region. Russia is by no means focused exclusively on China and is seeking additional Asia-Pacific customers. For example, at the annual meeting of the six-nation SCO in June 2006, Putin announced that 'creating a SCO energy club is a pressing issue, as is more intensive cooperation in transport and communications'.

For its part, China not only needs to increase its energy imports, but needs to diversify its supply, partially because 80 per cent of its oil imports at the moment pass through the Straits of Malacca. Again, this situation is not really new. Japan has virtually no oil or gas either and has thus been highly dependent on nuclear energy and Middle Eastern oil for decades. But, until the global economy becomes far less dependent on hydrocarbons for energy, China and the rest of East Asia will remain vulnerable to pressure from suppliers, including Russia.

Managing this situation and their relationship with each other will present Russia and China with some of their most important strategic tasks in the decades ahead. Both countries are likely to avoid too much dependence, and thus reduce risk, but both stand to reap huge benefits if they adopt an approach based more on economic cooperation and less on great power competition.

In contrast to Russia and China, the US strategic presence is remarkable given the natural limitation of the US–Central Asian relation. US attention increased from the mid-1990s, mainly because of the evolving shape of US–Russian relations, the rise of the Taliban in Afghanistan, and increased fears of Central Asian instability. Over time, the United States began to increase its political, economic and military inputs, encouraged Central Asian states to cooperate without the economic involvement of Moscow, and promoted the construction of the Baku–Tbilisi–Ceyhan oil pipeline to break Russia's control of the Central Asian energy export.

9/11 was a turning point in the fight against terrorism and religious extremism in Central Asia. With the emergence of Afghanistan as the epicentre of international terrorism and religious extremism, an international endeavour to fight this challenge became inevitable. This needed coordination and cooperation from all states in the region and beyond. Russia had been facing challenges and threats to its territorial integrity from its southern Autonomous Republic of Chechnya for quite some time. There, Chechen extremists with connections to their Afghan counterparts, have been waging a war against Moscow for a separate Chechen Islamic Republic. It was based on this backdrop that Moscow extended support to Operation Enduring Freedom. Although China has supported the US-led war against terrorism, it suspects that Western countries, especially the United States, has a hidden agenda for control of the natural resources of Central Asia and would like to encircle China from the western flank. The presence of the US military at Ganci airbase near Manas airport in Kyrgyzstan, just 200 kilometres from the Chinese border has further strengthened these fears. The unilateral military action by the United States and its allies against Iraq in 2003 is perceived by China as an assertion of unipolarity.

NATO's 'eastward enlargement' is another factor that has influenced Beijing's policy initiatives in Central Asia. It was expected that NATO would cease to exist after the end of the Cold War. However, Washington, along with its allies, decided to enlarge it by including new members from Eastern Europe. This enlargement is aimed at promoting democracy, human rights and civil society in the former Soviet political space. New democratic systems are projected as capable of addressing problems created by instability, transition and rising expectations.

A series of 'Color Revolutions' – the 'Rose Revolution' in Georgia in 2003, the 'Orange Revolution' in Ukraine in 2004 and the 'Tulip Revolution' in the Kyrgyz Republic in March 2005 – in the wake of rigged parliamentary and presidential elections created uneasiness in Beijing. These developments increased China's concerns about Uyghur restlessness being externally exploited.[57] China and Russia extended full support to Uzbek President Islam Karimov for his handling of the Andijon events of May 2005, and China was the first country visited by President Karimov after Andijon. The visit helped the Uzbek government face mounting international pressure for an international enquiry into the events in Andijon. An assessment emerged that the 'Color Revolutions' violated the sovereignty and threatened the legitimate governments of the Central Asian Republics. They also provided an opportunity for terrorist and extremist forces to manipulate the situation in their favour.[58]

China and Russia also have common interests regarding US efforts to promote democratic transformation in Central Asia. Both want to contain

US influence in the region and address non-traditional threats to security and stability. Instability in the region will have wide ramifications for both Russia and China because of the region's geographical proximity. This is addressed in the Treaty of Good Neighbourliness, Friendship and Cooperation signed by both countries in 2001.

The quest for energy security is also transforming China's engagement in Central Asia. China wants to reduce its dependency on West Asian (Middle Eastern) oil. If a conflict erupts over Taiwan, current oil supply lines would be seriously affected. China is working on new gas and oil pipelines connecting the Central Asian Republics to its pipeline network in Xinjiang. Projects are also under way for a network of roads and rail lines that connect China's west to Russia, Europe and West Asia.

Clearly, China's interests in Central Asia have widened from stability at the borders to encompass energy security, geopolitics and combating extremists, terrorists, as well as 'nationalist/separatist' forces.

For the present, counter-terrorism is also the primary interest of the United States as they view regional security in Central Asia as part and parcel with the so-called War on Terrorism. This policy is in fact a more robust continuation of the original US Central Asia engagement plan that included support for the Central Asian peacekeeping battalion (CENTRASBAT), combined training exercises and NATO's Partnership for Peace Programme (PfP) in the region. In addition to counter-terrorism, the strategic control of the Caspian energy as the world's most probable candidate for future energy extraction remains high on the American agenda.

Equally important is the geopolitical intention of the United States hidden behind its military presence in Central Asia. The abrupt US military presence in the name of counter-terrorism is to Russia an intrusion into its traditional sphere of influence and to China an intrusion into its strategic rear. In this way, it serves to monitor and constrain China, preventing Russia from restoring its control of Central Asia, propping up Central Asian independence from Russia and restricting Iran's influence in the region.

The new US presence has temporarily lessened the Central Asian states' dependence on their two larger neighbours. However, it is unclear whether future American economic and strategic interests will translate into direct support for these states in their fight against Islamist groups. Thus, the fact that no Central Asian state has pulled out of the group, signifies that their leaders believe that Russia and China are the best guarantee for regional security in light of the uncertainty hovering over the future presence of the United States in the region.

So, although the international community's focus on Islamist terrorism in the aftermath of 9/11 and the current war on terrorism has given the United States, which has traditionally been excluded from Central Asia, a key foothold in establishing its influence in the region, Washington holds only two primary aims in the area: first, develop Central Asia's rich oil and gas reserves; second, gain tactical ground to observe nearby political developments, especially in South Asia in shaping Indian–Pakistani relations. A US-controlled oil and gas pipeline running from Central Asia through Pakistan and India can bring much needed revenue to these states and the United States greater influence over the peace process in the subcontinent.

2 Shanghai Cooperation Organization

Security role in Eurasia

In addition to bilateral ties with Central Asian states, Moscow is paying increasing attention to regional organizations, including the Collective Security Treaty Organization (CSTO), Eurasian Economic Community (EURASEC) and the Shanghai Cooperation Organization (SCO). Russia's role in these organizations is not so much as facilitator of integration, normsetter or even 'banker', although Russia provides most of the funds for the CSTO. Instead, in many cases, Russia acts as a shock absorber, which helps to reduce or manage tensions between regional states and to promote the identity of Central Asia as a post-Soviet region (in contrast, for example, with the American vision of a 'Wider Central Asia', which would be part of South Asia rather than post-Soviet space).

Russia's participation in regional organizations has one important impact on its policies: in these multilateral formats Russia is increasingly confronted with the need to move away from unilateral leadership, shaped by a domination model, which was prevalent in its policies throughout the 1990s and even in the early Putin presidency, and to accept power-sharing as its new *modus vivendi*, with the rising regional powers, like Kazakhstan, and with powerful external players in the region. This power-sharing model was first tested within the SCO, which over the years, dating back to the SCO's predecessor, the Shanghai-Five Process, kept Russia engaged in Central Asia and helped to define Russia's agenda in the region while providing confidence-building and transparency in its relations with China in Central Asia. The SCO stands alone as the only organization in post-Soviet Eurasia to which Russia belongs without being a dominant leader or even the most powerful member. Instead, it has been following the agenda set mainly by China and increasingly by the Central Asian states themselves. Russia has been surprised by the fast pace at which the SCO has gained influence in regional affairs. As the SCO develops, Russia is constantly reassessing its attitudes towards the organization and its role among all the policy instruments available to Russia in the region.

There are a number of issues that both help explain the importance of the SCO for Russia and also raise questions as to the impact of the SCO's evolution on Russia's ability to secure its interests in Central Asia. In analysing these issues, however, one must bear in mind that Russia has yet to clearly articulate its interests and objectives in the SCO and strategies on how to achieve them.

It would be wiser to tackle things from the beginning. In 1996, when Beijing, in order to better serve its interests in Central Asia, inspired the 'Shanghai Five', a mechanism created in 1996 for settling border disputes between China, Russia, Kazakhstan, Kyrgyzstan and Tajikistan and protecting the security of each nation. As this mechanism was transformed in 2001 into a more permanent regional cooperation organization, the Shanghai Cooperation Organization (SCO), China acquired a security protection mechanism, an established channel for China to participate and maintain a dynamic and evolving posture in Central Asian affairs, and a platform to cooperate with Central Asian countries comprehensively. SCO institutionalization also reflected a strategic compromise and balance of interests reached between Russia and China as far as Central Asia is concerned, paving the way for mutual recognition of interests and strategic cooperation.

The SCO could evolve into a promising framework for building tighter trade, investment, cultural, environmental and technological relations between its member states. It would then become 'the region's authoritative voice'.[1] But this would require that the SCO operates as a legitimate vehicle for the collective interests of its members rather than as an organ dominated or directed by one or two states. In fact, the SCO was inspired to be a synergistic tool of Russian and Chinese foreign policy, a vessel by which these two powers could court Central Asian states into steadily growing military and economic relations while simultaneously coordinating policies to crush internal threats like militant Islamic movements. Russia and China want to use the SCO to eventually build a new regional security architecture that reinforces each other's territorial integrity while at the same time retrenching Western influence.[2] The leaders of the Central Asian states accepted the strategic Sino–Russian dominance over their region in order to gain support for their harsh domestic policies of severely repressing religious and political opposition movements.

Nevertheless, this didn't come without reward. By 2004 China had invested US$4 billion in Central Asia, excluding Kazakhstan.[3] Under the SCO umbrella, Beijing has set aside a credit of US$900 million for Kazakhstan, Kyrgyzstan, Tajikistan and Uzbekistan.[4] China has also brought Iran, Pakistan and India on board the SCO as observers. China has recently sealed a US$100 billion deal to develop Iran's giant Yadavaran oilfield near the Iran–Iraq border.[5] Besides Iran, Pakistan is another nation that is of key importance to China, especially for its strategic transit advantage, both land and maritime. In fact, Pakistan is China's 'Silk Route' to energy-rich and trade-hungry Central Asia, access to which Pakistan denies India despite persistent US intercession on the latter's behalf. In Southeast Asia, Pakistan is also China's bridge to Beijing-wary Indonesia, Malaysia and energy-rich

Brunei, all nations with predominantly Islamic populations. Beijing's major concern, however, is the Strait of Malacca, which is patrolled by Jakarta and Kuala Lumpur and through which three-quarters of Beijing's oil imports pass. Pakistan plays an indispensable role as an Islamic ambassador of good will for Beijing among Muslim-majority nations of Southeast and Central Asia.

The SCO's role in the Eurasian security balance

The motives underpinning the establishment of the SCO on the threshold of the twenty-first century included as already mentioned unprecedented achievements in settling the longstanding disputes along the 7000-kilometre border between China and the Soviet Union and its successor states; the successful implementation of confidence and security-building measures (CSBMs) in the border areas;[6] and recognition of the need for a more coherent response to regional security and economic development challenges generally.

The central distinctive feature of the SCO as a regional cooperation and security framework is that it enables Central Asian states, at least formally, to take part in generating regional approaches to cooperation and security on an equal basis with the larger regional powers. It is an opportunity that Central Asia has not had before in modern times. Even such prominent structures as the Organization for Security and Co-operation in Europe (OSCE), of which Central Asian countries are members, have been less appealing to the leaders of the states of the region. This is primarily because of a general lack of interest in the region in the OSCE and the local authorities' ambivalence over the prominent goals of democratization that are embedded in its agenda. Moreover, the pan-European security approach of the OSCE is perceived to be of little use for Central Asia, since it does not focus on regional ills specifically. It is also relevant that every other regional security or economic cooperation initiative excludes China,[7] although the country's growing significance for the region is beyond question.

Participation in consensus-based multilateral decision-making potentially elevates Central Asian foreign policy to a qualitatively new level after a period characterized by lack of focus and discipline or, to be more exact, reactiveness. On the face of it, regional cooperation in such a framework could have numerous benefits in terms of economic development and of establishing a more efficient security arrangement to fill the vacuum left after the collapse of the Soviet Union. Simultaneously, Central Asia is exposed to the potential dangers of falling into the orbit of Chinese or Russian domination at a time when China and Russia have tense relations with the West over both internal governance and foreign policy issues. This unique mix of prospects and challenges is one of the major elements that heightens the significance of the SCO as an actor in the international arena.

The fact that the SCO unites mainly non-democratic regimes (including the observer states, with the exception of India) has not failed to be noted and is one of the core reasons for the preoccupation in the West with the future of this new organization. As seen locally, the SCO's political agenda is not 'burdened' with democratization and human rights issues. Rather, it is predicated on diversity in patterns of political development and on the creation of an environment where states are free to pursue their respective internal models independently.[8]

It is clear that, in their interaction with large powers such as China and Russia, the states of Central Asia are significantly influenced by these two regional powers' agendas. On the other hand, the smaller powers of the SCO are still able to outline their national interests and security and economic concerns, and to articulate them within the frameworks provided by the organization. Given that the pivotal membership of both China and Russia in the SCO leads these two states constantly to seek common ground on a variety of issues, the role of the Central Asian members in the organization could be seen as an important potential feature of balance (a) internally in relation to the regional interests and broader aspirations that the large states seek to further through the SCO, and (b) externally in complementing or offsetting the impact of the SCO on the region's general international orientation.

An important starting point for exploring this issue is that the terms of SCO membership do not directly limit the Central Asian states' freedom to participate, together with non-SCO members, in other initiatives, programmes and undertakings aimed at establishing security and cooperation in the region. This is crucially important for the local states themselves, since the freedom to implement security policies with different partners maximizes the chances of building themselves a more effective, overarching security and development framework for the longer term. While further developing the substance of multilateral efforts for security, such varied relationships can also give Central Asian countries a certain leverage for maintaining more independent positions when interacting with the larger powers of the SCO. Perhaps the most evident example of this kind of Central Asian 'balancing' is NATO's Partnership for Peace (PfP) programme, in which all the Central Asian states participate.[9] There are, however, several other, no less significant undertakings, projects and organizations that strengthen the case: including the Central Asian military facilities currently used by troops of the US-led anti-terrorism coalition; the foreign military financing provided to local states by the US Department of State, and bilateral military-to-military training and exchanges; the OSCE's law enforcement training programmes; and efforts for technical interoperability between local defence structures and the West.[10] In addition, there are independent security initiatives taken by the Central Asian states such as the Conference on Interaction and Confidence-building measures in Asia (CICA) and the establishment of stronger ties with other outside actors not previously involved in cooperation with the region.[11] India, for instance, has been actively seeking ways to foster bilateral cooperation with Central Asian states, especially those that are viewed as potential energy suppliers.

The barely concealed internal contradictions within the SCO leave little room for the organization to evolve into a strong institutionalized alliance like NATO.[12] Although most analysts have supported this judgement with reference to underlying Sino–Russian tensions, there have been hints that implicit 'red lines' defined by at least some Central Asian states have also placed important limitations on the larger powers' ambitions. The fact that at least three countries of Central Asia either have established or plan to establish strategic partnerships with the United States is evidence enough; in fact, some Western military presence can be observed in all Central Asian states. Consideration of these facts should at least alleviate some mis-understandings about the intrinsic purpose and nature of the SCO as well as its current and potential evolution.

Uzbekistan was an ally, or 'strategic partner', of the United States until the May 2005 bloodshed in Andijan. A Declaration on Strategic Partnership and Cooperation Framework between the two states was concluded in 2002, just nine months after Uzbek President Islam Karimov had signed the founding documents of the SCO.[13] Kyrgyzstan, although a member of the SCO, still hosts a military base for the US-led anti-terrorism coalition forces. In spite of the fact that Kyrgyz President Kurmanbek Bakiev supported the often-cited SCO Astana Declaration of 5 July 2005 on scheduling the with-drawal of the US military from the region.[14] Kyrgyzstan reached an agree-ment with the United States in July 2006 on the further deployment of troops and facilities in support of Operation Enduring Freedom in Afghanistan, with no change of conditions for the continuing US military presence other than financial terms. More generally, the two states have maintained their friendly relations and mutual understanding on security matters.[15] In retrospect, the fact that Kyrgyzstan supported the Astana Declaration, implying closure of the US military base at Manas, may be seen as an example of *ad hoc* policy manoeuvring by weaker Central Asian states when confronted with pressure from larger powers in foreign policy matters. As later revealed by Bakiev, the initiative to adopt the headline-grabbing Astana Declaration came from none other than the President of the Russian Federation, Vladimir Putin.[16]

Kazakhstan's Foreign Minister, Kassymzhomart Tokayev, stated in an August 2006 interview in *The Washington Times* that 'the United States and Kazakhstan hope to sign a wide-ranging 'strategic partnership' accord when President Nursultan Nazarbaev travels to Washington in September.[17] This is hardly consistent with the interpretation of the SCO as an anti-West bloc, especially considering that Kazakhstan is the third largest SCO member and sits on significant energy reserves. Kazakhstan has also contributed person-nel for US-led coalition forces in Iraq. By sending 27 troops of the Kazakh peacekeeping battalion (KAZBAT).[18] as a part of the international peace-keeping operation in Iraq with a mandate to carry out humanitarian activ-ities, Kazakhstan signalled the emergence of a new Central Asian component in the political paradigms of the SCO – particularly symbolic given China's and Russia's clear disapproval of any involvement by their purported 'satellites' in the Iraq venture. Furthermore, in January 2006 an Individual Partnership Action Plan between Kazakhstan and NATO was finalized for ratification.[19] Kazakhstan thus became the first Central Asian state to assume the full status of a NATO partner country.[20]

An important general factor is that, in contrast to the CSTO or NATO, the SCO legal framework and foundations do not provide for collective defence against external aggression, and even less for the projection of military force.[21] According to Richard Weitz, the SCO 'lacks the internal cohesion and capabilities found in strong multilateral security institutions such as NATO'[22] Indeed, military cooperation is probably the most limited field of development within the SCO framework compared with border, law enforcement and anti-terrorism cooperation (although the last of these is hardly fully developed either). It is even difficult to imagine the SCO developing into a group that would move towards a military alliance at a later stage given the fact that China, the informal lead player in the SCO, has a formal stated position (and good practical reasons) to avoid such commitments. All the Central Asian states and their leaders share this position in practice, even if this is not always clearly articulated, because forming a military alliance would mean the end of their multi-vector external policy.[23]

The concern about a 'NATO of the East' being formed in Asia thus seems unfounded. In any case, the concern is odd because of the way that NATO's own agenda has been evolving to meet the challenges of a new world 'without dividing lines', profiling the alliance increasingly as a contributor to stability and security on a global level and for the general good. This makes it hard to argue that the creation of an organization that genuinely pursued similar goals from an Asian base should be feared per se. Such reasoning would be a reversion to the zero-sum East–West calculations of the cold war, from which NATO's own doctrine has consciously distanced itself. Rather, today's challenge for policy-makers is to see whether and how Western, Asian and other security initiatives can complement each other – and it would suit no one better than the Central Asian states if that vision of new modes of cooperation could be made real in the specific case of the SCO.[24] In this context it is worth noting that a majority of the SCO's practical activities and plans have reflected substantive priorities that resemble or echo, rather than contradict, generally accepted Western policy aims: for example, anti-terrorist exercises on the territory of Central Asian states, measures for countering trans-border crime and for border protection, high-level diplomatic contacts and other confidence-building measures, and other practical cooperation projects between the member states. There are, of course, exceptions, such as the joint military manoeuvres held by China and Russia in 2005,[25] which were difficult to see as a genuine 'counter-terrorism' exercise, even though it was called that. In fact, Chinese and Russian motives had more to do with signalling to the United States that it should not interfere militarily and strategically in what Moscow and Beijing perceive as their own sphere of influence. This exercise, however, was held outside the multilateral framework of the SCO proper.

Another aspect of balancing in the development of the SCO that is important for Central Asian agendas concerns the delicate interface between the SCO's regional endeavours and the aspirations of the larger members to project influence beyond regional borders. The broader role of the SCO as an instrument for the latter is more appealing for China and Russia than it is for their smaller neighbours, for obvious reasons that are closely linked with both of these two large states' belief in a multi-polar world and with the general dynamics of Chinese–Russian–US relations. As the larger members of the SCO struggle to increase their influence in the world as 'old' or 'emerging' power centres, they are impelled to bring more and more international aspects into the activity of the SCO.

Central Asian states SCO security policy

As one symptom of this larger vision, the SCO has sometimes clearly expressed an underlying goal to outbid other national or institutional players seeking influence in the region. The Fifth Anniversary Declaration of the SCO points out that 'What specific means and mechanisms should be adopted to safeguard security of the region is the right and responsibility of countries in the region' to choose, This would seem to identify the SCO as an attempt by its member states to build an independent regional approach to security and development, not dependent on Western guidance or protection schemes. At the same time, however, it may reflect a more positive realization by the regional powers and Central Asian states of the need to continue seeking and generating new multilateral security and development models for the area. The emphasis on 'independence' as a principle for tackling issues of regional security, economic development and cooperation can also be seen as a logical desire for policies and mechanisms that would accurately and effectively address the unique challenges faced by SCO members. Among other things, this could provide some excuse for the SCO's repeated refusal of observer status for the United States, which has elsewhere been viewed as a signal of 'anti-Western' orientation.

The Central Asian states themselves are clearly most interested in the SCO's practical undertakings for regional security and development such as confidence building, anti-terrorism activity, fighting drug trafficking and securing borders, trade and economic cooperation, investment projects, rehabilitation of transportation networks and exploitation of transit potential. Various Central Asian member states have made efforts, although never in a common front, to keep the SCO agenda focused on addressing these types of local challenge. On the other hand, the two larger SCO members and especially Russia have as one of their goals the prevention of the emergence of any kind of purely Central Asian cooperation framework in the area. One of the notorious examples is Russia's success in merging the Central Asian

Cooperation Organization (CACO) – the only exclusively Central Asian multilateral project to date – with the Eurasian Economic Community (EAEC), which is dominated by Russia in practice.[26]

Perhaps the most overt example of Central Asian agenda balancing comes from Kazakhstan, which has in general been successful in avoiding excessively intimate relations with either the West or China and Russia. Kazakh Foreign Minister Tokayev stated in a speech in July 2006 that, 'as an active member, Kazakhstan would work to keep the SCO a universal and well-balanced organization', thus implicitly assuring the United States that his nation would prevent China and Russia from generating anti-US policies in the SCO.[27] Although Kazakhstan's rich energy reserves help it to balance between the interests of major actors, a consistent approach to securing national interests is what has principally allowed the country to keep room for manoeuvre and to move towards the category of an independent international player rather than 'just' a post-Soviet state. Admittedly, the concessions to Kazakhstan made by important international stakeholders in pursuit of economic gains have also maintained a comfortable setting for President Nazarbaev's far from democratic internal policies.

Other Central Asian states have taken a less clear and consistent stance in defining the kinds of balance they seek by lobbying both in the SCO and elsewhere. The relative economic weakness of Kyrgyzstan, Tajikistan and Uzbekistan pushes them all towards a reactive foreign policy, with Uzbekistan in particular swinging from one extreme of alignment to another, depending on the changing context. However, another important reason why these three states fail to generate a more or less consistent stance is their shared preoccupation with sustaining current leadership regimes. There are some hopes that further economic development may help to overcome the syndrome of a short-sighted foreign policy and result in a liberalization of the domestic political situation in these states. It may be noted that in the July 2006 speech mentioned above the Kazakh Foreign Minister also spoke for many in the Central Asian political elites when he said that 'it is important to achieve success in the economic area and then to build up a solid middle class, which will serve as a pillar for democracy'.[28]

In sum, the so-called multi-vector foreign policy of Central Asian leaders has allowed them to manoeuvre between the interests of big powers, albeit rather ineptly, resulting in a very mixed pattern of international engagement in security and cooperation schemes in the region. At present, this suits the desire of Central Asian political elites to derive benefits from as many actors as possible while preserving the status quo in their respective countries. Although such an approach gives them flexibility to accommodate new drivers, such as the 'necessity to cultivate a solid middle class' or the emergence of new threats, it brings significant and cumulative dangers because it makes their foreign policy so tactical in nature, and thus highly sensitive to the slightest changes occurring in the region. Against this background one merit of the Central Asian states' participation in the SCO might be to help them develop more strategic approaches to various issues, especially to those agendas that are shared by larger powers within the SCO and beyond.

The security vision of the SCO is focused largely on Central Asia since it is seen as the region that is most vulnerable to threats of terrorism and extremism, both external and internal. Not only has this been made clear at the purely theoretical level, but the same message has been repeatedly conveyed in statements by member states concerning the crucial need for security building in the region. Various anti-terrorism training programmes and exercises, military-to-military contacts and intelligence links have been developed to help Central Asian states protect themselves from new threats and enable them to act effectively within a multilateral framework. Although it is clear that the two largest member states are concerned primarily with their own security, there is also an understanding among the SCO members that broader security can be served by protecting the most vulnerable links in the region. This coincidence of interest has not always been seen so clearly in the past, when the larger states seemed more inclined to contain the sources of danger within Central Asia so as to stop them spreading into their own respective territories.

Another important change, perceived especially since the 2002 Chinese–Kyrgyz joint anti-terrorism exercise, is that the Central Asian countries and larger states have rapidly moved from a pattern of bilateral interactions to using multilateral channels in the SCO.

Although bilateral relations with Russia remain important for some Central Asian states and Moscow-centricity still dominates the thinking of political elites brought up in the former Soviet system, it is difficult to overestimate the importance of any shift in this direction. In relations between such plainly asymmetrical powers – and as Russia's European and China's Southeast Asian neighbours have also found – a multilateral framework for security relations gives any individual smaller state the best prospects of preserving a more or less independent position.[29] No previous initiative or development since the Central Asian states obtained their independence had made real strides towards multilateralism, but even a cursory review of security cooperation in the region shows a trend for the defence- and security-related undertakings of the SCO to become more systematic and coherent in nature. Meetings of heads of law enforcement bodies, public prosecutors, customs authorities and ministers of defence are all designed to strengthen mutual cooperation and reciprocity between member states in the relevant spheres. A particularly striking step was the establishment of the SCO Regional Anti-Terrorism Structure (RATS) at Tashkent in 2004 as a permanent body of the organization, designed to coordinate the activity of member states' law enforcement agencies in combating terrorism, extremism and separatism. The decision to create such a structure was actually made as far back as the 2002 St Petersburg SCO summit, signalling that multilateral anti-terrorism activity was one of the driving forces for the SCO from the start.

In the SCO's first five years, Central Asian states hosted and participated in several anti-terrorist exercises under the auspices of the SCO security-building and anti-terrorism efforts. The first such joint anti-terrorism exercise was held in 2003, with phases in China and Kazakhstan and with the underlying aim of preventing Uyghur separatist operatives from crossing the border into Kazakhstan and using its territory to launch attacks against China.[30] (Uyghur separatists have been using this tactic for a long time, thus causing tensions in Sino–Kazakh relations.[31]) More broadly, however, this exercise was designed as a significant step towards strengthening security cooperation and confidence between China and bordering Central Asian states. Significantly, the exercise was multilateral, with almost all the SCO member states participating,[32] thus ensuring a broader involvement of the smaller states in anti-terrorism efforts.

On the eve of the SCO anniversary summit of July 2006, another multi-lateral anti-terrorism exercise was carried out on the territories of Kyrgyzstan, Tajikistan and Uzbekistan. The 'Vostok–Antiterror 2006' exercise was reportedly aimed at preventing terrorists from undermining stability in the countries concerned by attacking the strategic infrastructure. Administered by RATS, the exercise has been widely praised by SCO members, although objective external assessment is hampered by lack of information. More attention has generally been paid to the geopolitical repercussions of the occasion, since it symbolized Uzbekistan's return to the Chinese and Russian security camp after a falling-out with the United States.[33] At the fifth anniversary summit of the SCO, President Putin proposed another multilateral anti-terrorism exercise to be conducted in Russia in 2007. The exercise, which has become an annual tradition, was carried out in the southern Urals and was successful.

Since the issue of multilateral responses to trans-border crime, extremism and insurgency has been so central to the SCO enterprise, the general features of this cooperation and the issues it raises are worth reviewing here – although more specific details are addressed in the next section, on Central Asian interests. Although the outside world may sometimes suspect that concerns about instability in Central Asia have been exaggerated by authoritarian leaders to protect their own interests, there can be no serious grounds for doubting that the security challenges faced by the region are both real and substantial.

Under the pressure of declining economic and social conditions in some parts of Central Asia, the threat of radical movements that use terror as an instrument for achieving political goals has increased considerably. To take some examples that, although scattered and small in scale, give an accurate impression of the fragility of the environment: there has been evidence that operatives of the Islamic Movement of Uzbekistan (IMU) participated in the insurgency of 1999 in the Batken area of Kyrgyzistan, a series of terrorist attacks in Uzbekistan in 1999, the attempt in 2004 to assassinate Uzbek President Karimov, persistent post-civil war instability in Tajikistan, and the growing activity of Hizb-ut-Tahrir in the Ferghana Valley. Admittedly, the intensification of these internal security challenges could also be seen as the fruits of the oppressive authoritarian regimes in Central Asia combined with socio-economic inequality. Whatever their source, however, they create tangible dangers for stability in a region where ethnic tensions, resource management problems, poverty and unemployment are always present to aggravate the impact of any breach of order.

The case of the Ferghana Valley is one that particularly underlines the need for a more-than-national approach. This subregion is artificially divided between Kyrgyzstan, Tajikistan and Uzbekistan, splitting up its once integrated economic and social system in a way that accounts for much of the local turbulence and makes it a fertile area for Hizb-ut-Tahrir and similar extremist movements. If neglected, the valley could turn into a chronic cradle of terrorism, extremism and more general social unrest. Conversely, failure to make progress in normalizing security conditions in this case – and in other unstable cross-border communities – stands in the way of any positive effort by the region's states to develop the economy of such border regions through free cooperation, not to mention outside investment.

In face of these challenges, the Central Asian nations' defence and military establishments have witnessed a general decline since 1990, leaving the states barely capable of countering even a limited insurgency on their territories.[34] For example, during the IMU insurgency in the Batken oblast of Kyrgyzstan in 1999, the national armed forces were barely able to mobilize owing to dysfunctional coordination among units. Another example is the small-scale insurgency of six terrorists in mid-May 2006, which took Kyrgyz border and law enforcement agencies a lot of resources and time to neutralize, eventually leaving four Kyrgyz law enforcement officers dead and nine wounded.[35] This tragic event showed again how insecure and weak Central Asian establishments can be when facing even minor acts of terrorism. Closer cooperation between Central Asian countries should, in principle, be one of the most obvious ways to ease this problem, particularly in relation to transnational and trans-border crime.

Another reason for promoting close cooperation between Central Asian states is provided by the natural and political environment: its weak border security and inaccessible landscapes foster trans-border menaces, and the states generally lack good preventive policies. RATS, with its aim of developing and systematizing cooperation between law enforcement, border and intelligence agencies, provides a promising platform for countering manifestations of the new threats but also for confronting their underlying causes. Impressive results have been reported from the activity of RATS within the short period of two years since its creation. An official RATS report claims that 263 acts of terrorism and trans-border crime were prevented in the SCO area in 2005. However, the remit of RATS is not confined to active counterterrorism, and a good deal of its activity has been devoted to encouraging better information exchange, compiling intelligence data, and studying the root causes of terrorism, extremism and separatism.

At a meeting between Presidents Bakiev and Karimov in Moscow in early 2006, the leaders discussed progress and future cooperation between Kyrgyzstan and Uzbekistan in jointly combating new threats. They noted that closer cooperation had contributed significantly to recent successes in the Djalal-Abad oblast of Kyrgyzstan. Special forces there neutralized a group of extremists, some of whom are supposedly connected to the turmoil and bloodshed in Andijan, Uzbekistan, in May 2005. Although praised by the two leaders, however, the operations in question are reported to have resulted in dissent among local populations. Representatives of the Uzbek minority of Kyrgyzstan claim that they constituted a governmental crackdown on opposition and freedom of religion under the cover of a crackdown on terrorism. What is indisputable is that the two countries' leaders saw the episode as a crucial step towards normalization of Kyrgyz–Uzbek relations, which had deteriorated significantly after Kyrgyzstan handed over refugees from the Andijan incident to the UN High Commissioner for Refugees.

The SCO's security role in relation to Central Asian interests has often been seen by outsiders as a venture focused narrowly on the forceful suppression of certain surface manifestations of non-state activity, including some activities that would be considered legitimate elsewhere, as well as actual cases of terrorism and trans-border crime. There are some signs that this may be too simplistic a view. Anti-terrorism and conflict avoidance in Central Asia are, after all, in the interests of many outside actors as well, and the SCO has expressed – or at least indicated – its willingness to work more closely with other organizations, such as NATO, the OSCE and the European Union (EU), for a truly multilateral security framework comprising both interstate and inter-institutional coordination. At best, such overtures could be seen as opening a window for a higher level of dialogue and coordination in security-related areas – not limited to the methods of traditional, bilateral, 'great game' politics – between the East and the West in Central Asia.[36] More importantly, there are indications that some within SCO circles have grasped the need for a new, more comprehensive approach to security and anti-terrorism strategy. In his speech at the 2006 SCO anniversary summit, President Bakiev of Kyrgyzstan said that providing and maintaining security in the region should remain the prime long-term objective, but also that it should be achieved through increasing the well-being of the people.[37]

The contribution of the Central Asian countries to carving out this new approach is often underestimated by observers who assume that their agenda is totally dictated by policies made in Moscow and Beijing. The Central Asian practice of multi-vector foreign policy tends, in fact, to stimulate the emergence of more comprehensive approaches to security even when this is not the leaders' intention, simply because drawing in more outside actors also means bringing in their different security visions and priorities. Accordingly, it might be a mistake to underplay the potential that the direct ties between Central Asian member states and Western security organizations have for influencing the further evolution of the SCO itself into a constructive security partner.[38]

A point of specific concern for the Central Asian states' short-term security needs is the modernization of their armed forces, along with capacity building in law enforcement and border management. Central Asian leaders have recently been fortunate to receive contributions in this field from major powers, albeit generally aiming at building up anti-terrorism capacities rather than a robust traditional military posture. Most notably, Russia has taken steps to provide technical maintenance for Soviet-era equipment left behind on Central Asian soil and established an airbase in Kant, Kyrgyzstan, within the framework of the CSTO. China, as the leading actor of the SCO, stepped in with tangible support for law enforcement agencies in the form of patrol vehicles, communication equipment and individual supplies needed for law enforcement and border services.[39] As a result, today Chinese modifications of older Soviet vehicles are replacing old vehicles for patrolling the city streets and border areas of Central Asia. The United States for its part contributed millions of dollars for modernization of the armed forces and law enforcement agencies of certain states in the region.[40] The OSCE and NATO have carried out training for various units of Central Asian military, border and law enforcement authorities. Furthermore, there are initiatives such as the Caspian Guard[41] and the military base in Atyrau, Kazakhstan, both supplied with US equipment and substantial US funding.[42]

Apart from technical assistance, there has been a significant inflow of resource investment in various security-related sectors. Although this may not pass through SCO channels and indeed often dwarfs the impact of the SCO's own activities, it is arguable that the rise of the SCO has acted at least as a catalyst for new Chinese, Russian and Western technical, educational and financial support ventures aimed at strengthening Central Asian law enforcement and defence capabilities. The numbers of Central Asian military personnel going to Russia for training and study exchanges have increased significantly, and China is gradually opening up its law enforcement and military training institutions to Central Asian states.[43]

Since the SCO is not a mutual defence organization, it logically enough cannot provide Central Asian states with any military-related equipment or supplies. Accepting such assistance would in any case make a mockery of the non-bloc philosophy of the Central Asian members. This explains why outsourced assistance for the modernization of law enforcement, military and border services has tended to be provided through bilateral arrangements with the larger members. On the other hand, and apparently under Russian pressure, Kyrgyzstan and Tajikistan have increasingly often expressed support for the initiative for 'closer collaboration' between the defence ministries of SCO member states.[44] Russian aspirations in this regard have been articulated by Defence Minister Sergei Ivanov: 'Russia wishes to enhance exchange and cooperation between the two armies [Chinese and Russian], which accords with the long-term interest of the two countries and [is] beneficial to regional stability and world peace'.[45] It cannot be excluded that the creation of collective defence forces will at some time enter the SCO agenda, but it is clear that, at the least, China and Kazakhstan would be unenthusiastic about it.

Drug trafficking is another major security concern to all Central Asian elites. Although prevalent corruption is another very serious obstacle, actions and declarations in the SCO framework point to a growing realization among the political elites that drug trafficking, along with other types of transnational crime, severely undermines the development of the region.

Important documents and practical measures have been adopted to prevent further deterioration of the anti-drug capabilities of Central Asian states.[46] Some state leaders have rightly indicated that drug trafficking is turning into an issue of national security.[47] Strengthening anti-drug cooperation is also crucially important for China and Russia, which are becoming major drug markets. The increase in drug production from Afghanistan since 2001 is an obvious factor here, since this one country now accounts for 88 per cent of drug production in the world.[48] An SCO–Afghanistan working group on joint efforts to resolve issues of drug production and trafficking would seem to be a logical step for the interests of both SCO members and Afghanistan. President Rahmonov of Tajikistan stated during the 2006 SCO summit that it was in the interest of all the SCO states to help a friendly Afghanistan to become a stable and prosperous country without drug production.[49] He also advocated creating a separate SCO structure to work on this issue specifically. The eagerness of Tajikistan to push this issue is not surprising given that it is one of the Central Asian states that is most vulnerable (with Kyrgyzstan) to the drug threat. Thus, any SCO anti-drug agency would be expected to address Tajikistan as the top priority – no doubt bringing in additional contributions of aid from traditional donors.

Last but not least among the security implications of SCO-type multilateralism is the scope it gives for rapprochement between the Central Asian states in terms of confidence building. The challenge of mutual security relations has been a weak point for Central Asian states ever since the demise of the Soviet Union as a linking entity. Although recent progress has largely been limited to declaratory and paper measures of mutual reassurance, some practical steps are also being taken. One of these is the gesture made to resolve acute tensions on the Uzbek–Kyrgyz and Uzbek–Tajik borders in 2004, when President Karimov announced Uzbekistan's readiness to de-mine the border zone between these countries.

Other ways in which SCO activities have facilitated confidence building between the states of Central Asia include the steady increase in reciprocal contacts between law enforcement, political and military authorities, in terms of number, regularity and quality. The SCO has thereby helped to revitalize connections between Central Asian societies that had been historically closely linked in terms of political developments, cultural similarity and economic systems – not to mention geographical proximity. It is something of a cliché to relate the loss of these ties to the collapse of the Soviet Union and the subsequent emergence of Central Asian states seeking to define distinct identities: what is less often noted is that nothing arose to take the place of the former cooperation framework. In this perspective, the multilateralizing and confidence-building effects of the SCO seem to be in line with the interests not only of the current leaderships but also with the broader national interests of Central Asian states.[50]

Meanwhile, Central Asian political and military establishments are still suspicious of each other and reluctant to cooperate – even though this severely curtails the prospect for regional security and economic development. Perhaps the most tangible contribution that the SCO has made to Central Asia is to set the dialogue between local states in a regular and comprehensive format, which is an indispensable condition for confidence building and cooperation. Leaders meet at least annually, but there are many other levels of regular contact and dialogue within the organization, in spheres ranging from law enforcement and the economy to environmental issues. Considering the short- and longer-term benefits that opening up such contacts have brought for other regions in transition, it seems fair to conclude that the SCO 'process' may offer real benefits for regional stability and development.[51]

Central Asian states SCO energy and economic policy

In recent years, there has been an impressive increase in the resource transactions focused on Kazakhstan – at the crossroads of major energy projects – at a time when energy issues are at the top of all the SCO members' agendas (see Maps 2.1–2.4). For Kazakhstan itself, against the background also of vigorous energy competition between major actors in the Caspian basin, such developments hold out the prospect of decreasing its dependence on the Russian energy transportation infrastructure and the diversification of target markets.

Having officially joined the Baku–Tbilisi–Ceyhan pipeline scheme, Kazakhstan has secured its western route for energy transport, although it already has functioning northern and eastern arteries. Increasing access to major world markets is obviously in Kazakhstan's interests. Among the growing cooperative activities in energy between India and Kazakhstan, the possibility of a fourth, southern route being opened up should not be excluded, especially since this scenario is supported by major powers that do not favour an Iranian alternative for Indian energy imports.[52] The southern route for Kazakh oil would in turn influence all other countries that are located along the possible supply line.

President Putin recently initiated the creation of an 'energy club' within the SCO. Some commentators have argued that such a club would become a *de facto* 'rival OPEC' (Organization of the Petroleum Exporting Countries), possessing half of world natural gas reserves and almost a quarter of all oil reserves if the club came to include Iran. It is extremely difficult to predict what such a group would mean for the Central Asian countries themselves, but there are possible downsides to their overinvestment in energy as an economic driver, including exposure to the possible manipulation of local supplies for other powers' strategic ends and the growth of tensions both locally and globally. The events of early 2006, when Russian supplies of natural gas to Ukraine and the West were forcibly interrupted, showed how precarious pipeline transit and supply are. True, the diversity of routes and actors involved in Central Asia reduces the likelihood of such an incident arising there. Kazakhstan, the main oil producer in Central Asia, carefully follows the principle of diversity, thereby alleviating many of the concerns about the possible results of its commitments. Nevertheless, stability for long-term economic development will demand that Central Asia achieves diversity not only in energy routes, but also in the very structure of the economy: major oil producers in the region should strive to reduce dependence on energy exploitation and to develop industrial and service capabilities instead.[53]

The economic cooperation agenda of the SCO is probably the area with most undeveloped potential for Central Asian states. However, as these states are well aware, there are also some respects in which true economic multilateralism could be risky for their longer-term prospects.

The central idea of the programme for multilateral trade and economic cooperation between SCO member states, agreed by the prime ministers of the six member states in 2003, is that all the countries should work towards creating favourable conditions for the free flow of goods, services and technologies. China, with its large and vital economy, has understandably pushed hard for this aim, but the Central Asian countries and even Russia have shown corresponding caution: they see a more open multilateral market as removing the last remaining obstacles in the way of a *de facto* economic takeover of the area by China.[54] Central Asia's weak and immature economies and labour markets have good reason to fear opening the way for Chinese businesses and a cheap Chinese labour force, which would seriously undermine the growth prospects and perhaps even the survival of local enterprises. For similar reasons, Russia has repeatedly blocked China from achieving its own top priority in the SCO – an SCO free trade zone – and thus from taking a firm grasp on Central Asian energy reserves and markets.[55] The impact of such a sudden, ill-prepared economic opening would hit small and medium enterprises the hardest. There are, however, other, hidden, long-term risks, such as increasing the political influence of transnational corporate lobbies in Central Asia, which would eventually make Central Asian states economically dependent on China. Hence, Central Asian leaders prefer methods that involve direct investment in their own economic capabilities, rather than giving any early opening for competition with the mature business structures of larger SCO members.

With regard to investment, weaker Central Asian states are putting a major emphasis on the development of transportation infrastructure in order

Caspian Region oil pipelines

Caspian Region gas pipelines

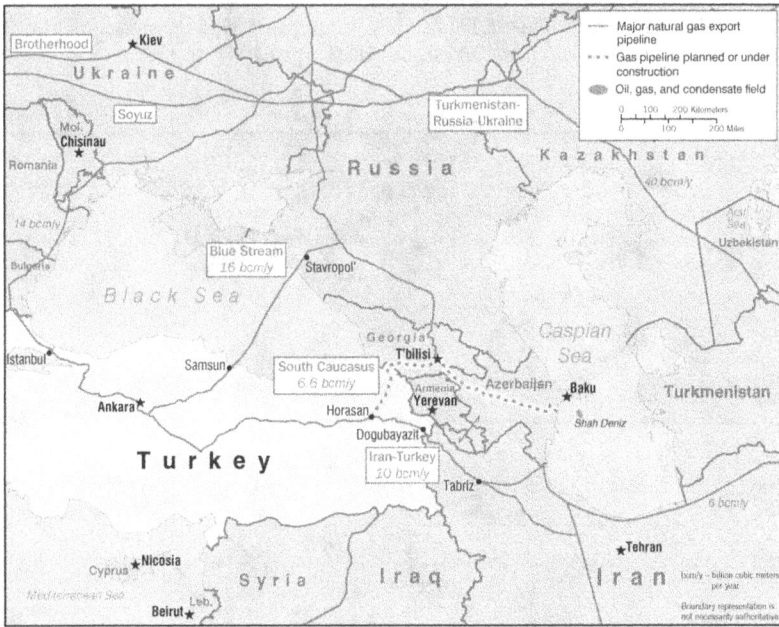

Map 2.1 Caspian region oil pipelines and Caspian region gas pipelines
Source: CIA maps (availabe at http://www.eia.doe.gov/emeu/cabs/Caspian/Maps.html)

Russia: Main Natural Gas Export Pipelines

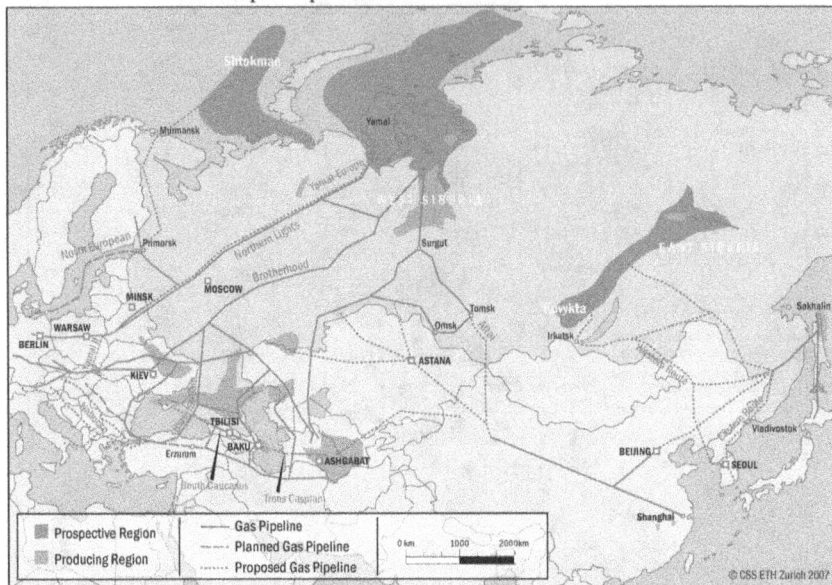

Map 2.2 Russia: main natural gas export pipelines
© Center for Security Studies, ETH Zurich, reproduced with permission. Map first published in: *Russian Analytical Digest*, no. 18, 3 April 2007, p. 13

Russia: Main Oil Export Pipelines

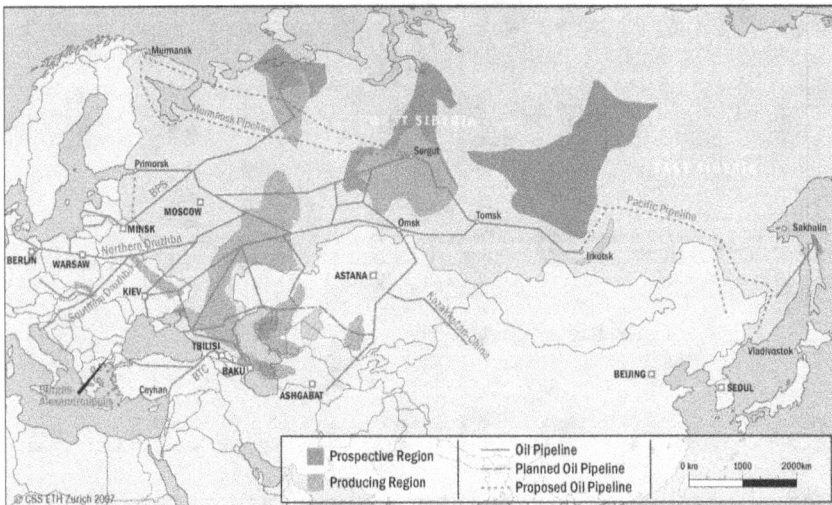

Map 2.3 Russia: main natural oil export pipelines
© Center for Security Studies, ETH Zurich, reproduced with permission. Map first published in: *Russian Analytical Digest*, no. 18, 3 April 2007, p. 12

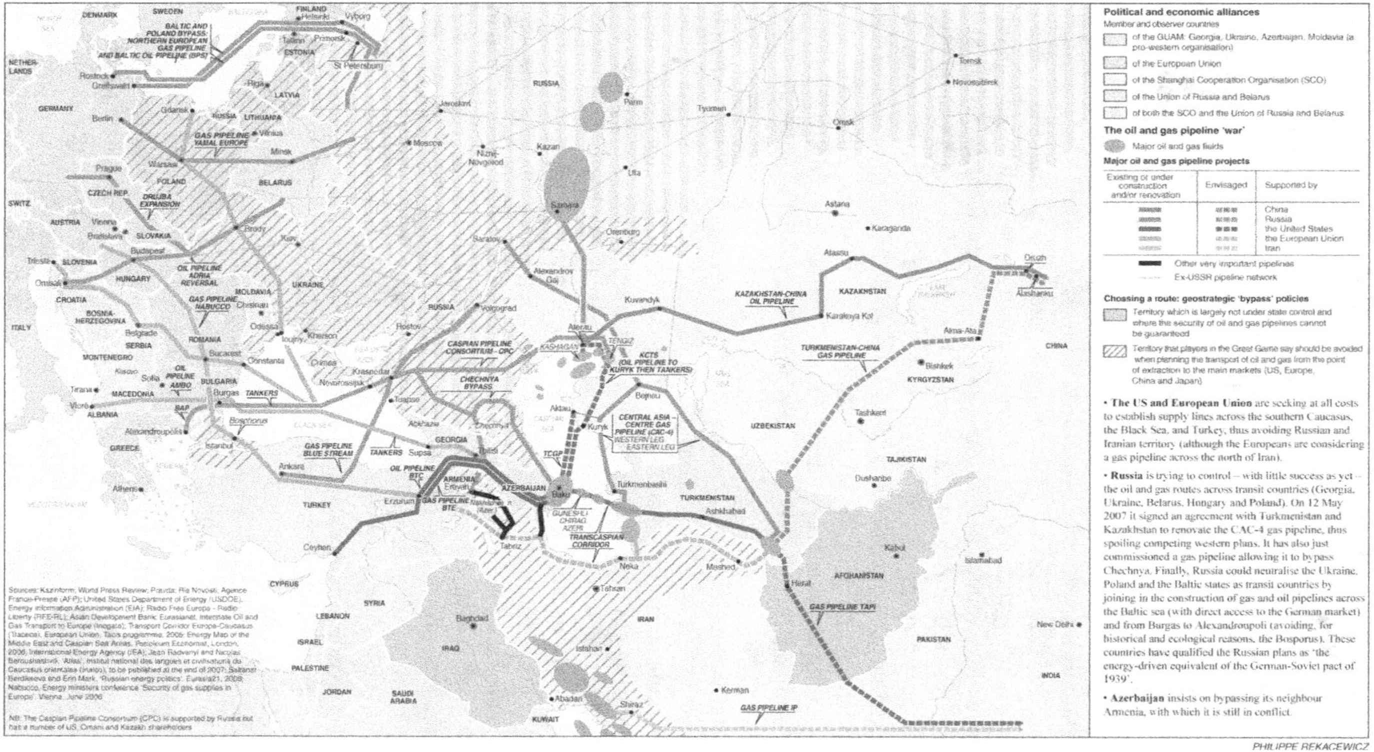

Map 2.4 Map of selected oil and gas pipeline infrastructure in the former Soviet Union
Source: Map by Philippe Rekacewicz, *le Monde diplomatique*, Paris, June 2007

to be able to exploit their transit potential. A broader concept for addressing this area has been developed within the SCO under the idea of 'restoring the ancient Silk Road' as a corridor between Europe and Asia. Although the motivation behind this project may largely be seen as a response to the Transport Corridor Europe–Caucasus–Asia (TRASECA) scheme, it also has a lot to do with the fact that there would otherwise be limited opportunities to firmly integrate Kyrgyzstan, Tajikistan and, to lesser extent, Uzbekistan into the SCO structures of support and subsidization.[56] China has, moreover, shown a clear interest in the construction of the Kashgar–Irkeshtam–Osh–Andijan railway, which has long offered the prospect of giving China its shortest route to Iran.[57]

The benefits that Central Asia's remote and land-locked states would derive from offering transit for a Chinese–Iranian trade route would include both immediate revenues and future prospects. Three Central Asian SCO members – Kazakhstan, Kyrgyzstan and Uzbekistan – would obtain their closest yet access point to the sea through Iranian territory. Pakistan has pointed out that it could offer another access point to the Indian Ocean for Central Asian states.[58] In connection with such schemes, all SCO members are working on measures to improve transport within the SCO area, but are also studying opportunities to join the European Highway transport agreement.

The construction of roads passing through Central Asia would require considerable investment, and there are signs that China is seriously considering making such investments. One of the supporting factors is the large (US$100 billion) gas deal between China and Iran, which is expected to be almost doubled in scale if ongoing negotiations are successful. Moreover, China appears to be very keen to find points of entry to even some of the most inaccessible Central Asian states. Turkmenistan, which is the only Central Asian state that is not a member of the SCO, recently concluded an agreement with China on gas sales and the construction of a pipeline to China's western provinces. The strategic importance of this artery goes beyond bilateral energy deals between Beijing and Ashgabat: the pipeline could be used for the transport of both Turkmen and Iranian gas to China, would affect existing energy schemes in the region and might have a tangible influence on global energy supply networks in general.

Logically, the most convenient route for such a pipeline would be along the Kashgar–Andijan road, although there are other proposals too. In any case, realization of this titanic project holds a significance for Central Asian transit potential that has made all national leaders passionately interested in the fate of this particular item on the SCO agenda. Unfortunately, the authoritarian leaderships of the weaker Central Asian states are all too easily sidetracked from providing consistent support for such undertakings by their search for immediate revenue to sustain their regimes. All too often, their public statements refer to the issues of developing transport capacity and transit potential only in superficial and general terms: something that is clearly at odds with their nations' longer-term interests. A more consistent approach would be most desirable, given that this is an economic area in which there is no conflict at all between their longer-term interests and China's.

The question of SCO enlargement

Misunderstandings about possible SCO enlargement drew unprecedented international attention to the SCO anniversary summit of 2006 and generated special concern in some parts of the West. The summit meeting itself, which did not change the SCO observers' status, proved the most dramatic predictions wrong: in fact, an enlargement of membership in the given conditions would have been doomed from the beginning. Upgrading the status of India, Iran, Mongolia and Pakistan from observer to member would boost the SCO's strategic scale and weight: the organization would represent half the world's population; its full members would include four nuclear weapon states, some of them known to have extremely tense external relations; and it would possess more than a quarter of global hydrocarbon energy reserves.

Yet there are also strong objections to enlargement that are perceived especially clearly by the Central Asian states themselves. Most obviously, admitting new members would diminish these states' own significance within the SCO and reduce their benefits by diverting more diplomatic and economic resources to the more strategically attractive new members. It would also bring China closer to realizing its larger Asian aspirations, thus inevitably distracting it from Central Asian affairs. The economic potential of the four current SCO observer states is incomparably higher than that of the Central Asian members, both as energy providers and trade markets. Central Asia could find itself relegated to little more than a transit territory for the economic undertakings of others. This role is, of course, also inherent in many Chinese and Russian ambitions for the region today, but the problem would be sharply aggravated in the event of SCO enlargement.

Kazakhstan spoke firmly against accepting new members, arguing that this would be difficult even in technical terms since the SCO lacks mechanisms to effectuate quick membership. Kazakhstan's actual motives for this stance reflect a mix of economic and geopolitical factors. For their part, and contrary to many views expressed outside the SCO, China and Russia are not pressing for early decisions on wider membership as they can see how profoundly their own invention – the SCO – could be affected. Both the Central Asian states and the larger powers of the SCO prioritize institutional strengthening and the realization of existing undertakings, which among other things can increase the attractiveness of the SCO as a cooperation framework for other players.

Another important aspect for Central Asian states is that, by siding with Iran in an organization like the SCO, they would be aligning themselves with explicitly anti-Western players in the region. This would have far-reaching implications for their relations with both Western and various local regional powers. It would mean the end of the multi-vector foreign policy that has served Central Asian political establishments so well. Most importantly, losing the support of the West would mean a deterioration of Central Asia's position as an independent actor both within and outside the SCO. China and Russia would obtain significant leverage to reinforce their own influence and preponderance. This helps explain why Kazakh President Nazarbaev expressed a striking degree of support for the authority of the United Nations when he stated during his recent meeting with Iranian President Mahmoud Ahmadinejad that, 'if the United Nations introduces sanctions against Iran, Kazakhstan will also have to obey'. This sincere and open position of the Kazakh leader also conveyed the general message from SCO members to Iran that Iran should not seek to burden the SCO with its nuclear problems.

Iran is, in fact, the most eager as well as the most controversial candidate for full SCO membership. It hopes that China and Russia would support its stand against US pressure. When underlining the possible benefits of Iranian membership of the SCO, however, President Ahmadinejad has also targeted the areas of key Chinese and Russian interest in the energy sector. At the 2006 SCO summit he offered to host a conference for the SCO energy ministers in Tehran in order to explore opportunities for further development of cooperation in the energy sector, including transportation and joint exploitation. Clearly, China and Russia are not ready to endorse Iranian membership, particularly not in reinforcing any sense that the organization is a 'club for dictators'; but this does not mean that specific Iranian proposals will be overlooked when they could serve SCO members' common interests in economic cooperation without political or security liabilities.

An other interesting point is the Central Asian states' nervousness about becoming too influenced by Chinese and Russian interests and about being manipulated by these large states for their own geopolitical aims. These fears have little to do with internal political affinities but more to do with Central Asia's long historical experience of being a periphery for one or more stronger states. If nothing else, Central Asia's present leaders are extremely committed to maintaining their sovereignty and independent position. The dilemma they face is that a more democratic orientation and greater openness to the West would be one of the most obvious ways to bolster their independent position vis-à-vis Beijing and Moscow.

The eventual outcome will depend on what is more important for Central Asian leaders – their independence or maintaining the status quo in domestic affairs – and predicting their choices is not easy. At present their behaviour indicates different priorities: Uzbekistan, for instance, opted to uphold its regime during and after the notorious events of May 2005 in Andijan, whereas Kazakhstan is making more consistent efforts to reinforce its independent position, in particular through closer connections to the West. The path eventually chosen by Central Asian political establishments could have a profound impact on the evolution of the SCO agenda. Either the latter will remain harnessed to protecting the interests of current authoritarian elites, or it could evolve to focus more on the real national interests of Central Asian states. In either event, it would be a mistake to see Central Asian interests as inherently or inevitably contradicting those of China and Russia: cooperation with neighbouring regional powers will always be a rational option both for security and economic development, and the SCO members' geographic closeness makes some kind of *modus vivendi* between them inevitable.

China's SCO political agenda in Eurasia and Central Asia

The political dimension of the SCO agenda is perhaps its most controversial but also its most unpredictable aspect. The organization, like its individual members, faces strategic choices for future development. China's and Russia's freedom to dominate the political agenda at present arises not just from Central Asian weakness but from the disengaged and often hostile attitudes towards SCO affairs that are prevalent in the West. It is worth speculating whether a greater Western engagement not just with individual Central Asian states, but with the evolution of the SCO as such, might help tilt the balance towards more positive scenarios.

In many aspects the history of Central Asia might have taken a much different course; however, as already mentioned, the events of 9/11 changed the security and geopolitical scene in the region when the United States deployed troops there and the Taliban regime fell in Afghanistan. These events highlighted Central Asia's strategic importance to the West as the 'geopolitical pivot' and 'shatter belt' of the extensive Eurasian landmass.[59] The region is no longer assumed to lie within the Sino–Russian sphere of influence, but finds itself once again in a 'great game' of geopolitics between major powers. Given Central Asia's rich strategic and physical resources, 'one can expect potential clashes of global interests of great powers for domination of the region'.[60]

As a result, the more Russia and the United States cooperated actively in Central Asia, Central Asian countries leaned politically to the United States, and Washington's influence grew, the more the SCO's role in regional security and China's influence was stemmed. In fact, no matter how much China has gained from the US campaign in Afghanistan against the Taliban and the ensuing blow to the operations of its own Uyghur separatist militants, US preponderance in Central Asia was a serious setback to the government that aspires to the role of Asian superpower.[61] Much to the alarm of Moscow and Beijing, SCO Central Asian members, particularly Uzbekistan, gladly welcomed US requests to station its military forces on their soil. This apparent lack of internal unity, compounded with SCO inability to mount a cohesive strategy towards the terrorist threat emanating from Afghanistan, has highlighted the blunt dominance of Sino–Russian interests within the organization, as well as its weakness as both a security mechanism and as a forum to combat the growing American influence in the region. In fact, the evolution of the SCO is the salient yardstick that measures how well Russia and China will coexist with each other as well as with the newly present United States. It represents the struggle to maintain Sino–Russian hegemony over Central Asia in the face of growing US interests and the stubborn presence of violent Islamist-oriented movements. It is clear that Russia, and especially China, want to use the SCO as an alternative alliance to the US military presence in Central Asia.

The SCO's creation in 1996 was a perfect interception of China's and Russia's interests in Central Asia, as it fused Moscow's long-standing quest to increase control over the region with Beijing's desire to create a multipolar world. They envisaged the organization as an instrument to ensure the safety of Central Asia from foreign encroachment by exerting dual hegemony over the region. China has long wished to develop the energy resources of the region in order to achieve civilian and military production targets over the next decades, but also to safeguard its western flank from intrusion from foreign powers, particularly as it faces US military installations or US-supported military forces on its eastern front via South Korea, Japan and Taiwan. The signing of the 'Good-Neighbourly Treaty on Friendship and Cooperation' between China and Russia (June 2001) codified the mutual support for each other's policies from the 1990s, and the SCO was a continuation of this trend.

It should also be noted that the so-called 'Shanghai process' (including both the original Shainghai Five and the SCO) is embodied in the framing of the new Chinese security concept – formally approved in 2001– which defines that security should be obtained by peaceful means, through mutual cooperation and on the basis of the principle that that 'security is mutual'. In other words, Beijing opposes the idea that any country can build its own absolute security upon the insecurity of others and supports the concept of multilateral security dialogue and cooperation.[62]

The creation of the Shanghai Five (later the SCO) was itself a seminal event. For the first time Moscow conceded that it could not maintain exclusive influence in Central Asia. Russia feared it was losing Central Asian governments to the United States, and that, most importantly, the spreading of radical Islamic movements supported by the Taliban would overwhelm governments in the region, meaning that the Kremlin would face the Taliban across its non-existent borders to the south. In this perspective, and considering Beijing as the least of several evils, Moscow allowed and even encouraged Chinese involvement in Central Asia. China was not so powerful that it could deny Russian influence in the region. In addition, Chinese economic and political resources could help prop up governments and prevent them from shifting preferences to Washington. Beijing itself could more effectively penetrate Central Asia with Moscow's consent, and prevent both the United States and Islamists from gaining influence there.

In fact, confronted with a dramatic expansion of the US military power ('hard power') all around China's periphery after 9/11, Beijing has responded by unveiling its 'soft power' strategy in the form of a diplomatic 'charm offensive', the notion of China's 'peaceful rise', and laid greater emphasis on economic integration and multilateralism. Although calling for an end to the Cold War-era US alliances with Japan, South Korea, Australia, the Philippines and Thailand, China has stepped up its efforts to establish a worldwide 'Coalition of Autocracies' with Russia, North Korea, Cambodia, Burma, Pakistan, Bangladesh, Nepal, Uzbekistan, Iran, Saudi Arabia, Sudan, Zimbabwe, Angola, Cuba, Bolivia and Venezuela – albeit under the rubric of economic interdependence and globalization.

With the United States bogged down in Iraq and Afghanistan, Beijing has been busy carving out a large sphere of influence for itself (i) by seeking to subdue Japan and Taiwan, and weaken the US–South Korean alliance in North-East Asia; (ii) by skilfully using multilateralism and economic diplomacy to establish a pro-China regional order in South-East Asia; (iii) by strengthening Beijing's military alliances with Pakistan, Burma and Bangladesh in South Asia to contain India and gain access to the Indian Ocean so as to secure trade routes and energy resources; and (iv) by making significant inroads in the South Pacific under the cover of a China–Taiwan contest for diplomatic recognition. In fact, courting the strategically located, resource-rich but isolated and turbulent countries run by authoritarian leaders while chanting the mantra of 'non-interference in domestic affairs' and 'peace and development' have long been the key characteristics of Chinese foreign policy. More importantly, China is now increasingly relying upon multilateral organizations to define limits to US global power, marginalize Japan, Taiwan and India, and have its foreign policy agenda endorsed by or imposed on global and regional organizations.

Particularly in Central Asia, China aims at the following strategic targets with the aid of the SCO: (i) strengthening security cooperation (especially against terrorism) with Central Asian states and promoting the stability of both Central Asia's and China's own western territory by cutting off the cross-border links between terrorist organizations; (ii) extending economic and trade relations with Central Asian countries and establishing a source of energy to meet growing domestic demand; (iii) broadening the cooperative dimension with Russia; (iv) creating a new diplomatic image for China by establishing a local model of multilateral cooperation; and (v) promoting an international processes of political multi-polarity.[63]

The Chinese and Russian view of the SCO

The presence of Russia and China among SCO members is the key reason why the SCO is increasingly taken seriously, although often with caution, by countries in the West and East. The SCO and its predecessor, the Shanghai Five, have provided a mechanism under which Central Asia's two most powerful neighbours can reconcile their interests and develop ways to coop-erate. Early observers predicted that there would be unavoidable Russian–Chinese rivalry or even conflict over influence in Central Asia. The SCO's ability to regulate this conflict has been, without a doubt, the most powerful testimony of the organization's success to date.

However, Russian–Chinese relations within the SCO are becoming increasingly competitive, rather than cooperative. As China moves from declarations towards promoting specific projects in Central Asia, including those focused on energy and infrastructure, increasing development loans, and signing contracts for strategic projects in the energy and water manage-ment sectors, Russia's role as a regional economic power, inherited from the Soviet Union, is diminishing.

At the same time, China has been more cautious than Russia about using the SCO as a tool for anti-Western, particularly anti-US, declarations, pre-ferring instead a quieter, but often more effective, diplomacy. Russia, on the contrary, has been the key engine behind the SCO declarations – such as those calling for NATO base withdrawal or member states pledging not to take steps that could damage the security of other members – which sought to openly challenge the Western presence and influence in Central Asia. Although Russia and China both oppose the US and NATO military pre-sence in the region, China is less concerned about engagement by the EU and Asian players, such as the Asian Development Bank (ADB).

Whatever we may think of the SCO in the West, I believe it would be useful finding out here first the Chinese and second the Russian point of view, because it will enlighten our spectrum of thoughts about the way the Chinese and the Russians are functioning within the SCO.

Pan Guang[64] explains that:

> The Shanghai process has pioneered attempts at building a new approach to neighbourhood security by means of mutual trust, dis-armament and cooperative security. Having solved, in a matter of a few years, the century-old border problems between China and the former Soviet states, this security approach already embodies great achieve-ments for the parties involved and offers potential to assist in other outstanding border problems, such as those between China and India, the South China Sea dispute, the Chinese–Japanese disputes over the Diaoyu Islands and part of the East China Sea, and so on. Moreover, the SCO has adopted a very broad perspective towards the definition and execution of security cooperation that has been highlighted by the way in which it has made the fight against drug-trafficking and cross-border crime its top priority: it has proposed the establishment of effec-tive mechanisms for the use of the mass media against new challenges and new threats; it has signed a joint declaration on maintaining inter-national information security; and it has given full attention to energy security, environmental protection, the protective development of water

resources and similar issues. Keeping an open mind towards the various contemporary non-conventional security issues, as well as the conventional ones, being in the framework of the SCO leaves China better positioned to play a growing role in global security cooperation. The SCO has helped to shape a new model of state-to-state relationships characterized by partnership but not alliance, as originally spearheaded by China and Russia. By endorsing a set of new rules regulating state-to-state relations in the post-Cold War era, the SCO presents a sharp contrast to the views of those who cling to a Cold War mentality, the pursuit of unilateralism and the strengthening or expansion of military blocs. The relationship between China, Russia and the Central Asian states – under the SCO umbrella – constitutes a close partnership with constructive interactions while stopping short of military alliance. The 2001 Chinese–Russian Treaty of Good Neighbourliness and Friendly Cooperation symbolized the initiation of a new stage in the bilateral relationship.[65] This treaty was the first between the two countries to be based on genuine equality and not on military alliance (...).

The SCO process has given rise to a new model of regional cooperation, characterized by common initiatives taken by both large and small countries, with security cooperation paving the way, a focus on collaboration for mutual benefit and the facilitating of cultural complementarity. This new model not only stresses cooperation and reciprocity in the economic sector but also emphasizes cultural exchange and mutual learning. Valuable experience for China's regional and cross-regional cooperation with many other countries can be supplied by the various activities pursued under this model, such as the establishment of the SCO Business Council and the SCO Inter-bank Association; the buyer's credit that China provides to other SCO members; the launch of the Huoerguosi Border Trade and Cooperation Centre between China and Kazakhstan; the SCO Cultural and Art Festival; the training provided by China for 1500 Central Asian professionals in various fields; and the strengthening of educational ties. They provide important input for the various proposed bilateral and multilateral free-trade programmes involving China (...)'.

More generally, the SCO process, with its successful practice and evolution, symbolizes the transformation of Chinese diplomacy from its traditional focus on bilateral relations towards the growing embrace of multilateral interactions. Prior to the Shanghai process, China chose mainly bilateral rather than multilateral channels for resolving its disputes with other parties. However, the SCO has now given China greater confidence in participating in and, in some cases, even initiating multilateral processes. For example, China is now an actor in the ASEAN Regional Forum (ARF) and an active participant in the '10 plus 1' ASEAN–China summits and '10 plus 3' meetings between ASEAN, China, Japan and South Korea.[66] 3 It hosts the Six-Party Talks on the

Korean peninsula and is a responsible player in the 'P5+1' efforts at resolving the Iranian nuclear problem.[67] 4 The beginning of the 21st century has seen China playing an increasingly active and constructive role in the multilateral arena.

As to Mister Mikhail Troitskiy:[68]

In terms of its overall role on the world stage, Russian policymakers want the SCO to continue to act as an important symbol of rebuke to Russia's might-have-been strategic partners in the West and as a bargaining chip in negotiations with the United States. The SCO's transcontinental nature and the mutual respect of sovereignty among its members are frequently cited by Russian observers as alternatives to a narrow policy focus on building alliances between Russia and EU countries or the United States – all the more so, given these partners' inclination to interfere in Russian internal affairs,[69] One of the symbolic concepts capturing the minds of Russian experts and policy-makers is that of creating an 'arc of stability' in the north of Eurasia. This 'arc of stability' is contrasted to the 'arc of instability' stretching along the SCO's southern rim – from the eastern Mediterranean through Iraq and Afghanistan to Pakistan and northern India. The instability in the latter arc is seen in Russia as largely the result of the US's flawed policies of intervening in Iraq, pressuring Iran and vainly attempting to build a viable state in Afghanistan.

Russia will strive for a balanced distribution of power within the SCO, thus hindering China's aspirations to win greater influence in Central Asia through the organization. Russia needs to assure its Central Asian partners that it is 'keeping an eye' on China's intentions *vis-à-vis* the region and stands by to provide Central Asian states with diplomatic backing should they need it in relations with China. On the same logic, any attempts by China to endow SCO bodies with even a restricted supranational mandate will meet with Russian resistance. Russia will strive to preserve the SCO's original design as an intergovernmental forum.

Finally, it should be appealing for Russia to establish itself as a 'bridge' between the SCO and Euro-Atlantic institutions, such as the EU or NATO, which have manifested their increasing interest in Central Asia. This move could serve to emphasize Russia's unique geopolitical position as a link between Europe and Asia, and raise its standing within the SCO itself (...)

The present Russian government clearly has a different idea of what democracy entails than does the Bush administration and will take opportunities to trump any card the United States may play. Nonetheless, some Russians are open to joint efforts to stabilize and develop Central Asia, provided that Moscow is afforded an appropriate say and share in any arrangement. To enlist Russia's assistance, the United States would need to be more consultative about the implementation of its limited goals in Central Asia.[70]

In strategic terms, Russia and China have increasingly diverging views on the future directions of SCO development. Russia is keen to keep the SCO as primarily a security organization, with only a limited economic role focusing on joint infrastructure projects. Russia seeks to use EURASEC as the key regional economic integration vehicle. China wants the SCO to evolve decisively into an economic grouping, which makes it easier for China to implement its business projects in the region, including those in the energy sphere and trade. China's proposals for the creation of a free trade zone within the SCO are seen as threatening for Russian and Central Asian state economies, which can hardly compete with China's economic power. This power has already displaced Russia as the key economic and trading partner for many Central Asian states. As this trend continues, Russia might start using the SCO mechanisms to limit China's economic expansion into Central Asia, rather than for the purpose of reducing the existing barriers through economic integration, the vision held by China.

Sino–Russian tensions are likely to grow and Russia will find it difficult to deal with China's rising influence and activism in Central Asia. The SCO is unlikely to help tackle such issues as migration, resource competition, and the increasing economic imbalance between China and its neighbours, including Russia. The SCO can be used by Russia and Central Asian states as a vehicle – a force multiplier – to contain and balance Chinese influence (just as the Shanghai Five process was used in negotiating border disputes). Such efforts against China could be implemented if the Central Asian states decide that their concerns over China's power outweigh the potential and real benefits from welcoming Chinese capital and assistance.[71]

As far as security is concerned, one role which the SCO could have played is to help translate some of its experience in addressing border disputes between China and post-Soviet states to tackle the existing border problems within Central Asia itself. Many unresolved border disputes represent potential sources of tension and even conflict and obstacles for trade and economic development. Closer ties with Russia helped to some extent to encourage some normalization in Tajikistan–Uzbekistan relations; however, this process is far from complete. At the same time, the withdrawal of Russian border guards from Kyrgyzstan and Tajikistan meant that Russia was no longer influential enough to help strengthen the border regimes. The SCO could have played some role in this issue but Russia is cautious to authorize anything that could imply some form of long-term presence of Chinese military or other security forces in Central Asia on a long-term basis.

Moreover, while keeping the security agenda – where Russia still enjoys greater power than China – among the SCO priorities, Russia is reluctant to empower the organization to such a degree that it could question the need for the CSTO, where Russia remains the undisputed leader. Unlike the SCO, which only established a working group on Afghanistan last year and has achieved few real results, the CSTO has been working on developing a concept of security belts against drug trafficking in Central Asia and reinforcing joint capabilities, which still remain rather weak and practically untested in real operations. China, on the other hand, is reluctant to see any merger, even on an *ad hoc* basis, between the SCO and CSTO, perhaps because such a union could strengthen Russia's role in the SCO.[72] Any prospective enlargement of the SCO, which could include any or all of the existing observers (India, Pakistan, Mongolia and Iran), will multiply security problems within the 'SCO area' while further undermining any chances for the creation of meaningful joint mechanisms to deal with them.

For many of the above-mentioned reasons, the SCO's security portfolio will remain limited. At the same time, its economic agenda is expanding, thus posing potential limitations on Russia's power within the SCO. Russia's key strategic economic interest in Central Asia is to gain control over its energy resources and its transportation routes to world markets. The recent deal signed between the presidents of Russia, Kazakhstan and Turkmenistan on the construction of a gas pipeline along the eastern shore of the Caspian Sea has been trumpeted as a key Russian geopolitical victory. Yet this approach contradicts the SCO agenda, according to which Central Asian states should have the chance to diversify their export routes. Not only China, as a SCO member, but also India and Pakistan, as observers, are determined to use SCO membership as a vehicle to get access to Central Asian resources and find ways to bring them into South Asia. The ideas of an integrated gas market or an alliance of gas-producing states, along the lines of the proposed gas OPEC, which was discussed by Putin and Iranian President Mahmoud Ahmedinejad on the fringes of the 2006 SCO summit in China, would not benefit all Central Asian states and therefore could not become an SCO project.[73] In those areas where the SCO as a regional institution can really contribute – such as regional infrastructure projects – China has so far demonstrated more interest and more willingness to commit funds than Russia.

Apart from the security and economic agenda, Russian support for the SCO is based on geopolitical considerations, first and foremost, its ambition to reassert itself as a major international player and to counter what Russia sees as the expansion of US influence in its backyard. For Putin, the SCO represents a powerful argument with which to back Russia's multi-polar world vision – also shared by China – and present the vision of an alliance between Russia, China and India. This idea has been floated by Russia since Yevgeny Primakov's time as Russian foreign minister under President Yeltsin as a counter-balancer to the United States and NATO. Although no such alliance can be created in practice for a variety of obvious reasons – such as continuing Sino–Indian tensions and India's close ties with the United States, as well it being a democracy – the SCO offers an opportunity to claim that such an alliance could be established within a wider framework. President Putin has been using the SCO as a powerful instrument to back up Russia's anti-Western rhetoric at home and to demonstrate that Russia and 'its allies' could present a real challenge to US and Western interests in Eurasia.

However, despite this campaign to promote the SCO, the organization is far from speaking with one voice in support of Russia's new zero-sum geopolitical rivalry with the United States in Eurasia. Despite the Astana declaration, US and NATO troops remain in Central Asia. They have a base in Manas (Kyrgyzstan) and continue to use facilities in Tajikistan and even in Uzbekistan, where German troops are stationed in Termez. Moreover, both Kazakhstan and Kyrgyzstan continue to expand their cooperation with NATO and the United States. Even China is reluctant to back strong anti-Western rhetoric as part of SCO declarations. In fact China has been developing a constructive and positive dialogue with the EU and gradually with NATO.[74] Moreover, any prospective enlargement of the SCO would mean that it will have even less appetite for any verbal confrontation with the West. Both India and Mongolia have close ties with the United States, which they value more than their relations with SCO member states, and Pakistan remains a strong ally in the US war on terror. Only Iran, which is in a state of cold war with the United States and has tense relations with the EU over its nuclear ambitions could move the SCO towards greater confrontation with the West, but its chances of obtaining full membership in the foreseeable future remain very low. Both Russia and China are reluctant to import the Iranian nuclear problem into the SCO umbrella. Sergei Ivanov, former Russian defence minister and by many analysts thought to have been the frontrunner to succeed Putin in the Kremlin, has made it clear that Russia will never endorse any collective security guarantees to Iran, as an SCO observer, should the West decide to take any military action against it.[75]

As Russia's relations with the West continue to deteriorate as a result of US plans to deploy missile defence systems in Central Europe or over Russia's decision to suspend its participation in the Conventional Forces in Europe (CFE) Treaty, or in response to Western criticism of Russia's domestic political developments, Russia could be tempted to use the SCO as a vehicle for reasserting its international role and to mount a strong opposition to Western policies. However, it is unlikely that other SCO members, including China, are open to a greater confrontation with the United States and the EU. On the contrary, they will be seeking ways to position the SCO as a partner to the West and to erase its image as a threat or an anti-Western political–military alliance.

The maintenance of security in Central Asia is a precondition for China to gain access to the most convenient energy reserves: Russia and the Central Asian states. For Central Asian states also, China is a huge potential market for energy sales and an important passageway to link up with the Asia-Pacific economic rim and the world market. On the other hand, China needs to be able to maintain Xingjian's stability and security cooperation with its Central Asian neighbours since both railroads and pipelines are vulnerable to terrorist attacks.

Notably, the perceived potential danger of Islamist militants is the main threat that binds together the regional security policies of the SCO countries. All its members share growing unease with Islamist-styled militancy or separatist movements, and that disquiet helped fuel the formation of the SCO. China faces Uyghur separatist problem in Xingjian. Russia wages its costly war in Chechnya while also uneasily observing public sentiment in its predominantly Muslim provinces, such as Tatarstan and Dagestan. Tajikistan, Kyrgyzstan and Uzbekistan all struggle with Islamist movements, such as Hizb-ut-Tahir and the IMU, fermenting in the volatile Fergana Valley.

Central Asian leaders have over projected the danger of Islamist militancy to justify their hard-line political tactics, but in reality Islamist extremists do not have the ability to topple the Central Asian governments. But it is also true that none of the SCO countries, besides Russia and China, can contain Islamist militants alone. Kyrgyzstan and Tajikistan in particular lack the domestic resources to permanently sustain any effective military campaigns against them. Such perception that Russia and China were the only powers that would contribute to the region's security compelled the Central Asian states to support the formation of the SCO in the first place. Yet, although the SCO proclaims terrorism and religious extremism to be of its primary targets, the group has not taken a single measure against any Islamist movement within its member states, besides establishing in Bishkek a regional anti-terrorism centre.

Things were made worse after the Andijan (Uzbekistan) revolt (summer 2005) and its brutal suppression by the Karimov regime. The SCO became an attractive partner for more states, including India, Pakistan, Iran and even Afghanistan. Russia and China felt sufficiently self-confident to push through a collective request to the United States to consider the withdrawal of its military bases from Central Asia. But concerned after the 'Tulip Revolution' in Kyrgyzstan redoubled their efforts to limit US influence as the example of Kyrgyzstan showed that the US presence could be mortal for the region's authoritative regimes. Uzbekistan, the Balkirev government in Kyrgyzstan and the Tajikistani government sided in favour of China, Russia and the SCO.

In spite of these successes and the over publicized 'Shanghai spirit' of coerciveness in strategic policies, Russia feels compelled to fight to maintain equal footing with China in order to return to Central Asia as an independent actor, rather than under the Chinese umbrella. For example, the choice of route for the new oil pipeline scheduled to provide energy resources to China in the Far East became a source of contention, for Moscow made a conscious effort to avoid dependence on a single customer by making a parallel proposition to Japan. President Karimov of Uzbekistan on the other hand, is trying to play Russia and China against one another in the same way that he tried to play Russia against the United States in 2004. There were also later refuted reports that China expressed interest in taking over the base in Khanabad once the United States vacated it.

Indicative also of increased diversity in Russian and Chinese policies, is the intrigue around the invitation of new observers and possible new members in the SCO. When Russia proposed to invite India, China immediately insisted on inviting Pakistan. The tentative enlargement of the SCO displayed both the Russian attempt to create a counterbalance to China within the organization and the Chinese attempt to counter-counterbalance that move. Only the invitation of Iran was by mutual consent, but again reflecting the personal strategies of the two countries *vis-à-vis* Tehran, and inspired by the motive of creating a multi-polar world. It seems the Kremlin is indecisive whether it genuinely wants to push the United States from Central Asia or whether it can live with the United States. Whereas Washington seems to fluctuate between denial and admittance of a great game, Moscow stubbornly sticks to the great game framework. Narrowly and pragmatically defined Russian interests, however, are not necessarily incompatible with US interests in the region. Paradoxically, the more players that are present on the scene (including China, India, Pakistan and Iran), the more stable the situation will be and the more likely it is that Russia will be able to advance its economic interests and prevent control over the region by an outside power. In the longer run, the US presence might become essential when Russia has to compete with China for influence in Central Asia.

In any case, US and Russian policies in Central Asia are a great game only to the extent that great powers are prepared to frame issues in that manner. Unless both the United States and Russia assume a different attitude towards each other's positions and interests in Central Asia, a Moscow–Beijing axis is likely to form and will create a geopolitical conflict with Washington. Especially if Central Asian states that have associated themselves with different great powers camps (Uzbekistan with Russia and China, Kyrgyzstan and Tajikistan more or less with the United States) try to involve their patrons in jockeying for power among themselves.[76]

Beijing's geo-strategic designs had been made evident when China made a proposal at the June 2006 SCO summit to sign a long-term Treaty on Peace and Cooperation that would effectively turn the SCO into the Eurasian collective defence organization along the lines of NATO. Although not signed, this Chinese move, coupled with the call made by the SCO in its 2005 summit to set a timetable for closing down foreign military bases in Central Asian states territory, has aroused concern that the China-dominated regional grouping could be positioning itself as a military bloc.

From this perspective, it appears to be significant that two regional powers of South-West Asia, Pakistan and Iran, are clamouring for full membership of the SCO As an inducement, Islamabad is offering 'an energy corridor and access to warm waters (Arabian Sea and the Gulf)' to Russia, China and the landlocked Central Asian member states, whereas Tehran is offering oil and gas in exchange for backing for its nuclear programme. Such a proposal could not escape a positive answer from energy hungry Beijing and Moscow, historically anxious to gain access to the warm, navigable seas of the south. As for the new states of Central Asia, they are not keen on Iran's or Pakistan's full membership, since they worry about Washington's wrath, and the Islamic inclination and pro-nuclear proliferation stance of Islamabad.

As for India, holding an observer status in the SCO, any long-term quest for full membership is negatively viewed by Beijing, partly because of historical animosity between the two Asian giants and because Washington, which sees the SCO as an attempt to forge a rival power centre, wouldn't welcome any such move from New Delhi, at a time when the US–India nuclear deal is under consideration in the US Congress.

In fact, restoring traditional linkages with its extended neighbourhood in Central Asia and beyond has been one of the primary strategic priorities of the Indian government because of its strategic location, proximity and of its energy resources. Central Asians themselves always perceived India's potential to be a countervailing factor in the delicate new geopolitical equilibrium in Eurasia. India has a positive perception of the potential of the SCO as an instrument for promoting regional economic integration, trade and ensuring energy security.

However, it maintains reservation on the political direction of the SCO. Even with the main objective of fighting terrorism, it would be an uncomfortable position for India if the Dalai Lama and his followers, members of the Falungong and people asking for genuine democratic rights in Central Asian republics were clubbed together as terrorists/separatists/extremists. Moreover, the often-raised objective of multi-polarity by China, constantly being used to counter the US influence in the Asia–Pacific, wouldn't fit well with the aforementioned rapprochement with Washington.[77]

Beijing on the other hand distrusts New Delhi and only welcomed it as an SCO observer when China was also admitted to South Asian Association for Regional Cooperation as an observer. In addition, China also brought Pakistan into the grouping. But while India participates in the SCO the Russian position in the organization is strengthened, since despite very weak bilateral trade (about US$ 2 million a year), 75 per cent of New Delhi weapons imports come from Russia. The two countries could cooperate militarily in Tajikistan, in the implementation of the north–south corridor, explore jointly oil and gas in Central Asia, and finally India could find adequate backing in its pledge for entering the SCO.[78]

In contrast, other scholars think that India should work for a separate regional organization,[79] and all countries which have a legitimate interest in the region cooperating on an à la carte basis should be included: the five Central Asian states, Afghanistan, China, India, Iran, Japan, Russia, Pakistan, Turkey and the United States. Russian uneasiness over increasing Chinese dominance in the SCO, complications arising with future enlargements, opposing Sino–Russian priorities for the organization, and most importantly the fact that none of the many regional organizations is able to accommodate all major players, argue in favour of this proposal.

As the global struggle for energy has intensified, Japan has also been alerted to the potential in Central Asia, especially since it lacks resources itself and is heavily dependent on the Middle East. Currently, 87 per cent of Japan's oil imports come from the Middle East, marking an urgent need for diversification of energy supplies. Central Asia presents a viable necessary, practical and effective choice for Japan to ensure a stable and sufficient flow of oil and gas supplies.

At the same time, by engaging economically and politically with this geo-politically important region, Japan could reinforce its strategic objectives of balancing China's influence in the Asia Pacific. Under these circumstances, Tokyo held the first round of the 'Central Asia Plus Japan' foreign ministers dialogue in Kazakhstan in August 2004, including Kazakhstan, Uzbekistan, Kyrgyzstan and Tajikistan (all SCO members), marking a big step forward in its engagements with Central Asia. On 5 June 2006, the second round of the dialogue was held in Tokyo, and the Japanese government announced that it would assist the Central Asian countries in building the so-called 'southern route' inland traffic network for future transportation of natural resources, 'including the construction of a road in west Kazakhstan, the road rehabili-tation between Bishkek and Osh in Kyrgyzstan, and the rehabilitation and modernization of airports in Kazakhstan, Kyrgyzstan, and Uzbekistan'. The ongoing projects invested by Japan also include the construction of a rail-road in southern Uzbekistan. As Japanese Foreign Minister Taro Aso said in his speech four days earlier concerning the dialogue, Japan hoped this 'southern route' would 'link Central Asia with the sea by means of a road stretching across Afghanistan'.[80] In late August 2006, Japanese Prime Minister Junichiro Koizumi visited Kazakhstan and Uzbekistan, and proposed the construction of pipelines from these two countries to the Indian Ocean through Afghanistan. In the foreseeable future, Japan will probably accel-erate its engagement with all the Central Asian countries while simultaneously keeping its eyes open to China's pursued strategy.

The increasing competition among the great powers over energy resources and their pathways will prove to have major implications for foreign policy formulation, and especially so in Eurasia. The close relationship between economic growth and energy supply makes developed countries worry about losing influence when challenged by rising developing countries, such as China and India. As stated in a report by the US National Intelligence Council: 'China and India's perceived need to secure access to energy sup-plies will propel these countries to become more global rather than just regional powers, while Europe and Russia's co-dependency is likely to be strengthened'.[81] Growing demands for energy will promote geopolitical and energy competition among the great powers that, in turn, will reinforce their perceived energy insecurity. This is however not to say that cooperation is impossible. In the words of one analyst: '[T]he rivalry between the United States, Russia, China, Turkey, Iran, and other regional powers since the early 1990s has focused on two dimensions – strategic considerations and hydro-carbon interests. To a great extent the former has been pursued in zero-sum terms with little room for compromise. By contrast, there has been some cooperation in the competition over energy resources'.[82]

Thus, the pace of economic globalization to some extent relaxes geopoli-tical competition and may prevent great power conflicts in the foreseeable future as well. Here, geo-economics emphasize the growing role of economic integration and interdependence where national interests cannot be pursued solely by military means but by economic expansion into foreign markets. Fortunately, great-power energy competition is still limited to the 'economic' level and penetration through investment and trade will continue to be the main choice for CEA countries and great powers in the 'great game'. Of course, if geopolitics and energy rivalry endanger the fundamental national interests of any great power, military involvement or conflicts may take place.[83]

As becomes clear from the next chapters of this book, Washington and Moscow have much more in common that is widely believed, and 'as an increasingly powerful China asserts itself in Eurasia and America scrambles to deal with the consequences, Delhi and Moscow still hold many cards'.[84] This could make possible the linking of the south and Central Asia through a close Indo–US cooperation in Central Asia, especially if Chinese expan-sion in this crucial region coincides with declining Russian influence. Improvements in India–Pakistan relations could make possible an overland route for India.

3 Clashes and coexistence between the three major powers in Eurasia

China and Russia, these two big neighbours in Central Asia, share a common interest in keeping other geopolitical powers out of what they regard as their 'back yards'. They have competing interests in controlling the energy resources and pipelines of the region: China in securing access as a user, Russia in controlling access as a producer and transit country. Businesses in both countries have an interest in gaining access to non-energy markets in the region, as well as owning key productive assets in the industrial and commercial sphere. Much of this is a reflection of genuine commercial interests, but national security and regional or geopolitical concerns may also be pertinent, especially when state-controlled enterprises are involved.[1] China and Russia share a much higher tolerance for state intervention in the economy than most other partners from outside the region. They also place a high value on stability in their immediate neighbourhoods, which for them means supporting the ruling elites and their power structures against any real or perceived threats from 'colour revolutions' or Islamic fundamentalist upheavals. Beyond this, China wants to assure that Central Asia harbours no support for possible irredentist movements in its Western provinces. Russia would like to maintain its long-standing role among the Commonwealth of Independent States (CIS) countries of the region, and has an interest in protecting the Russian minorities.

Short-term national interests also are reflected in the engagement of the EU and the United States in Central Asia. Access to Central Asia's energy resources is usually at the top of the list of concerns, followed by security concerns centred on the protection of NATO engagement in Afghanistan, and in the case of Europe concern about the drug trade and migration. Beyond this, EU and US support for democratic norms and liberal market principles is grounded in the belief that they will bring long-term economic benefits and stability to the region.[2] These interests are reflected in the US 'southern strategy' (which aims to provide Central Asian energy producers access to South Asian ports and energy markets and links the security of Afghanistan with that of Central Asia)[3] as well as in the elements of the new EU Central Asia strategy (which stresses along with stability in the region, the propagation of 'European values' and access to Central Asian energy resources).[4]

Following the end of the Cold War, US strategists began to pay more attention to the Central Asian region, and the Clinton administration showed particular interest in Central Asia's energy and economic potential. The Bush government also promoted massive and active involvement in Central Asian affairs both to restrict China's geopolitical rise and to gain influence in the region while simultaneously coveting Russia's Central Asian 'backyard'. This was perhaps primarily seen in the US support for the colour revolutions that have swept the region in the past few years, starting with the 'Rose Revolution' in Georgia in 2003, the 'Orange Revolution' in Ukraine in late 2004 and the 'Tulip Revolution' in Kyrgyzstan in early 2005. The domestic turmoil created by these revolutions also alerted the member states of the Shanghai Cooperation Organization (SCO) (China, Russia, Kyrgyzstan, Kazakhstan, Tajikistan and Uzbekistan), which demonstrated growing concern over this turn of events. Yet, the colour revolutions were followed by another incident that perhaps proved to have an even more profound influence over the regional geopolitics.

In May 2005, violence struck the Uzbek town of Andijan as insurgents freed a group of businessmen from a prison. The event is surrounded by uncertainty of what actually happened, but it is clear that it involved major bloodshed, which the Uzbek security forces were partly responsible for. The violent suppression of the uprising led to massive condemnation from the United States and other Western powers, which ultimately led the Uzbek government to demand a forced US withdrawal from the Karshi-Khanabad airbase, which it used for its Afghanistan operation.[5] Soon after, an SCO statement was also delivered demanding the United States to set a deadline for withdrawal from its bases in Central Asia as the situation in Afghanistan was assumed to have stabilized.

This event, combined with this year's stalemate in the Iranian nuclear crisis, also illustrated a dilemma for American foreign policy *vis-à-vis* Central Eurasia. As one expert noted,

> ... in the space of 12 months, Russia and China have managed to move the pieces on the geopolitical chess board of Eurasia away from what had been an overwhelming US strategic advantage, to the opposite, where the United States is increasingly isolated. It's potentially the greatest strategic defeat for the US power projection of the post-World War II period.[6]

Indeed, the geopolitical setbacks have prompted a policy review in Washington. In October 2005, Secretary of State Condoleezza Rice visited the Central Asian capitals to assess the new direction of US diplomacy. After returning, Rice ordered a revamping of the Central Asia desk in the State Department by merging it with the South Asia Bureau while simultaneously promoting the 'Greater Central Asia' concept to avoid US marginalization in the Central Eurasia (CEA) region. Considering the unprecedented

level of influence the United States had built up in South Asia, it was cal-
culated that the South Asian countries would serve its interests positively if
only they could be persuaded to play a proactive role in Central Asia.
Similarly, it was assumed that the Central Asian states would also rethink
their deepening involvement in the SCO if other options were provided.[7]

For centuries, Russia's control of the Central Asian region has had long-
term and profound geopolitical implications for other great powers. Even
though Moscow used natural gas as leverage to exert pressure on the
Ukraine in the winter of 2005 and has put increasing emphasis on energy
diplomacy, its foreign policy towards these countries is not driven primarily
by hopes of recapturing great oil wealth, but by geopolitical dominance. As
some experts have noted:

> Russian interests in the region are both broader and simpler. At the
> minimum, Russia has an interest in preventing these newly independent
> countries from falling under the dominance of any other regional power,
> for example, Turkey and Iran, or becoming a new frontier for the so-
> called hegemony of the United States. At the maximum, Russia would
> seek dominant influence over these countries' domestic as well as foreign
> policies. ... Energy is a means, not an end. Russia also has many cards
> to play short of military action.[8]

Russian President Vladimir Putin has carried out diplomatic, economic and
military measures to counterbalance the United States' growing geopolitical
role in Central Asia, where one means to do this has been through the continuous strengthening of cooperation within the SCO.

With regards to China, it has gradually given Central Asia increased
geostrategic significance since the end of the Cold War. As the United States
established a military presence in Central Asia and the United States carried
out preventive military activities against China in East and South Asia by
strengthening the US–Japan alliance, deploying more strategic submarines
and other deterrent weapons, and ingratiating with the Indians to counterbalance China's rising power, China's leadership has faced tougher geopolitical competition over Central Asia. Considering that China shares 3000
kilometres of border with the three Central Asian countries of Kazakhstan,
Kyrgyzstan and Tajikistan, its importance for China's stability should not
be underestimated. Besides, China's thirst for oil and natural gas to support
its booming economic growth requires Beijing to develop close and stable
relations with these countries, especially in terms of energy cooperation.

The United States is not the only energy rival of China in Central Asia.
China is increasingly competing with India, since both countries are struggling to ensure future supplies by either buying into new foreign oil and
gas fields or by signing supply contracts. In early 2005, Indian Prime
Minister Manmohan Singh said that his country could 'no longer be com-
placent' in its competition with China to secure international energy

supplies. When the China National Petroleum Corporation (CNPC) recently acquired PetroKazakhstan in 2005, outbidding India's state-owned oil company, the Oil and Natural Gas Corporation (ONGC), this further underscored the rivalry involved between the world's two largest developing countries.

Fortunately, both Beijing and New Delhi know they have similar energy strategies, acknowledging that traditional approaches to attain energy security may not be a solution to a forthcoming energy shock or shortage of supply. In April 2005, both parties reached an agreement on strengthening energy cooperation when Chinese Prime Minister Wen Jiabao visited India. Apart from the alliance established between China Gas Holdings and GAIL (Gas Authority of India Limited), India's largest energy conglomerate, the two countries are cooperating over the Greater Nile Oil Project in Sudan on oil refining and transportation, in which CNPC holds a 40 per cent stake and India a 25 per cent stake.

As reported by the Chinese Xinhua News Agency, the China Petrochemical Corp. (Sinopec) and ONGC also hold a 51 per cent and 29 per cent stake respectively in the development of the Yadavaran oil field in Iran. The CNPC is also negotiating with ONGC over joint investment in specific third-country oil projects. Since India supported the International Atomic Energy Agency's (IAEA) position over Iran's nuclear programme in 2005, Iranian criticism has made the proposed Iran–Pakistan–India gas pipeline uncertain. But this will also encourage India to deepen bilateral energy cooperation with China. Moreover, in 2006, India's oil minister Mani Shankar Aiyer signed an agreement to cooperate with China in securing crude oil resources overseas, the aim of which is to prevent fierce competition over oil to drive up prices. In the second round of the Sino–Indian 'strategic dialogue' held in Beijing in February 2006, both countries also agreed to cooperate rather than compete for global energy resources.[9]

Iran has been striving for a dominant role in Central Asia through control of offshore oil and gas fields in the Caspian Sea, but disputes with Azerbaijan, an ally of the United States, over the offshore fields have somewhat impeded full realization of Iran's strategy. Meanwhile, the dispute with the EU and the United States over its nuclear programme reached a stalemate in 2006. Since the EU, Russia, China, Japan and India have major oil interests in Iran, the Iranian nuclear crisis will present a vital foreign policy challenge to Mahmud Ahmadinejad's government.

Trying to examine the bilateral relations between the main external geopolitical actors in Central Asia, China, Russia and the United States, we conclude they are developing into a flexible triangle. China and Russia have a potentially greater common interest in their bilateral relations than in each of their relationships with the United States. This reflects the two countries' more similar power statuses as well as the fact that they have experienced many of the same gains and losses from the US military campaign in Afghanistan and its presence in Central Asia.

Cooperation against terrorism has enhanced both US–Russian and US–Chinese relations, as in the aftermath of 9/11 attacks Washington declared some separatist organizations in both Russia and China to be terrorist organizations. The three powers began sharing common views and interests in anti-terrorism. Russia opened its territorial air space to the United States, shared intelligence and, most important, allowed a military presence in Central Asia. China too closed its border with Afghanistan and shared intelligence with Washington.

Strategic competition in Eurasia

Nevertheless, there still exist elements of competition between the three players. The United States appears to have at least the potential objective of containing both China and Russia in geostrategic terms by its long-term military presence in Central Asia, even if the primary purpose of its deployment was to combat terrorism. This implication is of considerable concern to both Moscow and Beijing, in terms of the security of their periphery and their overall strategic interests. China now faces a US military presence around its north-eastern (the Korean Peninsula), south-eastern (the Philippine Islands, Singapore and the US military commitment to Taiwan) and western (Afghanistan) borders. Russia too has expressed its wish for the US troops to withdraw from Central Asia after the counter-terrorism war ended, and has tried its utmost to strengthen its military, political and economic influence in the Central Asian states. The very fact that Moscow accelerated its deployment at the Kant base in Kyrgyzstan during the Afghan war shows that, once again in its history, it reacts under the threat of encirclement, and therefore some degree of US–Russian strategic competition is inevitable, as shown in Ukraine, Georgia, Azerbaijan, and also Kyrgyzstan or Uzbekistan in recent years.

The same it is true in US–Chinese relations, as Washington's fear of Beijing's credible challenge to the United States' dominant strategic role in the Asia-Pacific region pushes the United States in a steady build up of strategic deployments in China's surrounding regions. At the economic level too, the United States has heavily invested in extracting and exporting Caspian energy resources to the United States and the West, to avoid heading towards China. The non-military (economic – mainly in the field of energy development and oil and gas pipeline construction – political and cultural) aspects of the competition among the three geopolitical actors in Central Asia may turn out to be the ones of most enduring influence.

This is true, given the fact that China, Russia and the United States all are too important – in various ways – to each other in fighting terrorism and in maintaining stability in Central Asia. US troops in Central Asia provide stability in such important regions of both China and Russia, for example Xingjian and Chechnya, and, given Washington's deep involvement in Iraq, countering the proliferation of weapons of mass destruction and other priorities, to afford upsetting their bilateral or trilateral relations in a confrontation over foreign policies. Washington wants to guarantee for itself the means of military access to the region for purposes of combating terrorism, and economic access to the energy competition in Central Asia. Russia, after failing to engulf Central Asian states through various multilateral institutions, cooperates with them in many fields, and has identified China as a partner capable of helping it to sustain its influence in the region.

Central Asia's importance to China's foreign policy and security again is not as important as Sino–US or Sino–Russian relations in terms of what the USA and Russia can contribute to China's political and economic priorities. China does not want to see any conflict in the region; therefore, it has supported the US-led military action against terrorism in Central Asia and Iraq. Given that in the midst of the anti-terrorism campaign the United States has become more reliant than ever on international, regional and bilateral cooperation, China has taken advantage of its geographic bordering with both Afghanistan and North Korea to promote its political utility to Washington. Beijing has also understood that by directly confronting Washington it risks losing opportunities for development through a stand-still in Sino–US economic and technical cooperation.

Currently, the SCO members are pushing energy cooperation forwards among themselves, which will surely affect the US's geopolitical role in Central Asia. A notable feature of the 2005 SCO Astana summit statement was that emphasis was also placed on resisting interference of outside forces by putting forward new geopolitical principles for CEA affairs. Moreover, at the 2006 SCO summit in Shanghai, all member states agreed to give priority to cooperation in the fields of energy and to 'play an independent role in safeguarding stability and security in this region'. Based on the SCO's rapid institutionalization, great-power competition is set to increase in the CEA in the years to come.

To weaken Russian and Iranian control of Caspian oil and gas, the United States has heavily promoted the newly inaugurated Baku–Tbilisi–Ceyhan oil pipeline running from Baku, Azerbaijan, to Ceyhan, Turkey, as well as a trans-Afghan natural gas pipeline running from Turkmenistan to Pakistan through Afghanistan, both bypassing Russian and Iranian territories. Moreover, the United States opposes India's plans to strengthen energy cooperation with Iran through the projected Iran–Pakistan–India gas pipeline and has also voiced its objections to the construction of the Atasu–Alashankou pipeline running from Kazakhstan to Xinjiang. With regards to Japan, not only it does compete with China over the Far East Siberian oil pipeline today, but also it has emerged as a player over Caspian oil and gas in recent years.

In fact, as the Soviet Union disintegrated, the United States announced its strategy of promoting US oil companies' investments in Central Asia and the Caspian Sea region. Backed by the United States, Turkey sought to gain access to Caspian oil by building the Baku–Tbilisi–Ceyhan pipeline. In the words of Brzezinski, the US strategy toward Central Asia in 1997 was guided by

> ... regular consultations with Ankara regarding the future of the Caspian Sea basin and Central Asia would foster in Turkey a sense of strategic partnership with the United States. America should also strongly support Turkish aspirations to have a pipeline from Baku in Azerbaijan to Ceyhan on the Turkish Mediterranean coast serve as major outlet for the Caspian Sea basin energy sources.[10]

There should be no doubt about the weight and significance given to the project from Western contractors and the states involved. The Baku–Tbilisi–Ceyhan pipeline was originally proclaimed by BP and others as the 'project of the century' where Zbigniew Brzezinski, acting as a consultant to BP during the Clinton era, urged Washington to support the project. It was obvious that the Baku–Tbilisi–Ceyhan plan had more political implications than economic considerations from the very beginning. Officials from the United States, Turkey, Azerbaijan and Georgia have always emphasized the geopolitical role of the Baku–Tbilisi–Ceyhan pipeline. This pipeline, it was argued, would strengthen the independence of the smaller Caspian states while impairing Russian influence in the CEA region. In 1998, in the presence of the US energy secretary, the presidents of Azerbaijan, Georgia, Kazakhstan, Turkey and Uzbekistan signed a joint declaration aiming to promote multilateral cooperation over the exploration and transportation of Caspian oil. As stated by Zhiznin: 'The BTC [Baku–Tbilisi–Ceyhan] pipeline was regarded as a strategic pipeline and political factors played a leading role in the declaration'.[11] In late 1999, during the Organization for Security and Cooperation in Europe (OSCE) summit meeting in Istanbul, the presidents of Azerbaijan, Georgia, Kazakhstan, Turkmenistan and Turkey in presence of US President Bill Clinton signed a series of political documents supporting the construction of the Baku–Tbilisi–Ceyhan pipeline and a cross-Caspian Sea natural gas pipeline. As Western specialists conclude, 'the building of the Baku–Tbilisi–Ceyhan pipeline constitutes a strategic milestone in post-Soviet Eurasia'.[12]

In September 2002, construction of the long debated 1,700 kilometre Baku–Tbilisi–Ceyhan pipeline began. It opened in May 2005 and with its total cost of US$3.6 billion it is one of the most expensive oil projects ever. As noted by Zha Daojiong: 'This is the first oil pipeline intervened directly and controlled by western countries, and this 'seeking far and wide for what lies close at hand' pipeline implies the American thoughtful motives of containing Russia and Iran.[13] In times to come, it is estimated that the Baku–Tbilisi–Ceyhan pipeline will have a capacity to transport 1 million barrels of oil per day. Needless to say, the Baku–Tbilisi–Ceyhan oil pipeline and its profitability may depend on the ultimate volume of Kazakh oil that is transported on this route. The United States has pushed for building a trans-Caspian pipeline that would give Kazakhstan the ability to pipe crude oil through the Baku–Tbilisi–Ceyhan pipeline.

In addition, the United States has been attentive to challenges presented by terrorist groups in CEA, as well as Russian and Iranian military presence in the region. On that basis, the United States is striving to get permanent access to bases in Georgia and Azerbaijan. This is something that is viewed as direct strategic provocation by the Caucasus countries' primary antagonists, Russia and Iran. For this purpose the Pentagon has put aside US$100 million for the launch of a Caspian Guard that purportedly is being set up to guard the Baku–Tbilisi–Ceyhan pipeline. Some of these funds are also reportedly being used to build a radar-equipped command centre in Baku.[14] The objective of the United States is 'to deny to a single state, other than the US itself, or coalition of powers not including the US, the capability to set conditions for accessing the energy resources of West and CEA'.[15] In a sense, to control the Caspian Sea would imply control of energy resources in this region, particularly exports from Kazakhstan and Turkmenistan, the two main targets of Chinese energy companies in Central Asia.

This strategy is becoming more evident taking into consideration another notorious pipeline schedule. In 1993, China became a net importer of oil products, and energy demand and imports have increased steadily since. Ten years later, in 2003, China's imports of oil increased 30 per cent over those of 2002 making China the second largest importer of petroleum after the United States, even surpassing Japan in 2004. In 2005, China's oil imports were expected to grow by 10 per cent to about 7 million barrels a day.[16] The trend of China's increasing import volumes is set to continue. China will inevitably have to strengthen its pursuit of energy to keep up with demand and the pace of economic growth. This has been partly achieved by seeking to forge more extensive energy ties with Kazakhstan.

In 1997, the news of the China National Petroleum Corporation's investment in oil exploration in Kazakhstan greatly surprised Western countries and spurred closer scrutiny of China's potential oil demand and the effects that this would have on energy prices.[17] The main focus of China–Kazakhstan energy cooperation has in recent years been the construction of the 3088 kilometre Atasu–Alashankou oil pipeline running from the Atyrau oil base in western Kazakhstan to Alashankou in China's Xinjiang autonomous region. In December 2005, the second cross-border phase of the pipeline running 962 kilometres was finished. In the words of William Engdahl: 'The pipeline will undercut the geopolitical significance of the Washington-backed Baku–Tbilisi–Ceyhan oil pipeline which opened amid big fanfare and support from Washington'.[18] Kazakhstan's Vice Energy Minister Musabek Isayev said on 30 November 2005 in Beijing that half the oil pumped through the new 200,000 barrel a day pipeline would come from Russia because of insufficient output from nearby Kazakh fields. That was interpreted as closer China–Kazakhstan–Russia energy cooperation – 'the nightmare scenario' of Washington.[19]

The Atasu–Alashankou oil pipeline represents a partial step into the massive reserves of the Caspian Sea, and especially the Kashagan oil field located in the north of the Caspian. As the connection between Kumkol and Kenkiyak is completed, the Atasu–Alashankou pipeline will have a direct linkage with Kashagan as the field is developed. In 2005, China imported 1.3 million tons of crude oil from Kazakhstan via the Alataw Pass in Xinjiang. Experts predicted the figure would climb to 4.75 million tons in 2006 and to around 8 million tons in 2007.[20] China is expected to become one of Kazakhstan's major target markets.

Chinese experts see three benefits derived from building the China–Kazakhstan pipeline and extending its energy ties with Kazakhstan: first, it will lessen China's dependence on oil from the Persian Gulf, greatly decreasing the risk of Middle Eastern turbulence to China's energy security; second, the inland location in Eurasia will make China's oil supply route safer; and, third, it will provide China with a long-term and stable land-based alternative oil supply.[21] As the project is completed, it will also represent a major strategic gain as it is ' ... the first time [China] have secured a source of imported energy not vulnerable to US aircraft carrier battle groups, as is the case with present oil deliveries from the Persian Gulf and Sudan'.[22] In late May of this year, oil began to flow to Duzishan of Xinjiang through the Atasu–Alashankou oil pipeline. Furthermore, in October 2005, the China National Petroleum Corporation completed a US$4.18 billion takeover of PetroKazakhstan Inc. after Washington blocked China's acquisition of Unocal.[23]

As a result of China's growing power, opportunities have appeared in recent years in which Russia gradually has come to accept China's strategic leverage in countering the American presence in Central Asia. Indeed, much strategic space could be found for China in the present regional power vacuum but coordination with other outsiders still remains a challenge for China's oil diplomacy. China has started to pay more attention not only to energy cooperation with Russia regarding the construction of pipelines from the Far East, but also in other projects. The construction of the China–Kazakhstan pipeline was undertaken on the assumption that it would not only carry Kazakh oil, but also transfer Russia's Caspian oil. As the Atasu–Alashankou pipeline opened, China considered asking Russian companies to help fill it until the Kazakh supply was sufficient.

However, the American policy towards Central Asia has affected China's room for manoeuvre. As a specialist on Central Asian affairs has stated, ' ... unlike Central Asia, Russia, Pakistan and India, China has made no solid gains from the changes in US policy after 11 September ... China's drive for influence in Central Asia will become harder now that the United States has ensconced itself in the region, and the American military presence on its western edge complicates China's strategic planning'.[24]

Apart from US competition, Japan has also become seriously concerned over the pace of China's energy cooperation with Central Asian countries in recent years and has launched countermoves. In the words of Zha Daojiong: 'Japan has the intention of constraining China's growing power through the means of transportation of resources'.[25] Nowadays, many oil giants from the United States, Great Britain, France, Italy, Canada, Russia and other countries have entered the fields of Kazakhstan, which will bring further complexities and uncertainties to China–Kazakhstan oil cooperation.

China's energy security in 'the Eurasian Balkans'

An undercurrent of instability and conflict owing to the growing political, economic and military competition among the great powers has in recent years made the Caspian Sea, Central Asia and the Caucasus a source of a power struggle that indeed may justify labelling it 'the Eurasian Balkans' to use the words of Brzezinski. For China's energy security, as stated in the National Energy Security Report:

> China is a neighbouring country of this [Central Asian] region. We must join the regional geo-economic and geopolitical activities for our circumjacent security and oil-supply security ... The rivalry between the United States (in Central Asia) and Russia will be getting rapidly intense. China should not withdraw from the (great-power) competition in this region for the safety of China's oil supply.[26]

Two key questions emerge from this: What are the alternatives for China's oil strategy towards the Caspian Sea region? How should China respond to great-power rivalries in Central Asia? China should adhere to the principle of relying on domestic resources to safeguard energy supply and it should study alternative ways to gradually increase its national oil reserve, rather than buy crude oil from the world market to fill its reserves when oil prices remain high. However, it has been said that

> [T]he idea that energy security can be improved by reducing import dependence is an obstacle to clear thinking ... The 'conventional vision' of continuing expansion of oil use with some loss of market share and without strongly escalating prices is a reasonable but fragile reference line against which to discuss the dynamics of the future.[27]

In fact, China's external oil dependency rate is getting higher, reaching 42.9 per cent in 2005.[28] In addition, the proven reserves of China will be exhausted in 14 years in terms of domestic oil supply.[29] The question is, when facing the threat of an energy blockade, how can Beijing ensure its oil security with international conflicts along the sea lanes of Asia, including the East and South China Sea, the Malacca Strait, the Hormuz Strait, and the Indian and Pacific Oceans? (see Maps 2.4 and 3.1). One of the main concerns of China's energy diplomacy is, according to a Norwegian report, 'to secure

Map 3.1 South East Asia and the Malacca Strait
Source: CIA World Factbook

access to energy for all parts of China at the lowest possible cost, either through domestic production or import'. The report also lists the various worst-case scenarios that will affect on China's oil strategy:

> In terms of threats to its energy security, China's policy makers have three major worries: sudden disruptions in provision of oil to the global market could trigger serious energy shortages and sharp price spikes; China might be affected by disruptions in tankers flows from unstable export-ing regions such as the Persian Gulf, Central Asia and Africa; Japan and

the United States might attempt to deny China vital oil supplies in the event of a confrontation.[30]

Under such geopolitical considerations, 'the construction of overland oil pipelines is seen as desirable in order to mitigate China's vulnerability'.[31] From this perspective, the Central Asian region would be China's preference for oil and gas supplies through overland pipelines.

Confirming this direction is China's growing investments in, and deepening political relationships with, energy-producing nations in Central Asia, in reality reflecting its perceived 'energy vulnerabilities' and a desire to ensure energy security by diversifying supply away from Middle Eastern sources. Geopolitically, one of the most important questions for China is also to 'stabilize the west side' and its western border.[32] The difficulty is how to maintain a stable situation in Central Asia when China's strategy towards its western neighbours in Central Asia has to consider the oil supply and geopolitical challenges simultaneously. Strengthening close energy relations with the Central Asian countries has remarkable implications for China's energy strategy, not least since the oil-rich Caspian Sea is regarded as the second 'Persian Gulf'. Therefore, China's close energy relationship with Central Asian countries will play an important role in improving China's economic growth.

In addition, the diversification of oil resources is an important component of China's oil security. The Middle East has been the main source of oil for China's imports, but it is the most turbulent region in the world, particularly after the US invasion of Iraq in 2003, which endangers China's energy security as China's dependence on oil from the Persian Gulf grows.[33] China has sought diversification by enhancing oil cooperation with oil-rich African countries, such as Sudan and Nigeria, Latin American countries, most notably Venezuela, and Central Asian countries such as Kazakhstan and Turkmenistan. Since the proportion of oil imported from Central Asia is relatively low, bilateral oil cooperation has great potential in the future.

Lastly, China's energy strategy shares the same feature of diversification with Central Asian countries. In order to maintain economic independence the former Soviet republics, and especially Kazakhstan and Turkmenistan, have carefully sought to navigate between the competing great powers, especially the United States and Russia, striving to avoid being played by any one actor against the others. China's entry into this region can provide new oil pipelines and further options for these inland states because of its role as a balancing force between Washington and Moscow.[34]

China should consider its strategy towards Central Asia from a geopolitical view and take the following measures. First, China should support the SCO to be not only an international organization for fighting the 'three evils' of extremism, terrorism and separatism, but also for promoting greater economic integration and energy cooperation. The deepening of political and economic cooperation under the SCO framework has been accelerating in recent years since China and Russia have regarded regional economic integration to be a primary interest for their own national security.[35] In terms of the 'Going West' development strategy, China's longest domestic pipeline, the 4,200 kilometre Tarim Basin to Shanghai gas pipeline, could potentially be extended to Kazakhstan and Turkmenistan, and even further to other Caspian states by linking up with the Atasu–Alashankou pipeline.

Second, China should work with Russia to improve the SCO's relationship with Turkmenistan and Afghanistan. Without the membership and participation of Ashgabat and Kabul (let alone observer status), the SCO falls short of its capacity to develop regional economic integration and energy cooperation. In a sense, Afghanistan is becoming the new 'colony' of the United States following the military intervention in Afghanistan. Turkmenistan, in turn, has pursued a foreign policy of neutrality and independence while facing growing security challenges from the south, especially from Iran and Afghanistan. As Iran gained observer status in the SCO in 2005, this will further promote regional integration and the feasibility of joint infrastructural projects. For example, the chances of building the proposed oil pipeline from Kazakhstan via Turkmenistan to Iran may be raised if this is coordinated through the SCO. Such a pipeline would further propel the prospects of regional integration and interdependence.

Meanwhile, China should reassess its foreign policy towards Iran considering the heavy oil dependence on that country. China currently receives 13.6 per cent of its oil imports from Iran, and in March 2004, China signed a US$100 million deal with Iran to import 10 million tons of liquefied natural gas (LNG) over a 25-year period. The deal was conditional upon Chinese investment in Iran's oil and gas exploration, petrochemical and pipeline infrastructure. For China–Iran relations, there is nothing more important than oil cooperation. The most urgent measure to be taken is for China to be involved in planning the construction of a pipeline from Iran to the Caspian Sea to link up with the planned pipeline from China to Kazakhstan.

Third, owing to the effects of geopolitics in the CEA region, China is better off exploring bilateral and multilateral oil cooperation when implementing its overseas oil strategy. There are arguments that China's growing presence on the international energy stage could ultimately bring it into confrontation with the world's largest energy consumer, the United States. The argument of 'China's oil threat' could hamper Beijing's efforts to improve oil cooperation among SCO countries if it neglects the establishment of bilateral or multilateral trust with the other external powers.[36] As stated by a group of analysts: 'Cooperation to achieve and share the benefits of certain major energy "projects", defined in the widest sense, could contribute to wider cooperation and put constraints on the development of conflicts'.[37]

Sino–Iranian energy security relations

It is this cooperation and these potential conflicts that the SCO is at least nominally entitled to assure and avoid respectively. However, much is dependent on the future course of Sino–Iranian relations, which spring from deep historical roots. It is noteworthy that China and Iran are the heirs to two great civilizations and centres of empire. During pre-Islamic times, Han envoys established contact with the Parthians and later the Sassanids, laying the foundation for lucrative commercial ties between China and Persia. In Islamic times, the Silk Road has served as the main thoroughfare through which Sino–Iranian cultural and trade relations flourished.

At every opportunity, officials from both countries invoke this ancient past relationship. These references should not be dismissed as empty rhetoric, for they are indicative of the way that in China as well as in Iran history and culture inform present-day conceptions of both nations and their view of their own power and status in the world. In this regard, the ancient Silk Road is associated with their respective past great achievements and wide-ranging influence. The determination to kindle their relationship with each other, therefore, reflects a common desire to recreate the past, not just commemorate it.

The past is also relevant insofar as both countries' historical experiences with other major players are concerned. Historical wounds, expressed in a profound sense of victimization and vulnerability, are deeply ingrained in Chinese and Iranian national consciousness. This is manifested in their commonly held preoccupation with issues of sovereignty and independence, in their desire to reclaim status and influence on the world stage, and in their aim of building a 'just' international order (i.e. one not dominated by a hegemonic power). In short, what might be referred to as a 'kinship of nationalisms' pervades the present-day Sino–Iranian relationship.[38]

Yet it is important to emphasize that these affinities have never been potent enough to drive the relationship forwards or to insulate it from the impact of divergent strategic outlooks or priorities. It is worth recalling that, in the contemporary era, Sino–Iranian relations have not always been cordial, but at the same time they have never been overtly hostile. A warming trend in Sino–Iranian relations began in the mid-1960s, against the backdrop of the Sino–Soviet split and incipient detente between the United States and Soviet Union. During this period, Beijing's reaching out to Asian and African countries intensified. Meanwhile, the Shah sought to gain a greater degree of independence from the superpower rivalry by developing a wide array of external relationships. The major turning point in Sino–Iranian relations came in 1971 with the Shah's decision to recognize Beijing as the sole legal government of China, leading to the establishment of diplomatic relations.[39]

Thereafter, Iranian and Chinese interests began to converge, with Moscow emerging as a common enemy.[40] China increasingly viewed Iran as a bulwark against Soviet ambitions in the Persian Gulf. And for a time, China and Iran shared with each other, and with the United States, the strategic aim of countering the Soviet Union. The transformation of the US–Iranian relationship from that of strategic allies to enemies, resulted in a sharp diversification of the Chinese and Iranian domestic and external policies. China, emerging from the Cultural Revolution, embarked on a bold effort to open up its economy, invoked the principles of peaceful coexistence, and declared an 'independent' foreign policy while maintaining a stable relationship with the United States. In contrast, the Islamic Republic of Iran exuded militant religious ideological fervour, embraced populist slogans and statist economic policies, waged a debilitating war with Iraq, and remained locked in a hostile relationship with the United States.

Thereafter, a combination of Iranian pragmatism and Chinese opportunism kept the relationship moving forward. The relationship was anchored in China's sale of conventional arms and ballistic missiles to Iran.[41] It is noteworthy that the Islamic Republic of Iran struck these deals in spite of its hostility to 'godless communism' and Beijing's heavy-handed treatment of the Uyghur Muslim minority. Similarly, the Chinese leadership, wary of Iran's fundamentalist Islamic message, nonetheless found it more prudent to engage than to confront Tehran, and sidestepped the issue of theocratic rule.[42]

It is important to emphasize that over the years, the United States has been the pivotal third party in Sino–Iranian relations, serving as both an enabling and a complicating factor. The US arms embargo and economic sanctions against Iran have indirectly benefited China. Pressure by Washington on its Western allies has reinforced Tehran's inclination to 'Look East' for both commercial and strategic partners. The prohibition on US companies from doing business in Iran has created space, particularly in the energy sector, which Chinese enterprises along with other foreign firms (e.g. BP, Royal Dutch Shell, and ENI) have competed with one another to fill.

Energy cooperation is the backbone of the Sino–Iranian economic relationship. Trade in crude oil is the core of energy cooperation. In 2005, Iran was China's third-leading foreign supplier (behind Saudi Arabia), satisfying about 14 per cent of its import requirements.[43] In January 2006, Iran replaced Saudi Arabia as China's number one source of imported oil. With respect to the benefits accrued to China, it is worth noting that Iranian crude oil not only helps meet skyrocketing Chinese consumption needs, but helps contain rising import costs through the purchase of the relatively cheap, heavy (sulphur-rich) oil that is plentiful in Iran (and Saudi Arabia).

China's growing appetite for natural gas in the form of LNG has provided a second energy link with Iran, which has an estimated 15 per cent of the world's natural gas reserves. In March 2004, the state-owned Zhuhai Zhenrong Corporation (a spin-off of NORINCO) agreed to import 110 million tons of Iranian LNG over 25 years, a deal worth approximately US $20 billion.[44] According to the terms of the Yadavaran project agreement,

Sinopec has committed to the purchase of 10 million tons per year of LNG over a period of 25 years, beginning in 2009. Iran's Deputy Oil Minister Hadi Nejad-Hosseinian estimates that gas exports to China will gradually increase to 40 million tons per annum.[45]

A third area of cooperation in the energy sector is upstream and downstream development. Participation by Chinese companies in such projects is part of the internationalization of their business operations and part of their global effort to obtain equity stakes in production, thereby enhancing long-term energy security. In August 2000, CNPC won its first drilling contract in Iran (to drill 19 gas wells in southern Iran), the first project of its kind put to international tender since the Iranian Revolution.[46] The most significant breakthrough in this area is the widely reported preliminary agreement (reached in October 2004) between the National Iranian Oil Company (NIOC) and Sinopec to develop the Yadavaran oil field, whereby NIOC would sell 150,000 barrels per day of crude oil to China at market prices over a period of 25 years when the field becomes fully operational. In June 2005, CNPC won a bid to develop the Khoudasht oil block in western Iran.[47]

For Iran, engaging Chinese companies in these ventures stems from a mixture of motives. The main commercial objectives are access to much-needed foreign investment capital and technology. These objectives dovetail with the strategic imperative of locking in an economic partnership with a major world power that holds a permanent seat on the UN Security Council – a potentially useful lever in countering US and Western pressure. The commercial benefits are evident in the June 2006 deal between the North Drilling Company (NDC) of Iran and China Oilfield Services Ltd (COSL), a CNOOC subsidiary, which signed an oil exploration agreement for management, repair and maintenance of the Alborz semi-floating platform being built by the Iranian Offshore Industries Company. This partnership will enable Iran to drill for oil in the Caspian Sea at depths that it otherwise would not have been able to.[48]

A fourth area of cooperation is the upgrading of Iranian refineries and the enhancement of oil recovery. CNPC is engaged in an oil recovery and extraction project to increase the production of Iran's Masjed Soleiman field based on a buy-back contract.[49] Iran and China also signed a preliminary agreement to construct a gas condensates refinery in Bandar Abbas, aimed at raising the production of gasoline, which currently constitutes 56 per cent of the refinery's output. The deal stipulates that Iran will own the gasoline produced at the refinery whereas China will export other outputs, and that Iran will assume ownership of the refinery after 25 years.[50]

China and Iran have found common ground in a fifth area – the construction of oil and gas pipelines. Chinese companies are involved in projects that will enable Iran to increase its swap deals. The Neka–Sari pipeline, built by a consortium of Chinese companies led by Sinopec and CNPC (completed in 2003), carries Russian crude oil shipped from the Caspian ports of

Astrakhan and Volgagrad from the Iranian port of Neka further into Iran. Another pipeline being built with Chinese participation will carry oil from the Neka terminal to a refinery on the southern outskirts of Tehran in the municipality of Ray.[51] China has an interest in expanding Iran's oil/gas pipeline network quite separate from whether or not its own firms help to build them. Consistent with its aim to develop alternative supply delivery networks.[52] Beijing hopes to receive the necessary guarantees from Tehran to build an oil pipeline from the Caspian Sea, at a length of 386 kilometres, to another pipeline in Kazakhstan that will be connected to China.[53]

China and Iran have been working separately and jointly to augment their capacity to handle the increased volumes of oil, gas and refined products moving from the Persian Gulf to East Asia. For example, in order to support the growth of LNG imports from Iran and other suppliers, China is building receiving terminals at Guangdong, Shanghai and Fujian. Meanwhile, China's main shipbuilding enterprises have won contracts to supply Iran with oil tankers. In 2000, for example, the Export–Import Bank of China (Eximbank) agreed to lend US$370 million to the state-owned conglomerates Dalian Shipbuilding Industry Corp. and the China Shipbuilding Trading Company Ltd, which had been contracted to build five oil tankers for Iran. At the time, this was the largest loan made by Eximbank since it was founded in 1994. Dalian recently delivered to Iran a fourth wide-bodied 300,000 ton VLCC oil tanker.[54]

It is perhaps useful to provide some context for understanding Sino–Iranian cooperation in shipbuilding. The penetration of the Iranian market by Chinese shipbuilding firms is part of their broader efforts to compete internationally.[55] Iran, which is seeking to expand its fleet of tankers and cargo vessels, appears to regard Chinese firms as welcome partners and seems inclined to privilege them over their competitors in recognition of the fact that China is likely to become a major LNG customer. The National Iranian Oil Tanker Company (NITC) plans to order another 35 vessels to be built by 2010, including 10 LNG carriers, a more complex ship that costs almost twice as much as crude oil tankers.

At the level of multi-party diplomacy, Tehran has sought to breathe new life in recent years to the Economic Cooperation Organization (ECO), in which China holds observer status. Another example is the SCO, whose fifth summit, held in Beijing in July 2005, was attended by First Vice President Mohammad Reza Aref. At the most recent meeting in June 2006, President Ahmadinejad urged members to join Iran in forging closer energy links.[56] In fact, there are several reasons for the United States to be attentive to, indeed concerned about, the consolidation of Sino–Iranian relations. Iran's vast energy resources provide Tehran with leverage that it is clearly prepared to use not just for economic gain but also to advance broader strategic objectives. China is susceptible to these enticements both because of the perception in Beijing that the country is experiencing an acute energy crisis and because of uncertainty as to how long Chinese energy companies, in the quest to lock in long-term access to Iranian energy resources, will be able to exploit Tehran's rift with the West.

The deepening of Sino–Iranian energy cooperation poses several challenges for the United States. The first challenge stems from Chinese business practices in pursuing energy deals, at least some of which tend to distort the market. The second challenge stems from the lack of transparency that prevails in many of the commercial dealings between China and Iran. This is particularly disturbing in light of the fact that among the Chinese enterprises most active in Iran are those that, besides being at least nominally state-owned and directed, have repeatedly violated the spirit, if not the letter, of China's pledges to halt the sale of missile and other sensitive weapons technology to Iran. The third challenge is Beijing's relatively high level of tolerance for Iran's non-compliance with non-proliferation treaty (NPT) obligations, which tends to feed the Iranian perception that it can play for time and probably avoid the sting of punitive sanctions.

> There is a much stronger perceived need and desire in Tehran than in Beijing to forge a full-blown strategic partnership aimed at countering the United States. Even where Sino–Iranian links are the strongest—in the energy sector—problems and limitations abound. As shown, the under-performing Iranian energy industry is in dire need of foreign technology and investment. China can only partially ameliorate these problems. Furthermore, the prevailing business climate in Iran, which is marked by protectionist policies and political uncertainties, is bound to discourage Chinese private sector investment in the areas where Iran arguably needs it the most—in non-energy labour-intensive industries. This brings us to the nexus between the high-stakes diplomatic manoeuvring over the Iranian nuclear programme and Sino–Iranian energy cooperation. More than four years have passed since Sinopec won the bid to develop the Yadavaran field. Officials from both sides have attributed the delay to technical obstacles – there are undoubtedly some, given the scope and complexity of the project. Yet there is reason to be sceptical about this explanation. Even with its propensity to assume high risk, Sinopec is not willing to sink billions of dollars into a project that could be destroyed in a potential military confrontation between the United States and Iran. That is why, oddly enough, China should have a stronger interest in supporting nuclear diplomacy rather than in subverting it. At some point this might require that Beijing choose to side either with Washington or with Tehran – a choice that until now Beijing has managed to avoid in the interest of cementing a less than perfect but nonetheless fruitful relationship with Iran.[57]

However, a few researchers and policy-makers have even argued that the competition between the United States and China is the beginning of a new Cold War. It is evident that China is gaining a greater role both in regional and international politics and this could create a military confrontation between the states, but with the current situation in Central Asia and in China the rivalry between the United States and China is not bound to become militarized.[58] It is important to point out that China has no reason or possibility to act aggressively against any state because of its bad finances and weak military organization. It is also important for China that nothing disrupts the international integration and domestic economic development since this could impact upon social stability in China. It is, moreover, in the interest of the United States to cooperate with China in the short-term as Washington is in need of China's cooperation in the Security Council of the UN and to create economic stability in both Asia and globally.

It is apparent that Central Asia will play a greater role in China's foreign policy in the future. It is, however, not a question of the classical problem of *Lebensraum* for China. Beyond the economic reasons the expansion also has political aspects. Domestically China would like to use the improved relations with the Central Asian governments to resolve the conflict with the Uyghur minority in Xinjiang, or to crush the rebels. To manage the situation in Xinjiang, China will need active help from the bordering states, both with closing the borders for rebels and with ending verbal and military support. In this aspect China, Russia, the Central Asian republics and the United States share a common interest, i.e. combating nationalistic Islam. Beijing has also realized that there are geopolitical benefits of a deepened relationship with Central Asia.[59] Dominance or strong influence in Central Asia could establish a cheap, fast and secure route for Middle Eastern oil but also stabilize the western borders of China, if China is willing to negotiate with the Uyghur rebels.

The Chinese policy will undoubtedly decrease Russian importance in the region; and the question is whether Russia has the resources to stop this development. As the situation in Russia appears to remain politically fragile and economically unstable, the answer has to be no.[60] Chinese attempts to take a more prominent position has become apparent as China controls large portions of the oil and gas fields in the region and is behind a large share of the investments in the region, but Chinese expansion is prevented by non-Chinese interests intended to limit Chinese influence in the region. China's efforts to dominate the region have been challenged by the United States following 9/11 and it will not be able to control the region to a degree that was possible before US intervention in Afghanistan, but China seems to have the potential to become the dominant power in the region. The extent of Chinese control will, however, not be possible to determine, as it will depend on the scale of American interest and investment in the region as well as on China's internal situation. China's intention is, however, to influence and control the Central Asian region to a degree that could be compared to a classical vassal relationship with Central Asia, where Beijing invests and provides security and receives political stability and influence in the region. This can be seen in the aggressive investment, military and political initiatives in the region that have been ongoing since the Central Asian states gained independence. The Chinese strategy is, however, not to dominate in a negative way, but rather to influence the states to the degree that they would, voluntarily or by necessity, view China as the main actor in the region once more.[61]

Truly, Chinese cooperation with Russia must be understood in light of their perception of the main threat and the assessment of Russian weakness. Many Chinese commentators view the US establishment of bases in Central Asia as part of a long-term US strategy of containment.[62] They view the differences between the United States and China as 'structural in nature'. They believe that the United States exploited the post-9/11 environment to establish strategic supremacy in regions, such as Central Asia, where previously the United States was not a major player. In contrast, Russia is viewed as a much lesser power than the Soviet Union and therefore a country with which China needs to cooperate in order to offset US influence. Together through the SCO they have enough strength to resist US penetration in Central Asia, something they could not have done separately.[63]

A common cause against the Americans provides the main stimulus for Sino–Russian cooperation. Once (and if) the United States withdraws, that cooperation should decline.[64] The differences between China and Russia are substantial and 'structural in nature'.[65] First, Russia has promoted the CSTO as the primary security organization in Central Asia. This contrasts with China's desire to give precedence to the SCO. Second, Russia has pushed economic integration through mechanisms that exclude the Chinese, such as the CIS and the Eurasian Economic Community. Moreover, China and Russia are perceived to be pursuing different objectives through the SCO. Russia for its part is viewed as mainly wanting by partnering with China to balance the West.[66] By contrast, China's goals are more specific and pragmatic. The Ferghana Valley, viewed as a hotbed of the so-called 'three forces' – separatism, extremism and terrorism – is only a mountain range away. Moreover, China views Russia, Kazakhstan and Uzbekistan as important sources of energy supplies, and the SCO provides a forum in which to engage these countries. Even here there are tensions since Russia would prefer to control access to Kazakhstan and Uzbekistan. Despite these underlying tensions, China realizes that it must manage its security relationship with Russia successfully in order protect its vulnerable north and west flanks. For the Chinese the SCO and multilateral relations are the fora of choice. The fear is that Russia may take its own independent course, or worse yet be seduced by the West as it was in the early 1990s. Chinese fears are not misplaced is this regard. As one Russian scholar has noted, Russia's approach to China depends on Russia's relationship with the West.[67]

The point of departure for an understanding of China's approach to Central Asia is Deng Xiaoping, who argued in the early 1990s that China should 'lie low and bide our time' [*taoguo yanghui*] and wait for opportunities for decisive action [*yousuo zuowei*].[68] China should take only that action necessary to assure peaceful development.

In sum, China, Russia and the United States have elements of both competition over security and energy affairs and cooperation in Central Asia. In fact, the perspectives of cooperation between the three players are greater than those for conflict given that Central Asia is regarded a second-order area in each of their strategic perspectives.

4 Is a strategic meeting of minds among Washington, Beijing and Moscow for the sake of Eurasia's stability realistic?

How can the security and energy security in Eurasia be discussed without first examining the relationship between the major powers in the area, Russia and China? To make things clear, Russia is the world's second largest oil producer, after Saudi Arabia, and China the world's second largest oil consumer, after the United States. Although bilateral trade-flow is still small, there is great potential inherent in the relationship. Old hostilities have been put aside after the final settlement in 2004 of a series of disputes along the 3645-kilometre border which had plagued Sino–Russian relations for centuries and caused war in 1969. Moreover, Beijing and Moscow have compatible views on separatism, Islamism, terrorism, democratization and stability.

The new Sino–Russian relationship is driven by trade and mutual economic interest. China's economy is the fourth largest in the world, with a gross domestic product (GDP) of US$2.8 trillion; in terms of purchasing power parity it is the second largest, with an output of US$8.6 trillion.[1] China has pursued a dual transition process, moving simultaneously from a planned economy to a market economy and from a rural, agrarian economy to a more urban, industrial one. In this process it has emerged as the world's second largest consumer of oil products at 7.4 million barrels per day,[2] a figure projected to at least double to 13.4 million barrels per day by 2025. Around 40 per cent of the growth in world oil demand between 2001 and 2005 came from China.

Russia provided 10.1 per cent of China's total oil imports in 2005. This amounted to 257,000 barrels per day, and was up from 29,700 barrels in 2000.[3] However, this figure is set to increase steeply, particularly if Russia's oil can provide China with a more secure foundation for its economic transformation than supplies from volatile Middle Eastern and African states. Energy reserves in western Siberia are estimated at up to 200 billion barrels, and those in eastern Siberia 50 billion barrels. In the Sakhalin region there could be 28 billion barrels. For comparative purposes, Iraq is thought to hold 112.5 billion barrels.[4] Rising global temperatures will in the future make it easier for Russia to access these resources.

Geography in the form of the shared Sino–Russian border has a crucial impact on the potential for trade between the two countries. For China, the strategic importance of access to Russian raw materials is great, because other assets are largely dependent on open waterways, particularly the straights of Hormuz and Malacca. These could be cut off in the event of a crisis over Taiwan or other major confrontation with the United States. Moreover, conflicts not directly related to China and beyond its control could result in supply disruption, for example a confrontation between Iran and the United States. Iran currently supplies 11.2 per cent of China's total imports and the Middle East as a whole supplies 47.2 per cent of total oil imports.[5] China sources 30.3 per cent of its total petroleum imports from Africa.[6] A crisis in these regions would have severe consequences for Beijing. By contrast, Russian supplies can arrive in China through their shared border or the Pacific, and therefore carry a different risk profile.

In fact, Chinese imports of raw materials from conflict-ridden countries in Africa, the Middle East, Latin America and Asia is a reflection of China's rising demand for imported raw materials, and a series of pragmatic decisions to channel Chinese investment to states where there is little competition from American and European corporations. China seeks to expand control over supplies of petroleum, minerals and other raw materials through equity investments, primarily for reasons of state and economic security.

This strategy has in a sense been encouraged by Washington, because it has sought to block Chinese bids for less controversial assets, such as the China National Offshore Oil Corporation's (CNOOC) US$18.5 billion attempted takeover of Unocal, on the grounds that China should not be allowed to take over 'American' resources. China has strong incentives to increase imports from Russia, even though the current political climate in Russia makes it unlikely that China will be allowed to make large equity investments.

The Beijing–Moscow–Tokyo equation

Most notably, whether Moscow favours Beijing or Tokyo in the construction of the energy transport infrastructure in Siberia will have important implications for the balance of power in East Asia. If China wins, this will both support China's claim to regional pre-eminence and promote the Russia–China axis; if Japan were to succeed, a more multi-polar structure would emerge in East Asia. The main issue is the route of a new pipeline to carry oil eastwards from Siberia. If the pipeline is laid directly from Siberia to China and does not reach the Pacific Ocean, the supply will be pre-eminently for China. If a pipeline is laid all the way to the Pacific Coast, for example to the port of Nakhodka, the oil could become available to any countries on the Pacific Ocean, including Japan and the United States. This option is more expensive, but gives Russia greater flexibility and less dependency on relations with China and the Chinese market.

In 2004 Japan seemed to emerge as the core partner for Russia in the construction of the Siberian energy infrastructure, after Beijing had earlier appeared to be Moscow's favourite. Tokyo was willing to guarantee financing for the project, possibly in the range of US$15 billion. The pipeline to Nakhodka would be the longest in the world: at around 4,180 kilometres, it would be three times the length of the trans-Alaska pipeline.[7] The pipeline terminus would be just one day away from Japan by tanker.

Putin had reasons to favour the Nakhodka pipeline, because Japan's deal promised greater net investment in Russia and because a pipeline to the Pacific would make Russia less dependent on China as a customer for its sales. Russia is concerned about monopsony, a situation in which there is only one buyer but many potential sellers – a concern further reinforced after the construction of a pipeline from Kazakhstan to Xinjiang in western China was finished in 2006.

However, the core reason why China fell out of favour in 2004 was the role that Yukos had played in exporting oil to China. Putin was displeased by Mikhail Khodorkovsky's political ambitions and his plans for privately controlled export routes for Russian petroleum products. Both in the Murmansk and in the Far East, Yukos seemed poised to play an influential role. The Yukos affair is an indication that internal dynamics in Russia can be extremely important to foreign policy outcomes. Although the episode was unfortunate from Beijing's point of view, China has been careful not to criticize what it regards as an internal affair of Moscow.

The pipeline to Nakhodka is yet to be built, and at present there is no final decision whether it will be. However, Russia appears to have decided to build a pipeline to Skovorodino only 70 kilometres from the Chinese border, scheduled for completion in the second half of 2008. This is set to include a spur to Daqing, and carry as much as 600,000 barrels a day.[8] The construction of the pipeline to Skovorodino strengthens China–Russia relations while simultaneously giving the Kremlin the option of extending the pipeline to Nakhodka. This allows Russia to maintain leverage over China and Japan.

The territorial dispute over the Kurile Islands north of Hokkaido continues to plague relations between Japan and Russia, which have yet to sign a peace treaty to end the Second World War. If there is no agreement on the issue, the pipeline to Nakhodka may not move beyond the planning board. If Tokyo is unable to settle its territorial dispute with Russia, and Beijing–Moscow relations remain good, Moscow may conclude that it has more to gain by constructing an additional pipeline to China. China, after all, is a market enjoying strong growth, and is unlikely to jeopardize future energy security by demanding renegotiation of price agreements once the pipeline has been built.

Natural gas cooperation in the massive Kovykta field, and perhaps Sakhalin, are likely elements in future Chinese–Russian energy cooperation. In April 2006 President Putin and Hu Jintao reportedly agreed on the construction of a pipeline from Kovykta to China and possibly South Korea, at an estimated cost of US$12 billion.[9] However, no formal decision on the project has been announced. Meanwhile, there have been significant increases in rail shipments of oil to China and a commitment to increase these further. Heilongjiang has been importing electricity from Russian hydroelectric power stations since 2004, and plans to import 18 billion kilowatt hours by 2010.[10] Sales to China decrease Russia's dependence on the European market and partially strengthen the Russian argument that it can turn to others if Brussels does not accept Moscow's conditions. China's energy consumption is predicted to surge from 1,675 terawatt hours in 2002 to 5,573 terawatt hours in 2030.[11]

Moreover, China's growing competitiveness does not represent any great threat to Russia compared with the United States and the EU. Manufacturing in the Russian Federation is weak and unlikely to recover, particularly given Russia's new wealth from natural resources and the lingering risk of Dutch disease. Instead China's cheap consumer goods present an opportunity to Russian consumers. Because of income from its exports of raw materials, Russia had a current account surplus of almost US$85 billion in 2005,[12] set to be even greater in 2006. For this reason Russia worries less about China's exporting power or the undervalued renminbi than do many other states. This means that a point of tension that characterizes Sino–US and Sino–EU relations is not present in the Sino–Russian relationship. China and Russia have acknowledged each other as market economies and China was among the first to conclude World Trade Organization negotiations with Russia in October 2004, indicating China's emphasis on building close trade relations with Russia.

A China–Russia strategic convergence?

Speaking now of the Russia–China military relation, we conclude that the United States is the silent party at the table in all China–Russia meetings, not in terms of pressure, but in terms of mutual interest on the part of China and Russia in constraining American hegemonic behaviour. Beijing's current starting point is 'one superpower, many powers'. Russia seems grudgingly to accept US primacy, but Putin has on numerous occasions made clear that Moscow would like to see a multi-polar world,[13] Beijing's current foreign policy discourse is centred on the 'peaceful rise' thesis, now rebaptized the 'peaceful development' thesis so as not to frighten anyone, but the underlying perspectives are in many respects similar.

Because both Russia and China are heavily armed, including nuclear arsenals, there is a balance of power. China's nuclear arsenal is far inferior to that of Russia and even more so that of the United States, but it is significant enough to decrease the attractiveness of a nuclear conflict for Russia.[14] In terms of conventional forces, China is superior to Russia. The chance that one state could seek to invade the other is low. Although many Russian actors do fear Chinese demographic and/or territorial expansionism in Siberia, occasionally backing up their fears with inflated numbers on Chinese cross-border migration, this aspect of the relationship may recede into the background as China increases in importance for Russia and on the world stage in so many other respects.[15] Moreover, both Russia and China are without significant allies.

China and Russia have expanded military cooperation. They have been collaborating on foreign and military intelligence since the early 1990s, and in 2005 they conducted their first joint war games. The exercise included 10,000 military, intelligence and internal security forces. Given China's reluctance to enter military alliances, it was a significant gesture to allow the games to be staged on Chinese soil. Russia and China have strong incentives to expand their military cooperation in a context where US military spending amounts to 47 per cent of the world total.[16] However, Moscow recognizes that Russian arm sales to China may represent a long-term strategic threat to Russia. Russian worries about this are reflected in Moscow's decision to sell its most advanced military aircraft technology to India rather than to China.[17]

Russia has been China's main source of arms since the end of the Cold War, and has accounted for 90 per cent of the estimated 165 billion renminbi in arms sales to China from the states of the former Soviet Union since 1991, according to a Pentagon report from 2004.[18] Moscow has sold Beijing advanced submarines, fighters, destroyers and missiles as well as strategic aircraft for troop movement and air-to-air refuelling. As the EU is unlikely to lift its 1989 arms embargo on China in the near future, and the United States is determined not to, Russia seems set to continue as China's main source of arms. The sale of sensitive technology from Russia to China still has considerable potential. Contracts worth billions of euros will be available as China pushes to expand its nuclear energy capacity. China plans to quadruple its nuclear output to 16 billion kilowatt hours by 2010, and double that figure again by 2015.[19]

The simultaneous demise of the Soviet Union and the rise of China fundamentally changed the dynamics in China–US relations. Washington stopped viewing China as an ally against Moscow, and began to see it as a potential rival. The United States is wary of the communist government in Beijing, and many senior actors in the US political landscape, especially among the Democrats, are increasingly sceptical of authoritarian trends in Putin's Russia. Putin, who initially built his political image on waging war on the Chechen separatists, has reasserted Moscow's right to appoint regional governors and effectively renationalized much of the petroleum industry. Beijing, on the other hand, is more comfortable with a relatively stable authoritarian Russia than the chaos of the 1990s, and feels vindicated in its decision to put down the rebellion in Tiananmen Square in 1989. The consolidation of what Putin calls the 'power vertical', i.e. centralization, has made Moscow a more reliable partner for Beijing.[20]

As far as the Moscow and Beijing stance towards separatism of restive minorities and independent politicized Islam, they share a fear; although Chinese Islamic separatists have not gone as far as some of their Russian counterparts. Given Beijing's policy of non-interference in the domestic affairs of other states, it has not at any point criticized Moscow for its war in Chechnya, and the war is highly unlikely to surface as a source of bilateral tension. China faces politicized Islam from the Uyghurs in Xinjiang, and Moscow does not feel uncomfortable with China's harsh treatment of the Uyghurs and other minorities, notably the Tibetans. The Taiwan issue is not a factor in China–Russia relations, unlike the case with China–US or China–EU relations. China and Russia will not criticize each other for their records on representative democracy, individual freedom or human rights.

The debate on Kosovo relates to two of the main discourses in both Russian and Chinese foreign policy: scepticism towards intervention in the affairs of other states, and the rejection of separatism. For Russia, negativity towards Kosovar independence is further fuelled by an underlying identification with Orthodox Christian, post-communist Serbia. Although China lacks the Orthodox Christian connection, the anti-interventionist and anti-separatist doctrines are strong enough to place China solidly on the Russian side of the important debate in contemporary diplomacy and international relations about whether independence is permissible for Kosovo.

The significant internal contradictions in Russia's position on separatism, underlined by its simultaneous crackdown on Chechnyan separatists and support for separatists in Abkhazia, South Ossetia and Trans-Dniestria, need not worry us unduly here. Although it partially undermines Russian credibility on separatism issues in relation to the West, it does not seem to pose a problem for the Chinese, and the leaders of the two countries are happy to talk almost identically about separatism.

Even more obvious is both countries shared geo-strategic interests. China and Russia have displayed coordinated reluctance to back the West in sanctions towards Iran. This illustrates how Moscow and Beijing can realize their national interests more effectively by cooperating in international forums in a way whereby neither is singled out as an obstacle to Western interests. China has billions invested in Iran's oil and gas fields and Iran is the source of 11.2 per cent of China's petroleum imports.[21] Russia also has several billion dollars invested in the country and wants to make more by reprocessing Iranian reactor fuel. Both sell advanced weapons to Iran. At the same time, China has vital security interests in the Middle East and Africa – with Iran, Syria and Sudan, among others. Russia also has strong historical ties to several Arab states not favoured by Washington, which allows for collaboration in areas where few other weighty allies can be found.

China and Russia have played an active role in the Six-Party Talks on North Korea's (DPRK) nuclear programme, but both have been reluctant to exert the pressure that Washington would like to see. North Korean nuclear weapons are not primarily pointed towards China or Russia, and Beijing and Moscow may benefit from the problems that North Korean nuclear weapons cause the US–South Korean alliance and in relations between South Korea and Japan. Seoul believes that US rhetoric towards North Korea has been unnecessarily aggressive, whereas Washington has been frustrated with Seoul's efforts to push ahead with industrial zones in North Korea despite Pyongyang's disregard of commitments to nuclear disarmament. North Korean nuclear advances may therefore weaken US–South Korean relations without representing a substantial threat to China and Russia.

In the aftermath of 9/11, the United States established a network of jumping-off bases across Central Asia. The ostensible rationale has been the fight against terrorism and support for operations in Afghanistan. However, and particularly when coupled with Washington's rapprochement and strengthened military cooperation with India, these developments are often interpreted as being motivated by containment of China and especially Russia. Moscow's and Beijing's calls to have the bases closed have succeeded in Uzbekistan, but fallen short in Kyrgyzstan. The US presence has a direct impact on the political processes of the states in the region, and Beijing and Moscow consider this a potential threat to their security. As long as Washington maintains a presence in Central Asia, Beijing and Moscow are likely to find that they have more to gain by uniting in seeking restraint on US power than by seeking mutual confrontation.

In a long-term perspective, in particular in the case of decreased US interest in Central Asia, it is possible that the area could become an arena for competition between Russia and China. For most of the post-Cold War period, Central Asia has largely been left to Russia, for historical reasons and because Russia has claimed it. But with China increasingly active in Central Asia, albeit mostly in the energy sector, Russia may at some point feel challenged. However, the United States does not seem intent on abandoning the region, and is attempting to extend the energy corridor that already exists between Azerbaijan, Georgia and Turkey to Turkmenistan and Kazakhstan. In this perspective Chinese–Russian relations in Central Asia are likely to remain mostly congruous, united by the external threat that US influence is seen as posing to Russian influence over, and Chinese access to, the Caspian basin's vast natural gas deposits.

Considering the substantial complementarities in the energy sector, cooperation has great potential for the region. There have been several attempts at bilateral and trilateral energy cooperation, and even some cases of multilateral energy cooperation such as ASEAN+3, the SCO, and the Northeast Asian Economic Forum. A serious problem with these programmes to date is that they do not take into account the interests of all actors, including the national sources of natural resources, the refining points, and the transit countries for oil and gas. Successful integration needs to include all available actors in a truly multilateral forum. There have been several suggestions on how best to accomplish regional cooperation on energy issues.[22] But as yet there are very few actual mechanisms in the region to make such cooperation real. The geostrategic aspect of energy greatly complicates matters, with Moscow, for example, keeping Beijing's proposals for a true 'strategic partnership' in energy at arm's length.[23]

There are no organizations in Eurasia today that have the credibility needed to bring about such cooperation. Most states acknowledge the need for further cooperation. For example, China developed a strategy for energy security in the 1990s called the 'Pan-Asian Continental Oil Bridge', which would link Japan with the Middle East by means of structures that would have been under Chinese control.[24] From a Chinese perspective this was seen as positive, since the regional economies would become tied to one another. Others in the region viewed this as a bold attempt by China to dominate regional markets. Doubtless, any state that controls the energy transit routes would have significant power in the region.

The picture is further complicated by the fact that major external actors would view strengthened energy cooperation on the Eurasian continent with suspicion since it would, over time, integrate participating states both economically and politically. Such a Eurasian energy bloc might decrease the political and economic influence of the EU, Middle East states, and, most important, the United States. If such a grand project is to succeed, it needs strong external support similar to that received during the formative period of the European Coal and Steel Community (ECSC) project. This will also further the interest of the Euro-Atlantic community.

The year 2005 was critical for the region. In the wave of serious unrest in both Uzbekistan and Kyrgyzstan in 2005 and widespread concern within the Russian political elite that this could lead to regional contagion, the Kremlin refocused minds on how to engage with emerging post-Soviet realities in the near-abroad Central Asia. Russia realized it should use multilateral structures to retain a guiding role at the cost of allowing deeper and broader Chinese engagement within the region. As the communiqué from the SCO 2007 summit indicates, the organization received a broader role in the ensuing foreign policy adjustment.

The Kremlin faces the following strategic, economic and political imperatives in Central Asia: (a) defend its porous southern border, (b) face off the perceived threat of encirclement, (c) abate Zhrinovskyite nationalists at home, (d) project Russia's great power status internationally, (e) secure access to regional resources and markets and, finally, (f) combat Islamic fundamentalism intrusion in its own Muslim republics. Because it realized that the brutal use of military means in Chechnya or the actions of the Russian forces in the Tajikistan civil war only created an enduring source of regional instability, the Russian government was forced to reassess its reliance on traditional approaches exercising hard power and search for effective and binding cooperation with Central Asian regimes.

Russia has encountered limited success in the use of multilateral organizations in Central Asia (Eurasian Economic Commonwealth – EEC, Collective Security treaty Organization – CSTO, Central Asian Union – CAU) in its effort to engage Central Asian leaders in a multilateral framework with itself, mainly because of the structural weaknesses of the Russian economy. In the post-9/11 geopolitical arena, searching for new levels of influence within Central Asia, and increasingly concerned by the US military presence there, the reactivation of the GUAM (Georgia, Ukraine, Azerbaijan and Moldova) group and the effectiveness of US support for regime change in Georgia, Ukraine and Kyrgyzstan, Russia has decided to engage with the SCO. But the SCO differs in that it balances the interests of the two major powers in the region. This move marks a significant departure from previous policy, because in allowing China to having an equal role in engaging the Central Asian regimes, Moscow is coming close to legitimating the view that Beijing's interests in the region are equivalent to its own.

For Russia, the benefits associated with engaging the SCO in its relationship with Central Asia can be divided into two categories – the explicit and the implicit. The explicit benefits include the ability to present a united front in dealings with the United States, a renewed regional focus on combating insecurity and extremism, and the opportunity to broaden and deepen economic ties. Some of the potential implicit benefits, such as the protection of individual regimes, are even more far reaching, and are currently still emerging. For example, despite previous criticism of Moscow's plans for Central Asia, Uzbek President Karimov has fallen more fully into the Russian camp following the Andijan incident, when he received strong support from Moscow and Beijing. This success of Russian foreign policy indicates the role the SCO seems best fitted to play, as a guarantor of mutual support between both states and regimes.[25] This was also true when Russia was given the green light by the Kyrgyz government to more than double its military forces in its Kant base. Russia used the SCO so that its base should not be treated equally by the new Kyrgyz regime.

Equally important from the Russian perspective and a significant strategic breakthrough, was the strength of the 2005 SCO summit resolution calling on US forces to leave the region; a sign that Beijing and Moscow have agreed to use the SCO as their vehicle for opposing the US role in Central Asia. Moscow can present its demands much more forcefully to the United States by coordinating its message with Beijing and ensuring that it is mirrored in regional capitals. An alternative analysis explains the same calling of 'determination of the date' of Western military withdrawal as Moscow's bowing to Beijing's demand.[26]

Indicative of the role Russia wishes the SCO to play is the calling of the Organization as guarantor of regional stability both in Central Asia and in the Far East (2003 Russian Defence Ministry White Paper). In 2005, the first-ever joint Sino–Russian military exercises were held, on Chinese territory. However, Russia has been careful not to let the regional balance in Central Asia tilt too far towards China. Although Beijing has been pressing for the SCO to move towards establishing a free trade area, Russia has been blocking that, fearing China's clear advantage. In general, of the two fundamental areas of SCO activity, security and development, Moscow has been emphasizing the former. But even in the security role of the SCO, Moscow has been very modest in its evaluation. The Organization's security role is to give moral and political support to its members, and facilitate exchange of information. As President Putin noted, the SCO is not the place to discuss defending against aggression and excluded any possibility of military operations conducted under the auspices of the SCO.[27] Earlier in the same year (spring 2005), Moscow gave a negative answer to an even theoretical possibility of a Chinese military presence in Central Asia, replacing US forces after evacuating the base in Uzbekistan.

Truly, in spite of the fact that counterterrorism, maintaining stability and promoting development in Central Asia is in the common interest of all three major powers, there remain obstacles to cooperation. First, the problem of US 'legitimacy' in the region. The term 'legitimacy' is not used in its meaning in international law, but rather as an indication that the US presence in Central Asia has not been recognized and accepted by Russia and China. At the beginning of the war in Afghanistan, the United States promised that its presence would be temporary and would not endanger China's or Russia's interests. But as the present state of affairs show, US troops will be deployed in Central Asia far into the future and China and Russia will persist that the United States keep its promise.

The second obstacle to cooperation is that China, Russia and the United States have not forged any form of mechanism or mechanical framework for their relations in Central Asia, mainly because there doesn't exist a foundation on which the three powers can engage directly. There is no appropriate channel for dialogue and no platform for cooperation. Although the SCO and other mechanisms of dialogue and cooperation exist between China and Russia, there are none between China and the United States, between Russia and the United States, and among China, Russia and the United States. What the three major powers in Central Asia need ultimately is a multilateral cooperation framework consisting of dialogue, communication, consultation and collaboration. This presumption is not only feasible, but also desirable. China, Russia or the United States do not have the intention or will to pursue confrontation. This is the fundamental precondition that can prevent confrontation among three powers in Central Asia. One way or the other, there will be no stable equilibrium of power in Eurasia without a deepening strategic understanding between America and China.

It is in the political and strategic interests of all three major external powers in Central Asia not to compete with each other, because this would allow the various destructive forces in the region (religious terrorism, drugs production/trafficking) to use the rivalry of the external powers their own benefit. And the institutional structure of the SCO leaves the way wide open for this. The SCO is based upon the principle of non-alignment, in other words not targeting a third country or any other region; it seeks a constructive working relationship with the West. It places no restrictions on member states expanding their relations with others, and in that way it offers flexibility and adaptability. Thus, the Central Asian state's military cooperation with the United States should not be considered as abandoning the

SCO. In any case, the constructive relationship between the United States and SCO member states and the US military presence in Central Asia leaves little possibility for the organization to seek dominance in Central Asia, nor as a tool used by China and Russia to eliminate US influence in the region. On the contrary, it has provided new opportunities for the three powers to cooperate with each other.

In case of a US and its NATO allies failure in Afghanistan and military withdrawal, Russian and Chinese security is definitely not going to be improved. As Dmitri Trenin notes: 'As to the SCO, it needs to open itself to the United States as an observer, especially since the US cannot be seriously excluded from region-wide discussions. In that way, more mutual confidence could be ensured not only between Russia and America, but also, and more importantly, in the 21st century global context, between America and China'.[28] The United States' limited participation in SCO activities would raise the status and influence of the Organization and will help it to turn into a truly region-wide political and security organization. But another analyst is of the opinion that in that case the SCO could decentralize into an organization with multiple centres of power, and thus make it irrelevant.[29]

Considering the above, we believe that a realist perspective can be employed to understand China–Russia strategic convergence. According to both classical and neo-realist theory, a unipolar order is inherently unstable, and the emergence of a sole dominant power will lead other powers jointly to oppose the hegemon. Hans Morgenthau wrote that states are seeking domination, but that the balance of power leads to the restoration of equilibrium.[30] Kenneth Waltz argued that the instinct for survival in international anarchy 'stimulates states to behave in ways that tend toward the creation of balances of power'.[31] Realists essentially presume that negative feedback is the rule in international politics, and that deviation from equilibrium automatically sets in motion countervailing forces to re-establish it. Waltz, writing about the United States in the 1990s, argued that '[u]nbalanced power, whoever wields it, is a potential danger to others'.[32]

For leaders in Beijing and Moscow this appears to be true, as they have watched Washington's invasion of Iraq and its unrelenting support for Israeli policies. In the period following the collapse of the Soviet Union, Russia has generally remained relatively close to the United States, behaviour that might be described as bandwagoning. Moscow, however, is increasingly disappointed with the results of its attempts to stay close to the West. At the same time, Western governments increasingly appear to conclude that Russia is unlikely to become democratic in the near future, and regard its regime as having more in common with that of China than with, for example, the situation in Poland.[33]

So, we reach the conclusion that there are key factors which bring Russia and China together. The two states have complementary economies, shared concerns about US power, fear of more Orange/Rose/Tulip revolutions, and common interests in the Middle East and Africa. There are, however, several significant obstacles to closer cooperation between Russia and China. The most significant weakness in the relationship lies in Russia's concern over China's dominance, particularly in connection with Siberia, which it is feared could fall victim to Chinese expansion – Manchuria in reverse. Russia is currently wary of both Chinese migration and economic dominance in Siberia.

At the level of global politics and trade, the divergent prospects of the two states may complicate Sino–Russian relations. Russia is a has-been super-power, now most likely to play a role as a regional power. Even at that, it is often weak and humiliated, as with its bungled attempt to halt the Orange Revolution in Ukraine. China, on the other hand, is rapidly emerging as a major player in global politics. At the same time, China is consolidating its position in lower- and medium-end goods while emerging as a manufacturer of high-end goods. Russia's economic resurgence lacks this broad base, and is built almost entirely on export of raw materials. As we have argued, this means that the two economies are highly compatible, but it also gives China the dominant role in the relationship. There has been a tipping of the geo-economic balance between the two countries compared to that between the Soviet Union and China.

China and Russia are unfinished international actors: Russia because it is still in the process of redefining its post-Cold War identity and reasserting state control; and China because it is industrializing, urbanizing, growing rapidly and opening to the outside world. Russia is taking important lessons from China about the assertion of state control in strategic sectors of the economy, which in turn signals compatibility of methods and shared worldviews.

Institutionalization of the Beijing–Moscow relationship remains low, but a pattern of regular consultation between top leaders has evolved. Russia and China also meet annually for bilateral military and technical cooperation talks, and have continued to develop the SCO, founded in 2001. China–Russia strategic convergence is a discernible trend that will gain further momentum. However, strategic convergence should not be confused with an alliance, and China and Russia are not perfect strategic partners. Developments inside China and Russia are crucial to how the relationship develops. Key questions are whether political stability will prevail and whether rapid growth can be sustained.

Trenin argues that a Sino–Russian alliance could occur only as a result of 'exceptionally short-sighted and foolish policies on Washington's part'.[34] China and Russia are not pro-Western, but neither are they definitively anti-Western. Paradoxically, if an alliance, or something resembling an alliance, were to be formed this could lead to a breakdown of the relationship in the medium to long term. China and Russia both command sufficient resources and sophistication to be significant global powers in their own right, and they certainly consider themselves as such. China was unwilling to subordinate itself to Russia for more than a brief period after the Communists came to power in 1949, and Russia would refuse to subordinate itself to China.

The most likely scenario is Sino–Russian strategic convergence based on a relationship of mutual self-interest. Trade and investment between China and Russia are set to continue to grow rapidly, particularly in the energy sector, further enhancing the significance of the relationship. Although Beijing and Moscow have common interests in placing restraints on the power of the United States, the creation of a fully fledged anti-Western alliance is unlikely to prove viable in the short term. Russia and especially China are both dependent on open access to Western markets to sustain growth.

The realist prediction that unbalanced power is inherently unstable, and the emergence of a sole dominant power will lead other powers jointly to oppose the hegemon, cannot be confirmed. However, if Beijing and Moscow find that the US hegemon does not allow them the space they need as they re-emerge as world powers, they will have strong incentives to deepen their mutual strategic ties. If Washington were genuinely committed to allowing the concurrent rise of China and Russia as world powers, despite their inherent challenge to Washington's own power, China and Russia would have limited incentives to cooperate, and mutual fear would be the overriding feature in the relationship. Both would seek to work closely with Japan, as a counterweight to the other's power. However, the United States has been unable to provide China and Russia with the reassurance they would like, and they may be in the process of turning to each other for collaboration.

The development of China–Russia strategic convergence does not necessarily mean that China and Russia are turning their backs on the West, but it does represent a challenge to US hegemony and could change the world order. The year 2008 will be decisive, with presidential elections in both Russia and the United States in which neither of the present incumbents can legally participate. That same year, the pipeline from Russia to China is set for completion. One scenario is that the US–Russia relationship could deteriorate rapidly in the wake of the Russian presidential election if a member of the Petersburg ruling circle is anointed the new president. The resulting tension between Russia and the United States could drive Russia into the embrace of China. Alternatively, fresh presidential faces on both sides of the Atlantic could spell renewed cooperation between Russia and the United States, lessening the significance of the Russia–China axis. The Beijing Olympics will also take place in 2008, and China will do everything it can to avoid confrontation with the West, but at the same time it welcomes close ties with Russia.

Recently, the EU also seems to be prepared to format a geo-strategic approach towards Eurasia. Because the SCO has competence on energy matters, it could become relevant for Europe's energy security. The membership of the SCO includes two of the largest global energy producers outside OPEC, Russia and Kazakhstan, as well as two of the largest consumers, China and India. Europe will continue to depend on Russia for oil and gas imports and could in the future compete with China over Eurasian energy resources. So a dialogue between the SCO and the EU on energy security could provide a forum for their members to discuss issues such as the transparency of domestic energy sectors and the diversification of energy supply routes. The two bodies could work together to develop strategic projects involving energy transport to China and Europe.

The EU has launched a major initiative towards Central Asia just as its sources of supply for natural gas are increasing.[35] However, demand will outstrip supply by 2012, so the long-term prospects still look bleak. At a landmark meeting of the EU troika with the foreign ministers of the Central Asian states in Astana on 28 March 2007, the German Foreign Minister Frank-Walter Steinmeier said, 'The EU aims to diversify its energy policy. This is why it is necessary to increase our contacts with Central Asia'.[36]

Central Asia also lies astride a major transit route for illegal drugs from Afghanistan to Europe. Around 65 per cent of Afghani opium transits Central Asia en route to Western Europe.[37] Apparently over 90 per cent of the heroin in the United Kingdom originates in Afghanistan.[38] Thus drugs and the drug economy pose a serious problem for Europe.

Energy security, drugs, transnational terrorism, the need to assure the continuing relevance of NATO and their own armed forces as well as real humanitarian concerns were among the factors that led European countries to support NATO's increasing involvement through the International Security Assistance Force (ISAF) in Afghanistan. The European presence in ISAF shows a clear commitment to Central Asia as well as Afghanistan. It is obvious that the EU does have direct, clear and immediate strategic interests in Central Asia. And those interests have to be taken seriously since Russia provides over a quarter of the EU's natural gas, the majority of which Moscow presents as Russian and resells it at a significant mark-up to the Europeans.

However, Europe's interests in Central Asia and the Caucasus lack the intensity generated by shared history and geography peculiar to Russia's stake in these regions. Europe also lacks the global ambition of the US approach to them. Europe's concern about Central Asia has been largely that of a remote regional power without a compelling rationale for more active involvement there.

Of course, it is in the interest of the so-called 'new Europe', or countries of Eastern Europe with first-hand experience of Soviet occupation, to support democratic change in the former Soviet lands as a means of countering Russian influence. Georgia, following the 'Rose revolution' has been the leading beneficiary of this policy.

In Afghanistan, the deployment of European allies has given Europe a new interest in Central Asian security affairs, but it has yet to translate into a more active involvement there on the part of the Europeans. This is also due to limited absorption capacity by regional governments of security assistance. As far as energy matters are concerned, Europe has taken a back seat to the United States, even though it will benefit from Caspian oil and gas far more than the United States. Europe – with the notable exception of Eastern Europe – has tended to see this issue more as a matter of commerce than strategy.[39]

The United States and Russia will be the key actors in the Central Asian region for the foreseeable future. Europe will remain in a supportive role. Despite US–Russian differences about Central Asia, it has been increasingly clear that competition is likely to hurt all involved. Russia no longer has the means to act as security manager in its borderlands. But it can still act as a spoiler.

The United States, with help from Europe, plays an indispensable role in Central Asia by continuing to secure Afghanistan. Russia was and is unable to fulfil that mission. It has a big stake in the United States succeeding there. Moreover, in Central Asia, Russia and its regional partners have to contend with the prospect of a resurgent China. The United States could prove a useful partner to Russia and Central Asia in that context.

But cooperation requires compromise. For Russia and the United States, it means recognition of each other's interests. For Europe, it entails accepting greater international responsibilities. For Russia and its local partners in Central Asia, it involves recognizing that reform is necessary for the sake of long-term stability. For the United States, it calls for recognition that democratic change could lead to protracted instability and that it needs to be promoted with caution.[40]

All of this is self-evident in the abstract, yet little of this has been recognized and accepted in the real world. Words have consequences and could cast a long shadow over bilateral relations. A new Cold War is not on the cards. But the future of the area around Russia has emerged as one of the most contentious issues in US–Russian relations. What it would take for the parties to act as responsible stakeholders, recognizing both stakeholders' rights and responsibilities, is not clear. The sooner the need for this change is recognized and acted upon, the better it will be for all concerned.

5 The nexus between energy, security and maritime power and SCO's role in China's energy security

China's two decades of rapid economic growth have fuelled a demand for energy that has outstripped domestic sources of supply. China became a net importer of oil in 1993 and it is projected that it will need to import some 60 per cent of its oil and at least 30 per cent of its natural gas by 2020. To appease its thirst for energy, Beijing is making intense efforts to ensure energy security that include investments in overseas oil exploration and development projects, discussions about the feasibility of several transnational oil and gas pipelines, plans to establish a strategic petroleum reserve, construction of refineries capable of handling crude oil from the Middle East, development of the natural gas industry, and the gradual opening of onshore areas to foreign companies for exploration and development.

China's energy security activities can be explained in terms of Beijing's long-standing fear of dependency on foreign energy as it regards oil imports as a strategic vulnerability that could be exploited by foreign powers seeking to influence China. As the United States is perceived by many Chinese as uncomfortable with China's rising power, the government views the United States as the primary threat to China's energy security and wishes to minimize the vulnerability of its oil supply to American power. They regard their country as being especially vulnerable to American power in a world in which the United States is the sole superpower. More explicitly, the Chinese government is uncomfortable with the fact that the US navy dominates the sea-lanes, stretching from the Persian Gulf to the South China Sea, through which the bulk of China's oil imports must pass. There is a concern that if Sino–US relations sour, the United States could use its superior military power to disrupt China's oil supply. Some even suggest that Washington has already implemented an 'energy containment' policy against China, the objective of which is to weaken China by gaining control of the energy resources in western China and blocking Beijing's access to oil imports.

Energy security, and particularly oil supply security, has become a major concern for the Chinese government over the past several years. The focus of this anxiety is the vulnerability of seaborne energy imports. At present, China lacks the naval power necessary to protect its sea-lanes of communication (SLOCs). Beijing fears that during a national security crisis ships carrying energy resources could be interdicted by hostile naval forces. Any disruption to the free flow of energy resources into China could derail the economic growth on which the Chinese government depends to shore up its legitimacy and pursue its great power ambitions.

China's heavy use of the Malacca and Lombok/Makassar straits in Southeast Asia is emblematic of this concern. The Malacca Strait is a narrow and congested waterway separating Indonesia and Malaysia, with Singapore located at its southern tip. As the shortest route between the Indian and Pacific oceans, the strait is one of the world's most important waterways. More than 60,000 vessels transit the strait each year, carrying 25 per cent of global trade. The Lombok/Makassar Strait passes through the Indonesian archipelago and is used mainly by very large crude carriers. In terms of volume of oil shipped, this route is of near-equivalent importance to the better-known Malacca Strait.

For China, the strategic significance of these straits increases every year. At present, approximately 60 per cent of China's crude oil imports originate in the Middle East, and this figure is expected to rise to 75 per cent by 2015. Oil from the Persian Gulf and Africa is shipped to the People's Republic of China (PRC) via the Malacca or Lombok/Makassar straits. Over the past few years Chinese leaders have come to view the straits, especially the Malacca Strait, as a strategic vulnerability. In November 2003 President Hu Jintao declared that 'certain major powers' were bent on controlling the strait, and called for the adoption of new strategies to mitigate the perceived vulnerability.

Over the past 18 months the Malacca Strait has attracted the attention of security analysts for reasons other than China's oil supply security. During 2003–2004 the straits witnessed an upsurge in pirate attacks. Perceived lax security in the strait engendered concerns that transnational terrorist groups might link up with pirates to disrupt maritime traffic and hence global commerce. International criticism led the littoral states (Indonesia, Malaysia and Singapore) to step up strait security through the establishment of coordinated air and naval patrols. As a result of these and other initiatives, the number of pirate attacks in the area declined in 2005. Yet piracy and other transnational threats in the strait remain major concerns. Owing to sensitivities over sovereignty, Indonesia and Malaysia have firmly rejected the idea of external powers such as the United States, Japan or India permanently stationing military forces in the strait. They have welcomed help from external powers, however, in the form of capacity building, intelligence exchange and training.

As a heavy user of the Malacca Strait, the PRC has a vested interest in the elimination of transnational threats in the waterway. Yet Beijing remains uneasy at the prospect of a greater role for external powers in securing the strait. Chinese security analysts have accused the United States and Japan of using the threat of terrorism as a pretext to expand their naval presence in and around the strait. The PRC has also watched with concern India's enhanced presence in the area, especially the modernization of military facilities on the Andaman and Nicobar Islands, located near the northern entrance to the Malacca Strait. Nevertheless, China does not want to be left out and has offered the littoral states its assistance to improve security in the strait. At a meeting held in Jakarta in September 2005 to discuss strait security, Ju Chengzi, director general of China's Ministry of Transportation, said the PRC government was willing to assist the littoral states with capacity building, technical support, training programmes, hydrographic surveys and navigation aids (Xinhua, September 7, 2005).[1] More specific details have yet to be released.

Meanwhile, China is pursuing a number of options to mitigate its dependence on oil imports and reduce the country's strategic vulnerabilities. In an effort to reduce import dependence, the PRC continues to rely on domestically produced coal for its energy needs. Beijing has also emphasized energy conservation and efficiency, the expansion of nuclear power generation, and the development of alternative and renewable energy supplies. In 2004 construction began on four strategic petroleum stockpile (SPS) facilities on China's eastern seaboard capable of stockpiling 20–30 days' supply of oil imports. Two more are likely to be built in Guangdong province and another on Hainan Island.

China's overland energy provision

China's interest and investment in the development of Central Asian and Russian energy resources can be explained by the Chinese perception that these regions are less vulnerable to US power than is the Persian Gulf and the sea-lanes connecting it to the South China Sea. The Chinese even seem not to be annoyed by the US military involvement in Central Asia as they consider it not directly threatening China's energy security. Although the United States is a competitor for Central Asian energy resources, its ability to threaten China's oil supply from this region is limited. Geography dictates that Central Asia's energy cooperation with China is likely to be greater than the one with the United States.[2]

The lack of a strong US military presence in Central Asia explains China's enthusiasm for the proposed 3,000-kilometre-long oil pipeline between China and Kazakhstan, as it would provide Beijing with an oil supply route that avoids the sea-lanes dominated by the US navy and passes through regions where China's land power has the advantage. China freed from this serious strategic vulnerability, would not feel so much pressed by the United States and Japan. In addition, China's investment in Kazakhstan would be a means for China to expand its influence there. In addition, this pipeline would help to foster political stability along China's Central Asian border, which suffers from the Uyghurs separatist ambitions, by promoting their economic enfranchisement by investments in energy development projects in Xingjian province. Because of these characteristics, the Chinese government overlooks various reports that dismiss the pipeline as economically infeasible, not so much for its cost of US$3.5 billion as for fearing that the combined reserves of the Aktyubinsk and Uzen fields were not sufficient to justify it.[3]

The same motives make appealing to Chinese policy-makers the development of the Siberian energy resources. A group of Chinese oil experts have called for the construction of a 'pan-Asian continental oil bridge' (1996), which would consist of a comprehensive network of pipelines linking suppliers in the Middle East, Central Asia and Russia to consumers in China and possibly Korea, Japan and Taiwan. Such a system would increase the availability of oil on the world market and oil trade between the countries involved, possibly supplying East Asia with up to 20 per cent of its oil needs, not to mention the benefits for security in Eurasia.[4] The two countries are discussing the construction of an oil pipeline from Angarsk in Siberia either to the northern provinces of China via Mongolia or to the north-eastern provinces, avoiding Mongolia. Whereas Russia's Ministry of Fuel and Energy is in favour or the first route because it is 170 kilometres shorter, Chinese officials prefer the second because of the lessened political risk. The pipeline, estimated to cost US$2 billion, is expected to transport around 220 million barrels of oil per year. Nevertheless, whatever the route to be chosen, in this case the views are not unanimous. Many political figures in China fear that in the event of a Sino–Russian crisis Russia would stop the flow of energy resources to China.

In its anxious search for energy supply for its booming economy, Beijing seeks to apply hegemony in Central Asia in its right as a developing economy and a key component of a pan-Asian land bridge for energy and other goods. Thus, it is written that China

> Should become a guide and a kind of courier station for the Central Asian states in their dealings with the Pacific countries and guide them to more economic cooperation and trade contacts in the Pacific. The 'second Eurasian bridge' is an important route for China to guide the Central Asian states through the Pacific ... China should ensure that the economic development of its north-western part is connected not only with that of Central Asia but also with overall economic development in Eurasia. Looked at in this way, there is stronger motivation and greater scope for its economic relations with the Central Asian states.[5]

China's economic and trade policies aim to tie Central Asian states in to expanding trade with the PRC and give them significant economic motives for not supporting Xingjian's unrest lest Beijing terminate that lucrative trade and investment. Thus China aims at securing critical political advantage vis-à-vis weaker Central Asian governments who need the Chinese market by putting an end to unrest in Xingjian, and also create a sphere of relationships, if not influence, that constrains local options *vis-à-vis* Beijing. China has sought to use major domestic energy corporations to extend political influence into Kazakhstan. Under these circumstances, it is not surprising that energy-producing Central Asian states are wary of what Chinese objectives might be above and beyond purely market relationships.

This wariness about Chinese objectives is exacerbated by the peculiarities of China's approach to the energy issue. First, although China's preferred instrument for most political transactions in Central Asia is the SCO, it has not figured in Beijing's energy acquisitions. Despite its talk of multi-polarity in world politics, China will not multilateralize discussions about its access to energy. Instead it prefers bilateral discussions with energy producers, because it is in that way that it can most effectively maximize its leverage upon the individual producer.

Second, China's policies aim at maximizing the reliability of long-term supplies through control of the product or of equity shares in the producing company from wellhead to terminal. It seems that the key driving force from the Chinese government point of view is the desire to enhance the security of the country's petroleum supply through owning both the resource in the ground and, where relevant, the transport network.[6] China seeks a percentage of annual oil output by becoming a direct investor or shareholder to shield it from significant price fluctuations for oil imports. Building up a strategic petroleum reserve also aims to ensure reliable supplies at accessible prices. Even when buying pipeline networks at home and abroad, China is looking to control the oil and gas shipped from Central Asia, the Gulf and Russia.

China's willingness to provide military assistance, missile or nuclear technology to energy producers, e.g. Iran, Saudi Arabia and Sudan, even to commit its own forces beyond its borders to Central Asian states as stipulated in the 2001 treaty creating the SCO, suggests a potentially forceful reply or increased support for missile and even nuclear proliferation in reply to threats to its energy supplies.[7] Such an approach makes Central Asian states nervous. It also raises Russian fears, because Russian control over Central Asian energy, monopolized production, refining, pipelines and sales, is necessary for Russia's sustainable economic growth and freedom of manoeuvre in world politics. Thus, Russian contemplation of long-term trends connected with China's economic activities in Central Asia is influenced by its knowledge that only China has the long-term means and local presence to challenge Russia's presence in Central Asia, even if it now accepts Russian leadership there.[8]

Beijing's activity in Central Asia raises fears also in the Kazakhstan. Kazakhstan, historically a borderland between Russia and South Asia, is now equally so between western China and the expanded post-Soviet Middle East stretching from North Africa to the South Caucasus. This country is nowadays part of an emerging triangle in East Central Asian geo-economics along with Russia and China, in which energy cooperation is a linchpin but, as we shall see, the ententes themselves go far beyond energy.[9] China has met with every conceivable kind of obstacle to the objective of obtaining reliable supplies from and access to Kazakh energy sources. Beijing has encountered Kazakhstan's and Russia's growing insistence on national and state control of their valuable strategic assets and the Kazakh population's irritation at the presence of Chinese managers and companies overseeing their workers and owning their land, and Russian opposition to China's direct presence in Kazakhstan's markets. Astana's reaction has turned increasingly negative with legislative and political pressure being brought to bear upon the government to take control of energy firms, so that Kazakhstan's most strategic asset, energy, does not pass into foreign hands.

Equally negative has been the Russian officials' reaction to being merely China's source of raw materials and have demanded equal status in eco-nomic–technological exchanges with China.[10] These officials also blocked the sale of Slavneft to China, successfully destroyed Yukos, the company that favoured a direct Russo–Chinese sale of oil and a pipeline from Angara to Daqing and the partly Japanese-subsidized extension of the pipeline to Nakhodka. The Chinese would then have to buy from Japan rather than directly from Russia. Russia also resists Chinese moves towards equity shares, and hence ownership or control in Central Asian energy markets, and the potential independence of Central Asian producers. Hence monopoliza-tion of energy sales from Central Asia is an essential component of Russian neo-imperialism there and in regard to China one of Russia's few options for gaining some leverage *vis-à-vis* its ambitious Asian neighbour.

China's strategic energy quest: a role for the SCO?

What follows is an account of China's strategic interests that are developing around its quest for energy resources in the regions of the Indian Ocean, South China Sea and the Caspian Sea. This account may explain the length and breadth of China's grand geo-strategic endeavours in its quest for securing energy assets, thus securing its continuous economic revival.

The Indian Ocean region (South Asia)

The Indian Ocean provides major sea routes connecting the Middle East, Africa and East Asia with Europe and the Americas. Four critically impor-tant access waterways in the Indian Ocean are the Suez Canal (Egypt), Babel Mandeb (Djibouti–Yemen), Strait of Hormuz (Iran–Oman) and Strait of Malacca (Indonesia–Malaysia). The Indian Ocean carries a particularly heavy traffic of petroleum and petroleum products from the oilfields of the Persian Gulf and Indonesia. Larger resources of hydrocarbons are being tapped from the offshore areas of South Asia, Iran, India and Western Australia. An estimated 40 per cent of the world's offshore oil production comes from the Indian Ocean, which no nation dominates yet.

China has long nursed hopes to extend its reach into the Indian Ocean to pursue its diverse interests: first, it wants to secure the SLOCs for its very substantial commerce across the Indian Ocean. Second, it seeks to secure further waterways, such as the Strait of Malacca, through its access to the Indian Ocean in order to have uninterrupted energy supplies. Third, it wants to be able to neutralize any potential hostile action to choke off its energy shipments across the Indian Ocean or the Strait of Malacca.

The realization of these interests hinges on Beijing's access to the Indian Ocean, access that is gaining growing importance in its strategic thinking. The importance of the Indian Ocean thus continues to shape Beijing's strategic relations in the South Asian region, which is home to the Indian Ocean. China has built alliances with nations that are vital in helping to build greater access to the Indian Ocean. Of these, Bangladesh, Pakistan, Sri Lanka and Myanmar stand out because of their geographical proximity to the Indian Ocean. Although Myanmar is a member of the Association of Southeast Asian Nations (ASEAN) and is geographically located in Southeast Asia, its aquatic placement is in the Indian Ocean region rather than the South China Sea region. Bangladesh occupies the Bay of Bengal; Pakistan sits on the shores of the Arabian Sea; Sri Lanka is an island nation on the Indian Ocean; and Myanmar's coast meets the Indian Ocean. All these nations can bridge China's presence in the Indian Ocean, where India currently is the major player due to its geographical proximity, a proximity that works to the disadvantage of China. Beijing, however, hopes to make up for this disadvantage by deepening its alliance with Bangladesh, Pakistan and Sri Lanka.

Pakistan is of paramount maritime importance for China as the leading steward of the Arabian Sea at the mouth of the Indian Ocean. China, together with Islamabad, began to build a deep-sea port in 2002 in Gwadar, a village in Pakistan's south-western province of Baluchistan along the Arabian Sea coast. The Gwadar port signifies the summit of the Sino–Pakistani strategic partnership.

The port will serve five Chinese ends: first, it will ensure safe shipping for China's energy imports from the Persian Gulf, which supplies 60 per cent of its fuel needs. Second, in the event of any hostile action to block its energy supplies through the Persian Gulf, the Gwadar port will serve as a safe alternative supply route. Third, it will eventually become the substitute passage for all of Chinese shipments through the Persian Gulf and the Strait of Malacca, where China is totally dependent upon the goodwill of the United States and its allies who police it. Fourth, as the Gwadar port sits opposite the Strait of Hormuz, through which the bulk of the world's energy resources, importantly Japanese fuel imports, are shipped, it will give China a strategic lever to retaliate in case its shipments are obstructed elsewhere. Fifth, above all, the port provides China a strategic foothold in the Arabian Sea and the Indian Ocean. Its presence on the Indian Ocean will further deepen its strategic influence with major South Asian nations, with which its relations are already thriving.

China's arrival in Baluchistan is even more meaningful for the latter's untapped wealth of hydrocarbon, mineral and metallic resources. Baluchistan sits on estimated reserves of 29 trillion cubic feet of natural gas and 6 billion barrels of oil. China is building a vast network of road and rail links, including a US$200 million coastal highway running from Gwadar to Pakistan's primary naval base in Karachi. The coastal highway will connect Gwadar to western China, including its Muslim-majority autonomous region of Xinjiang, through the Karakorum Highway. China wants its energy shipments from Central Asia and the Middle East, especially (lique-fied) natural gas from Turkmenistan, Qatar and Kuwait, tankered to Gwadar and then piped or trucked to western China through the Karakorum Highway.

The South China Sea (East and Southeast Asia)

Unlike the Indian Ocean region, the South China Sea region is perceived as China's home turf. Yet China has several challenges even here. Most of these relate to the contested ownership of the South China Sea, especially its islands and their surrounding waters, which boast of immense untapped natural resources, especially natural gas and oil. Thus, the battle in South China Sea region is about natural resources as well as the critical shipping seaways.

China and Taiwan have laid territorial claims to the South China Sea and all its islands, reefs and rocks. Yet their claims do not go uncontested. Many of China's Southeast Asian neighbours are rival claimants to an assortment of islands in the South China Sea, which is bordered by China and Taiwan in the north, Vietnam in the west, Malaysia, Indonesia and Brunei in the south, and the Philippines in the east. China's neighbours also assert their claims to the waters that surround the contested islands. The major conflict, however, is over two sets of islands: the Xisha (Paracel) Islands and the Nansha (Spratly) Islands. All of the Xisha (Paracel) Islands are contested among three countries: China, Taiwan and Vietnam, although only China has physically occupied them since 1974. The Nansha (Spratly) Islands, on the other hand, are claimed by Brunei, China, Malaysia, the Philippines, Taiwan and Vietnam. Most of these claimants occupy several of the Nansha (Spratly) Islands, which will subsequently be referred to as the Spratlys. China occupies eight, Taiwan one, the Philippines nine, Malaysia nine, and Vietnam three. Brunei lays territorial claims to several of these islands, but occupies none.

The total area of the Spratlys is less than three square miles, but each is important as the basis for staking claims to the surrounding waters as an exclusive economic zone (EEZ), which under the United Nations Convention on the Law of the Sea (UNCLOS) extends to 200 nautical miles from the territorial sea. China bases its claim to the Spratlys through its history by invoking their ownership by successive Chinese dynasties. Beijing points to the fact that the international community has continued to accept its sovereignty over these islands since China's independence in 1949. Yet many authorities believe that the Chinese claim of sovereignty over the disputed islands is inconsistent with UNCLOS, which limits sovereignty claims to 12 nautical miles.

Nonetheless, it is not just the islands and their surrounding waters that drive the disputants' territorial claims; it is their sub-surface natural wealth, which lies unexplored in the waters surrounding these islands, that fuels the contested claims. According to the US Energy Information Agency, the South China Sea has proven oil reserves of 7.8 billion barrels. Current oil production in the region is over 1.9 million barrels per day. According to a 1995 study by Russia's Research Institute of Geology of Foreign Countries, 6 billion barrels of oil might be present in the Spratlys in addition to vast reserves of natural gas. The Chinese media describe the South China Sea as the second Persian Gulf. Some Chinese specialists have asserted that the South China Sea could contain as much as 150 billion barrels of oil and natural gas. In the Spratlys, which are the most contested territory, the exploratory work has yet to be done to quantify proven oil reserves.

Besides its natural wealth, the South China Sea is equally important to Beijing as the primary seaway for energy shipments, especially those from the Middle East. In recent years, the South China Sea has become one of the world's busiest international sea-lanes. More than half of the world's annual merchant shipping traffic sails through the Straits of Malacca, Lombok and Sunda. Crude oil, liquefied natural gas, coal and iron ore make up the bulk of shipping traffic. Over 100,000 oil tankers, container ships and other merchant vessels transit the straits each year. Oil tankers carry over 3 million barrels of crude through the straits each day. Over 9.5 million barrels of oil per day flow through the Straits of Malacca alone. More importantly, major East Asian nations such as Japan, South Korea and Taiwan have over 80 per cent of their oil imports shipped through the South China Sea. The estimated volume of future fuel shipments across the South China Sea further enhances its strategic significance and makes the Strait of Malacca a major bottleneck in the world's oil transport system. Given its congestion, insecurity and China's near-total dependence on it, leads one observer to describe the Strait of Malacca as China's dilemma.

Because of its unequalled strategic significance, the South China Sea and its islands, especially the Spratlys, are hotly contested between China and the neighbouring East- and Southeast Asian nations. All but Brunei have backed up their respective claims with a military presence on at least one of the Spratlys. Although their claims to EEZs overlap, all six claimants – Brunei, China, Malaysia, the Philippines, Taiwan and Vietnam – invoke UNCLOS in support of their claims. China, Taiwan and Vietnam claim even part of Indonesia's territory in the Natuna Island area.

The Caspian Sea region (Central Asia)

The disputes over natural resources and strategic seaways mark interstate relations in the Caspian Sea region as well, where many Central Asian nations are claimants to the natural resources of the Caspian Sea basin, of which Azerbaijan, Iran, Kazakhstan and Russia are the most important. Although China has no such claim to the Caspian Sea basin's natural resources, it has emerged as a major potential consumer of these resources, and as such it is making large investments in their development. The region's natural wealth in general has set off a race among its potential consumers who are scrambling for the largest chunk and a monopoly of control.

China is seriously interested in the Caspian Sea hydrocarbon resources and has even reported an interest in a pipeline to the Arabian Sea, with a view to importing gas and oil by super tanker.

China's gateway to Central Asia is its only Muslim-majority autonomous region of Xinjiang. Trade between Xinjiang and the five Central Asian states accounts for 40 per cent of the total trade between China and Central Asia. Xinjiang's trade with Kazakhstan alone was valued at about US$3.3 billion in 2004, which accounted for 73 per cent of China's national trade with Kazakhstan. Xinjiang is critical to Beijing's future for its vastness, geographical proximity with Central Asia and above all its immense natural resources. The Tarim Basin alone has proven reserves of over 1 billion tons of crude oil and 59 billion cubic metres (BCM) of natural gas. These oilfields are expected to provide 50 million tons of crude a year by 2010.

China's engagement with the nations of the Indian Ocean, South China Sea and Caspian Sea regions sufficiently demonstrates that its quest for energy resources is defining its economic and strategic alignments. In the Indian Ocean region, it is employing economic diplomacy to strengthen its relations with the key nations in the region – Bangladesh, Pakistan and Sri Lanka. It has bound them with strategic and defence pacts. In the South China Sea region, China is deftly deploying both coercive and cooperative diplomacy to assert its territorial claim to the South China Sea and its islands, reefs and atolls.

Beijing's measured use of force, duly tempered with its willingness to negotiate, has worked to its advantage in defusing potentially fraught conflicts with Indonesia, the Philippines and Vietnam. The use of force, however, showed China's willingness to raise the stakes in defence of its territorial claim to the South China Sea. Yet its readiness to back down and seek a negotiated settlement to its disputes with Jakarta and Manila served to confirm its credentials as a responsible power. Above all, it successfully brought major contenders in the South China Sea into a cooperative framework of joint exploration and exploitation of its resources, all the while standing by its sovereignty claim over the entire South China Sea.

In the case of the Caspian Sea region, China moved fast to settle its border disputes with its smaller neighbours such as Kazakhstan, Kyrgyzstan and Tajikistan, which went a long way to secure its energy supplies, as all of its Central Asian neighbours are either energy-rich nations or strategically located to serve as transit points for their shipments. Beijing's energy diplomacy infused the region with a massive inflow of capital investment, especially in energy infrastructure building. To further integrate Central Asian nations with the region's economic and strategic interests, China deftly used the SCO, which was founded in 2001, as a major diplomatic instrument to create a 'multipolar world'.

However, there is a major struggle looming between China and the other major country in the organization, Russia, in the strategic preponderances set by Russia and China regarding the true purpose of the SCO. While China wants it to become an international institution analogous to NATO or ASEAN, Russia, as well as Iran, floated the idea of an 'SCO energy club'. In 2004, China proposed creating a common market within the SCO area with the corresponding complex of changes in the tax, customs, immigration and other legislations. Although the proposal was supported by Kazakhstan and Kyrgyzstan, it was rejected by the Kremlin. One could make a risky – the SCO is still very young – but still analogous comparison to the prospects continental European member states of the European Union attribute to the Union, i.e. a political, economic and military co-federation, and the ones attributed by the United Kingdom, i.e. an economic union of sovereign states.

Some analysts argue that in the long term, the strategic race for the world's energy may result in regional tension and even trigger a military clash. In fact, although the SCO refutes the charge of striving to be 'NATO of the East', its security agenda and joint military exercises indicate otherwise. I argue that as Central Asia remains prone to internal and external fissures, there are too many contradictions and geopolitical fault lines in the Eurasian 'heartland' to allow for the formation of a NATO-like military alliance. In addition, to US–Chinese rivalry over security and energy, as we have already seen, there exist similar undercurrents between Russia and China, China and India, and China and Japan.

As for the Central Asian states, their ties with the United States, Japan, India and others provide them with leverage to lessen the overbearing influence of their neighbouring giants (China and Russia). Since they do not want to replace Soviet with Chinese domination, they view the US presence in the region as an insurance policy against any future bid by China and Russia to reassert control. From this point of view, the US-planned creation of its own 'Greater Central Asia' initiative, a grouping of countries friendly to American policy that will serve as a counterweight to the SCO, a GUAM of the east maybe, could be in the right direction.

Others argue that while courting Central Asian states, other major powers in Eurasia need to remain vigilant about Beijing's geopolitical machinations. Major energy-dependent democratic economies (the United States, Japan, India, South Korea and Taiwan) need to chalk out a common strategy to foil China's attempts to 'lock up' oil, gas and mineral supplies for Beijing's exclusive use in Central Asia, Russia, Africa, the Middle East and Latin America. While the United States is preoccupied with the war on terror, a confident and assertive China is busy steering regional and global multilateralism along the lines of the SCO to serve Beijing's strategic expansion goals and weaken the power and influence of its perceived competitors and rivals. China is redrawing geopolitical alliances in ways that help propel China's rise as a global superpower. But then, does the SCO pose a real threat to the security of Eurasia?

Despite protestations of mutual identity of interests and eternal friendship in high-level Sino–Russian meetings or in SCO institutions, the reality in energy and economics has been actually mutual suspicion and tough bargaining. The Chinese also face a dilemma. They can rely largely upon Russian energy but then would depend on a state they perceive as increasingly unreliable. Russian leaders want to sell China this energy because they want the market and the leverage on China that it provides, since otherwise they can only use arms sales as leverage *vis-à-vis* China. But doing so then angers Japan and leaves Russia dependent upon a single, monopolistic consumer. Although the most recent evidence suggests that the Siberian pipeline will probably go first to China and only then to Japan, Russia's constant flirtations with both states make this an inherently unstable situation that could deteriorate for both political and economic reasons.[11]

Truly, the connection between energy, foreign relations and security is growing closer and the rivalry for influence among the great powers and Central Asia's neighbours continues apace. In conjunction with these trends, recent Russian, Iranian and Uzbek proposals that the SCO becomes or creates within it an 'energy club' take on a new meaning.

At the most recent summit of the organization (Astana, June 2006), Russian President Putin has suggested launching an SCO 'energy club' or 'gas OPEC', which would probably do for natural gas what OPEC has done for oil: cut production and drive up prices. An Asian 'energy club' would accumulate the efforts of the producers, transporters and consumers of oil, natural gas and electricity in a self-sufficient energy club. In particular, prospecting, extraction and transport of oil and natural gas, and development of mainline electricity networks for transfer of excessive power to neighbouring countries. In the fifth session of the Council of the Heads of States–members of the SCO (Dushanbe, 15 September 2006) Japan, which hopes to take over the initiative, proposed its own version of an 'energy club', by way of creating a mechanism for consultations in East Asia with the participation of Russia, China, Japan, South Korea and the 10 member states of ASEAN, aimed at ensuring their interests in energy security.

Russia, from its part, has steadily implemented a strategy formulated in 2002 to set up a gas cartel in the Commonwealth of Independent States (CIS) that would be dominated by Russia. This cartel would allow Russia to set the global market price for gas and to exercise uncontested influence over the gas policies of other producers in Central Asia, i.e. Turkmenistan, Kazakhstan and Uzbekistan. Indeed, by late 2005 the head of the Kremlin had already come most of the way to achieving this cartel, relegating these other gas producers to more or less exclusive dependence upon Russian natural gas pipelines and subordination to the Russian producer and distributor Gazprom, now an arm of the Russian state. This domination is essential to the continuation of the current domestic economic and political status quo in Russia, as well as to Moscow's recovery of its coveted great power status abroad.

Kremlin is evidently interested in taking part in multilateral cooperation within the framework of the SCO 'energy club' that would make it part of the process of diversification of export channels and decreasing prices and political risks on global oil and gas markets. However, Chinese attempts to gain a foothold in the energy sector of Turkmenistan, Kazakhstan and Uzbekistan are beginning to pose a threat to Russia's position in Central Asia, based on the monopolistic ownership of gas pipelines to Europe. In response, Russia seems to be favourable towards the idea of SCO expansion in Iran. Iranian officials have been urging the Kremlin to form an oil and gas arc. Russia and Iran have the largest reserves of gas on the planet, and Russian-leaning Turkmenistan and Qatar are not far behind. If successful, a Russian–Iranian hydrocarbon cartel could cause a major power shift, as Russia is also the world's second–largest oil exporter, whereas Iran is a founding member of OPEC. These two countries would be able to exercise the same power in this new cartel that Saudi Arabia possesses in OPEC. Moreover, such an energy club would counter Saudi Arabia's leverage in respect of oil while dominating Asian gas markets. It might allow Russia to provide Iran with needed help in developing its refining capacity.

Here high-profile business meets high-stakes strategy. Iran wants to buy security by leading China to believe it will become what Saudi Arabia is for the United States, while promising the Russians access to future nuclear energy markets. Beijing wants to expand energy and transportation cooperation and build economic power without premature confrontation with the United States while positioning itself as the rational intermediary between Washington and Tehran. If Iran can be prevented from producing nuclear energy on its own and must depend, as it is the case now, on imported gas, this would certainly increase Russia's clout over it.

However, ever since the start of international negotiations with Iran over its nuclear programme some three years ago, China has worked actively to dilute the effectiveness of any global response. It has done so initially through its vociferous opposition to Iran's referral to the United Nations Security Council, and more recently by its resistance to the imposition of multilateral sanctions against Tehran.

China's obstructionism has been driven by its emergent energy needs. This has made Tehran an indispensable energy partner for the PRC. Home to approximately 10 per cent of proven world oil reserves and the world's second largest reserves of natural gas, Iran is a *bona fide* energy superpower. Beijing's engagement with – and investment in – the Islamic Republic has reflected this reality. In 2004, the two countries reached agreement on two massive accords, granting Chinese firms extensive rights to develop Iranian oil and natural gas reserves estimated to be worth some US$100 billion over the next 25 years. A flurry of additional deals has followed, and today Tehran and Beijing boast an energy partnership valued at some US$120 billion or more.

The benefits of this partnership are hardly one-sided, however. Iranian officials remember well the experience of the late 1990s, when low world oil prices and international isolation brought their country's economy to the brink of collapse. As a result, the Islamic Republic has embarked upon an ambitious effort in recent years to diplomatically and economically engage foreign nations, more often than not through its chief export commodity: oil. The burgeoning partnership between Tehran and Beijing is a testament to its successes on that front.

Although energy represents the primary driver of contemporary coopera-tion, mutual opposition to America's primacy in world affairs serves as an important secondary force. In the post-Cold War era, officials in Beijing have expressed their commitment to a multi-polar world in which American influence is diluted, and have pursued partnerships with nations antagonistic to the United States as part of this effort. As numerous observers have noted, China today has embraced a 'balancing' strategy designed to frustrate US policy through robust international diplomacy. Although it is doing so most directly in Asia, the Chinese government has increasingly sought Middle Eastern partners for this venture as well. Cooperation with Iran, the emer-ging geopolitical centre of gravity in the post-Saddam Hussein Middle East, has consequently emerged as a major point of political focus.

These sentiments have been echoed in Tehran. Ever since the Islamic Revolution of 1979, the regime in Tehran has viewed the United States as its principal enemy. For just as long, Iran's ayatollahs have sought external partners for their anti-American regional and international policies. This focus, moreover, has deepened dramatically since the start of the War on Terror. The US-led campaign against the Taliban in Afghanistan in 2001, and the subsequent removal of Saddam Hussein's regime in Iraq two years later, may have eliminated Iran's chief ideological and military adversaries. But it also raised fears among Iran's ayatollahs of a dangerous encirclement, and of the possibility of a similar US-driven transformation in their country. Iran has responded by seeking to strengthen its international partnerships, with China emerging as a major area of Iranian attention.

These trends have found their expression in an increasingly robust pro-liferation partnership, and in the integration of Iran into Chinese-dominated security structures.

Iran is likewise expanding its links with the SCO. Beijing appears to be receptive to Iranian efforts to expand its role in this grouping. Such a union, however, would have major benefits for both sides. Iran, facing a looming confrontation with the United States over its nuclear programme, is eager to obtain a measure of collective security. China, meanwhile, has a vested interest in securing its most important energy partner against external threats. And while Iran's immediate membership is not likely as a result of both institutional and political constraints, the potential of such an expanded bloc, if and when it does materialize, would be immense. An SCO incorporating Iran 'would essentially be an OPEC with bombs'.

From Moscow's standpoint, Iran's participation in such a cartel would be very promising, as Gazprom has indicated its desire to participate in building an Iran–Pakistan–India pipeline and providing gas in South Asia, contributing to a north–south transport and trade network. This is a plan that attracts a lot of attention to Indian and Pakistani policy-makers, because if these countries – already SCO observers – join the organization they might get a more favourable rate at which to buy gas. India might save US$300 million annually on its energy costs, and Pakistan needs the pipeline as a way of getting both natural gas and transit fee revenues estimated at US$500–600 million. It is also planned to link it to the Yunnan province in China. Moreover, this project seems to entail fewer political risks, as the Indian authorities do not intend rejecting the pipeline on security reasons, despite the fact that the pipeline runs across Pakistan.

That there are tremendous gains from an Asian oil and gas union is obvious, not only in terms of bringing states together in the long run, but more importantly in the short run there are economic improvements and visible economic gains for the states involved. The benefits could be divided into political trust, economic development, deregulation, environmental improvements, decreased political reliance on oil exporters, increased national security, etc.

Politically, increased energy diversification and increased energy security would be a tremendous asset. By decreasing its reliance on one, or a few states, each individual actor would have more possible actors to trade with at more financially sound levels. This is high on the agenda of most states, but fear of strengthening other actors have hindered this much-needed diversification, a diversification that could be gained through Russian, Central Asian and Iranian oil and gas.

The economic implications of increased cooperation among the Eurasian states would be tremendous. Enhanced regional cooperation would decrease the reliance on oil transportation by sea and the reliance on Middle Eastern oil, which today is the most important provider of oil in Northeast Asia. The current waterways are not the most direct routes because of the water depth in the Malacca Straits, which forces the prices up. Opening up the Central Asian and Russian energy resources to Northeast Asia would thus significantly decrease the economic costs for the regional economies, as well as increase investments in the economically weaker Central Asian states and Russia.

Unfortunately, lack of trust between the different actors, internal economic considerations, and failure to open up the economies and energy sector because of sovereignty fears have limited the avenues for cooperation. What is needed is political commitment and strong economic incentives for the regional economies and non-state economic actors to integrate and work closely together. Each state has its own strong commitment to this, but they are rarely compatible with other states unless they are directed towards a third state. In fact, it has been noted that the key problem in realizing such an energy-cooperative network are the issues of coordination and distrust. The competing countries have, to date, depended on their own limited solutions in pursuing their own cooperative measures bilaterally without concerted policy directions between countries and often at the expense of their neighbours, thus producing animosity. Thus, we note that realist thinking and zero-sum game strategies are very apparent in the thinking of many policy-makers. This has made it very difficult for any structure in the region to overcome the lack of trust. To accomplish this it is necessary to rely on an organization that has an excess of political capital and currently there is no such organization in Eurasia.

One organization that is partly an exception is the SCO, which is well positioned to initiate such cooperation over energy in an effort to improve political relations but more importantly to improve the economic situation for all actors. This is possible because of the strong political commitment China and a few Central Asian states have placed in the organization. China has to further this organization as the primary multilateral organization in the region; however, this is something Russia and Uzbekistan are less enthusiastic about. Russia would like to promote the CIS as the primary organization in the region, as it controls this organization, whereas Uzbekistan would like to engage the Central Asian states, either bilaterally or in a truly Central Asian organization that it would dominate. However, in order for the SCO to act as the vehicle for an oil and gas union, the SCO would need to include some of the more important energy consumers such as South Korea, Japan and even possibly Taiwan and production states such as Iran in order to make it economically viable. There are currently very few economic incentives to further such a plan and the capital investments involved are so large that the private sector would be reluctant to cover all the cost by itself.

It is without doubt that states that control transit routes to consumers will have increased influence in the region. Politically they would be able to impact the foreign policy of the states dependent on the transit. This is one reason that Japan and Taiwan have opted for sea transportation rather than a Chinese pipeline and why the Japanese proposed a pipeline from Angarsk to Nakodha, which skirts around Chinese territory. Politics not economics was the key factor of consideration in such a pipeline. This proposal has taken precedent over the Daqing initiative proposed by China, and it is less than half as expensive to construct compared with the Nakhodka pipeline. However, political and other economic considerations in Russia have made the Japanese initiative a more likely option, even if the Chinese will do anything in their power to prevent this from happening.

Challenges to an Asian oil and gas union are many, and politically there is growing conflict over influence in Central Asia and Northeast Asia. China and Russia are engaged in a more or less open conflict over influence in Central Asia. The traditional Russian influence is decreasing and China is attempting to move into this region rapidly; the last thing Russia wants to do is to assist China in this strategy. The CIS. and the SCO have thus been put in a position where they could potentially be forced to compete with each other. Until now, political considerations from both Russia and China have made it worthwhile cooperating and decreasing the US influence in the region. Neither organization has become so strong as to create any concern in Moscow or Beijing. It will not be until the political relations between Russia and China are tested that the SCO will be baptized. Bilateral relations between China and Russia will to a large degree determine the future of the SCO, at least until it has become so powerful on its own that it can distance itself from regional power struggles. The question is of course whether the SCO will ever be allowed to distance itself from national considerations.

Northeast Asia suffers from a situation that in essence is the same as that which is witnessed in Central Asia between China and Russia. China and Japan are engaged in a regional power struggle, whereby China is increasing its political influence in the region at the expense of Japan. In both regions there is a feeling in the United States that China should not be given carte blanche to exert unchecked influence. This attitude is closely connected to the dissatisfaction of China's close relations with so-called 'rogue' states, specifically in communist North Korea and Islamic Iran. In the economic field there is also concern over how China's growing economy is casting a shadow over its neighbours: the Chinese economy is rising at a rate that is truly worrisome for states that have traditionally been stronger, such as the United States, Japan and, to a certain extent, Russia.

Moreover it is imperative for many smaller economies that they are not dominated by a growing Chinese economy. This said, the concerns of China are likewise many and focus on energy security, fear of being surrounded by hostile states and a strong concern for domestic economic development. The Chinese leadership believes that this can only be accomplished by increasing international contacts and economic integration, while maintaining Chinese sovereignty and measures to protect its national security considerations.

Iran is a state that cannot be ignored from a pan-Eurasian energy cooperation viewpoint. It can be perceived either as a problem or as an advantage, depending on which perspective we look at it from. Although China, Japan and most Eurasian states are positive towards the inclusion of Iran in the Eurasian energy network, such a move will most certainly alienate the United States and may even create a dispute with the United States over time.

Iran would however serve Eurasia positively, as it would increase the flow of oil to Eurasia and possibly make the pipelines economically sustainable more quickly. The Eurasian economy could be sustained to a significant degree with Iranian oil, even if pipelines full of Iranian oil will spur political instability, for the United States will work against the use of such pipelines. One argument in favour of Iranian participation is that incorporating Iran into a multilateral institutional framework would create conditions for a more moderate Iran through interdependence linkages. On the other hand, this would of course also give Tehran some degree of political legitimacy and render sanctions useless, if sanctions are a primary objective.

The SCO energy club, unique in uniting both energy producers and key consumers, would certainly constitute a rival to any US-organized plans to utilize Turkmen gas to supply Afghanistan, Pakistan and India through a new pipeline that bypasses both Russia and Iran, seriously limiting Turkmenistan's manoeuvring ability for a more independent stance over setting prices for its gas exports against Russia's monopolistic-desired role in Asia's, and thus the world's, gas markets. Uzbekistan, another Central Asian gas producer, has also taken a positive stance regarding the creation of such an energy club. Such an outcome would be the next major step in the far-sighted and profoundly important global Russian strategy. But the game is hard, and there exist many unpredictable players.

In the case of Turkmenistan, President Niyazov repeatedly attempted to reduce the tight control of the Kremlin and Gazprom on his country's gas supplies. In April 2006 he proposed the development of a pipeline stretching 2,500 miles (4,000 kilometres) from the Amu-Darya River basin, passing north through Uzbekistan and Kazakhstan to Shanghai and strategically sidestepping Russia. He committed to deliver 30 billion cubic metres of natural gas annually to China for 30 years. China will assist in constructing the pipeline, scheduled to be completed in 2009. With China's agreement to pay in US dollars, the deal is certainly preferable to Russia's grip on Turkmenistan's export routes.

Considering that the Energy Research Institute of China anticipates a 7 per cent annual growth rate in natural gas use between 2000 and 2020, Turkmenistan is probably heading in the right direction. If Turkmenistan can break free of Russia's monopoly on its gas exports, then the Kremlin would no longer be able to dictate how much gas it can export, where these exports can go, and how much it can charge for the gas. As the supply of gas to China's might diminish the amount of gas Turkmenistan sells to Russia, Niyazov would have the power to demand higher prices from Russia. Since Moscow resells Ashgabat's gas at two to three times the price it pays, the deal with Beijing may seriously impact Russia's foreign currency earnings as well as diminishing the strategic value that Gazprom plays in the region. However, the survival of the deal depends on the outcome of a complicated and evolving relationship between Russia and China.

In March 2006 important energy deals were signed during Putin's visit to Beijing, and the construction of two huge gas pipelines was agreed. The first is 1,700 miles (2,800 kilometres) long, stretching from Russia's Altai field in Western Siberia to China and will supply 30 billion cubic metres a year by 2020. The initial gas flow is scheduled for 2011, that is two years after the Turkmenistan pipeline is due to open. In addition, the Russian pipeline will be shorter and built on existing paths and structures. The second pipeline, will send 30 billion cubic metres of gas to China from Eastern Siberia and like the previous one is expected to cost US$5 billion. However, the two great powers are engaged in a complex courtship that involves overt cooperation combined with underlying competition. Although Turkmenistan is not an SCO member, if the Russian energy club initiative is implemented and the organization becomes a critical regional player, Niyazov will probably have to abandon his beloved neutrality and reconsider his position and join hands with the others. One thing that is true, is that to date the real energy cooperation game is occurring outside the SCO framework.

In sum, many external actors view the development of an Asian Oil and Gas Union with suspicion as it will not only increase the economic strength of the actors involved, it will also integrate these actors economically as well as politically over time. The formation of such a bloc is perceived as a threat by many actors as it will decrease the political and economic influence that the EU, the Middle East and, most importantly, the United States will have over Eurasia. If such a grand project is to succeed, it needs strong external support.

Unfortunately, not only is there visible economic rivalry between Beijing and Moscow, especially in regard to energy, there is also a subterranean, or masked, but real strategic rivalry that makes the unbreakable strategic partnership of the two countries against American pretensions in Northeast and Central Asia an anomaly.[12] China indeed has had limited success in securing reliable energy supplies under its control from Russia or Kazakhstan. Consequently, in view of the centrality of this issue for China's domestic stability, its global foreign policies and for regional developments in and around Central Asia, the future course of its quest for Eurasian energy supplies must and surely will exercise a profound impact upon energy markets and upon China's internal stability and its international affairs in general.[13]

Conclusions

Although China has been primarily a continental power throughout its history, the country's 11,000 miles of coastline and more than 5,000 islands make it a maritime nation as well. First, China relies on its extensive river network for communication, commerce, and energy production.

Second, coastal waters provide China with critical maritime highways, as do the regional waters of East Asia, the third category of maritime dependence. These seas are of course international bodies of water, and link China to friends and opponents, both current and potential. Hence, any evaluation of East Asian military power must include these linkages between China and Russia, Korea, Japan and the nations of Southeast Asia, all of whom are members of ASEAN. The United States by virtue of its omnipresent naval and air forces throughout the Pacific Ocean and adjacent seas is linked directly to maritime China.

Finally, the oceans of the world are increasingly vital to China's continued economic growth and national well-being, especially under the aegis of 'comprehensive national power' and 'peaceful rise' so frequently trumpeted by Beijing.

China's regional maritime arena includes the Yellow, East and South China Seas, and the region from Japan and the Korean Peninsula in the north to the Strait of Malacca in the south. China's interests in these waters by definition present international issues. China shares maritime boundaries and disputes with North Korea, South Korea, Japan and Vietnam, as well as maritime disputes with the Philippines, Brunei, Indonesia and Malaysia. The South-east Asian nations' concerns could provide a point of leverage for the United States to counter China's increasing influence in the region.

The world's oceans increasingly concern Beijing, since they are necessary for China's continued economic growth, consolidation of its status as a world power and hence continuation of the Chinese Communist Party (CCP) regime in power. China already deploys the world's second largest merchant marine, trailing only Panama's 'flag of convenience' fleet.[1] China's shipbuilding industry is also among the world's most robust, with the largest shipyard in history under construction in the Shanghai estuary. This city is also the principal container port for Northeast Asia, and the third largest in the world. Its maritime importance to China is matched by Hong Kong, which is the maritime doorway to the southern half of China, and the world's busiest container port.

China's 2004 White Paper on National Defence directly addressed the importance of national security interests in the coastal and regional maritime areas.[2] The defence of national sovereignty, territorial integrity, and 'maritime rights and interest' were all discussed in this White Paper as 'national security goals'.

These maritime interests in turn include energy resources, both proven and estimated, that are increasingly of vital importance to China. The White Paper also notes the 'priority [of] the building of the Navy, Air Force and Second Artillery force'. Chinese army strategists also appear to view the American presence in Japan, Taiwan and the Philippines as forming a 'blockade' of China's legitimate maritime security interests.[3]

It is worth mentioning that the Central Asian member states of the Shanghai Cooperation Organization (SCO) represent one of Beijing's most significant efforts at multilateralism and delineate the theatre most likely to require the help of the People's Liberation Army (PLA) in the realm of protecting continental energy resources. Xinjiang's energy resource infrastructure, including the Tarim Basin fields, is conceivably a target of Uyghur separatists.

Beijing has built more than a half dozen major pipelines; others are under construction or being planned.[4] As demonstrated by T. E. Lawrence in the Middle East during the First World War and currently by the *Ejercito de Liberacion Nacional* in Colombia, pipelines can be difficult to protect.[5]

However, the PLA is perhaps most directly involved in China's search for energy security through the its role of securing SLOCs and ocean bed energy fields. Here, the United States is viewed as the likely force that will have to be countered.

The whole matter is a security question of the outmost importance, considering that China's hunger for energy has become a driving factor in contemporary world politics and a precondition for sustaining China's continuing high economic growth, which is the government's major task and the basic rationale for its continuing legitimacy. Indeed, Chinese officials approach the question of reliable access to energy from a geopolitical oblique strategic standpoint. Chinese energy policy, accordingly, has been a political and strategic rather than market-driven policy.

The requirements of ensuring energy security, e.g. by keeping the Malacca Straits open and preventing America or other states from preventing Chinese energy flows of gas, oil and electricity, apparently drive Beijing's long-term military modernization. China's policy-makers fear that energy vulnerability gives America a political weapon with which to 'contain China' or that strife in the Gulf and elsewhere in the Indian Ocean, if not Taiwan, could cut off its vital energy resources. There exists a remarkable nexus between energy, security and maritime power that actually makes things move in Eurasia that are in Central and Northeast Asia. On the other hand, Russia, although essentially partner of the SCO, has systematically obstructed China's efforts to obtain independent access to Central Asian oil and gas fields or businesses, not to mention any hope of equity ownership in Central Asia or in Russia.

It would be difficult for even the US military to interrupt China's SLOCs over which international energy flows, but to the eyes of the Chinese army planners these appear vulnerable too. Should the United States attempt physically to interrupt either SLOCs or overland pipelines, it would almost certainly mean directly attacking China, directly attacking other nations (hosting pipelines and pumping stations), interfering with the peacetime passage of third-country tankers at sea, or all of the above.

The SLOCs are most vulnerable not on the high seas, but at transit points through narrow straits, including Hormuz, the 9-Degree Channel, Malacca, Luzon and Taiwan. The most likely tactic for an opponent to employ would be a blockade of Chinese oil port terminals, or of these bottlenecks. Such actions would be acts of war against China and other nations, and also would likely not succeed in significantly reducing China's overall energy supply.[6]

The US Navy will protect these SLOCs for the foreseeable future, but a Sino-American crisis (over Taiwan for instance) might drive Beijing to decide that its army had to be capable of defending these SLOCs. The way for China to preclude this eventuality is to resolve Taiwan's status peacefully and to develop continental pipelines as the primary avenue for accessing foreign oil sources. Failing that, Beijing would have to make a major change in national budgeting priorities to build a navy and air force capable of protecting the extended SLOCs that carry much of China's imported oil and natural gas. This degree of the Chinese army growth is inhibited by several factors.

First, Beijing's national priorities continue to fall under the rubric of 'rich country, strong army': developing China's economy and ensuring the welfare of its people remains the government's and the Chinese Communist Party's top priority. Second, while Taiwan remains the most sensitive issue between Beijing and Washington, the present economic and political situation on the island, US and Chinese interest in keeping the issue within peaceful bounds and common interest in the campaign against terrorism, all mitigate against the reunification issue deteriorating to the point of hostilities. Hence, Sino–American relations should remain peaceful, if frequently contentious.

Third, there is little indication that the Chinese military's strategic paradigm is going to change significantly in the near future. The armed forces remain dominated by the army, with the navy only as strong as specific maritime-associated national interests justify. Current modernization of the Peoples Liberation Army seems fuelled by increased national revenues rather than by a reordering of budgeting priorities within its structure.[7]

The current Beijing's maritime strategy is one of offshore defence, meaning that the PLA Navy (PLAN) will strive to 'maintain control over the maritime traffic in the coastal waters of the mainland' and the resources in those waters.[8] Defining this area of capability is not easy, but perhaps the most reliable approach is to look at specific missions and sea lines. This approach yields formidable ocean areas for the PLAN to defend: all of the South China Sea, the western half of the East China Sea, the waters extending from the Chinese coast to at least 100 nautical miles east of Taiwan along a line from the Philippines to Japan, and all of the Yellow Sea.

Continued constructive relations with the nations of Southeast Asia should relieve Beijing of concern for commanding the seas of the narrow Malacca Straits. Defence of more distant SLOCs, from the Malacca Strait between the South China Sea and the Indian Ocean, to the Hormuz Strait from that ocean into the Persian Gulf, would require a quantum leap in the Chinese army's capabilities. Conceivably, however, China could choose to deploy its army units as part of a multinational force.[9]

As for the vast Indian Ocean distances between Hormuz and the Malacca Straits, China faces a wary India with a formidable navy of its own. Beijing's policy in Southeast Asia, an area to which Beijing is devoting increasing political and economic resources, is motivated by its concern for the Indian Ocean SLOCs on which China depends for so much of its energy imports. At the same time, India is trying to establish a stronger political and naval presence east of Malacca, evidenced in New Delhi's increased attention to ASEAN and the 2001 deployments by the Indian Navy to East Asia, from Singapore to Japan. These events, combined with Indian naval strength in the Indian Ocean, pose a classic problem in maritime strategy for Beijing: its most important source of petroleum imports, the Persian Gulf area, lies at the end of very long SLOCs that are dominated by the navy of a potential enemy.

Beijing apparently has decided not to build a navy capable of patrolling these long SLOCs to the Middle East. Instead, Beijing is forming supportive relationships with the nations bordering those routes, from Vietnam and the Philippines to Saudi Arabia.

Given China's significant draw on Middle Eastern–Southwest Asian oil, a prolonged war in that region might well seriously disrupt the outflow of petroleum products. To forestall or ameliorate that eventuality, Beijing is engaging in diplomatic activity both to signal its interest in the welfare of the Arab states and to offer mediation services in the Israeli–Palestinian conflict. This activity backs up and possibly extends Beijing's activities with petro-leum companies in the region, including investments or extraction activities in Iran, Iraq, Kuwait, Saudi Arabia, Egypt, Sudan and Somalia.

Unrest in Southeast Asia also has the potential to disrupt the maritime oil flow to China. The political situation in that region is so fractured, however, as to make effective multilateral action against freedom of navigation extremely unlikely. Even if the Malacca Strait–South China Sea route were interrupted, oil could be shipped via alternate routes at an acceptable increase in cost.[10] These options include rerouting tankers through other straits in the Indonesian archipelago or completely around Australia. Other alternatives currently being discussed include building a canal or pipeline across the Kra Isthmus, a pipeline north through Burma or through Thailand to China.

Despite rhetoric about multi-polarity, China has thus far shunned multi-lateral discussions within the SCO about its access to energy, preferring to making bilateral deals with the Central Asian states, Russia, Iran, India or Pakistan, either about the acquisition of energy fields and businesses or the construction of pipelines. The results have been very varied indeed. The SCO, a primarily security mechanism, hasn't yet reached its limits as far as energy security is concerned.

Recently, China has hinted that it expects the SCO to set up an energy working group to study proposals for the construction of pipelines among the members.[11] It seems that China is reconsidering its entire energy strategy, and besides starting its own strategic reserve and making major gas and oil deals with several countries around the world, is reconsidering things on a multilateral basis as well. That might suggest a growing interest in multi-lateral energy associations and a certain scepticism about the virtues of Beijing's previous unilateralist policy. Evidently, China stands at the cross-roads of a new energy policy, perched between the old statist, dirigiste and mercantilist paradigm and a newer, more market-friendly one.

The idea of forming a gas OPEC, essentially establishing a cartel among natural gas producers that could control global prices and output, has been given much attention. It was even argued that the observer status of Iran in the SCO was misleading: this great exporter of energy products being a *de facto* member. The was supposed to avoid the SCO being labelled and demonized as an anti-American or anti-Western military grouping.[12]

However, since Russia and the Central Asian Republics deliver most of their natural gas via pipeline rather than converting it into LNG and operate under long-term contracts, it would be difficult to coordinate any-thing on a global or even regional level.[13] More importantly, it is unlikely that countries like Russia or Turkmenistan would be willing to hand over decision-making power over their energy policies to a multilateral organiza-tion. And although many commentators pointed to the fact that Iran has the second largest gas reserves in the world, Iran's gas production is very small compared with its potential. The notion that a gas cartel would be built upon the foundation of the SCO seems the most far-fetched assertion of all. A gas cartel, or even a gas coordination mechanism to minimize competi-tion, would be to the disadvantage of China as it seeks to incorporate more natural gas into its energy mix. Why would the Chinese allow the SCO to form a gas cartel that would then be used to set higher prices for China? Especially at a time when it cannot come to agreement on how much it should pay for Russian gas and is probably eager to see more competition, not less?[14]

But this is not only true of a gas OPEC. When officials and experts talk about an 'energy club' or 'cooperation and coordination' within the SCO what some of them really want are mechanisms to defuse potentially damaging competition among producers, consumers and transit states. What could this 'damaging competition' entail other than a more open market where China is able to have greater choice as to who it gets its energy from and how much it pays for it? It doesn't seem very likely that China would buy into such a scheme.

Indeed, in order for the SCO to act as a vehicle of energy security in Eurasia, the organization would need to open itself to the United States as an observer, especially since the United States cannot be seriously excluded from region-wide discussions. In that way, more mutual confidence could be ensured not only between Russia and America, but also, and more importantly, in the twenty-first century global context, between America and China.

Notes

Introduction

1 Mehdi Parvizi Amineh and Henk Houweling, 'Caspian Energy: Oil and Gas Resources and the Global Market,' in Mehdi Parvizi Amineh and Henk Houweling (ed.), *Central Eurasia in Global Politics: Conflict, Security and Development* (Koninklijke Brill NV: Leiden, the Netherlands, 2005), 77–78.

2 Guy F. Caruso and Linda E. Doman, 'Global Energy Supplier and the U.S. Market,' *Economic Perspectives* (May 2004). More information about Caspian Sea region oil and gas production and export, see Mehdi Parvizi Amineh and Henk Houweling, 'Caspian Energy: Oil and Gas Resources and the Global Market', pp. 87–88.

3 Zbigniew Brzezinski, *The Grand Chessboard: American Primary and its Geostrategic Implications* (Basic Books, 1997) Chapter 4 and 5. Brzezinski also regards Afghanistan, Iran and Turkey as part of the Eurasian Balkans in this book.

4 Svante E. Cornell, 'Eurasia Crisis and Opportunity,' *The Journal of International Security Affairs*, 11 (Fall 2006), 29.

5 Mehdi Parvizi Amineh, *Globalization, Geopolitics and Energy Security in Central Eurasia and the Caspian Region* (The Hague: Clingendael International Energy Program, 2003), 209.

6 A central reason for 'energy security' was that the 1973 oil crisis represented a triple threat: day-to-day life was disrupted; there was an economic threat; and there was a political threat. See John Mitchell with Koji Morita, Norman Selley and Jonathan Stern, *The New Economy of Oil: Impacts on Business, Geopolitics and Society, Energy and Environment Programme* (The Royal Institute of International Affairs and Earthscan Publications Ltd, 2001), 176.

7 Nicklas Swanstrom, 'China and Central Asia: a New Great Game or Traditional Vassal Relations?' *Journal of Contemporary China*, 14, 45, November 2005, p. 1.

8 Niklas Swanstrom, *China and Xinjiang after September 11*, Nordic Institute for Asian Studies, No. 3, 2002.

9 Dilip Hiro, *Between Marx and Mohammad: The Changing Face of Central Asia*, (London: Harper Collins Publishers, 1994); Arthur Wardron, *The Great Wall of China: From History to Myth* (Cambridge: Cambridge University Press, 1990).

10 Peter Hopkirk, *The Great Game: The Struggle for Empire in Central Asia* (Tokyo: Kodansha Intern, 1994); Zbigniew Brzezinski, *The Grand Chessboard* (New York: Basic Books, 1997); Samuel Huntington, *The Clash of Civilisations and the Remaking of World Order* (New York: Simon and Schuster Cop., 1996); P. Stobdan, *China's Central Asia Dilemma* (http://www.idsa-india.org/an-jun8–7. html.2001).

11 Swanstrom, China and Central Asia, p. 571.

12 Ibid.
13 Sergei Troush, China's Changing Oil Strategy and its Foreign Policy Implications, CNAPS Working Paper, The Brookings Institution, 1 July 1999 (http://www. Brook.ed/fpcnaps/papers/1999_troush.htm).
14 Swanstrom, China and Central Asia, p. 582.
15 Ibid.
16 Ibid.
17 Hamish Robertson, China and United States Develop Relations, *The World Today Archive*, 14 November 2001.
18 Swanstrom, China and Central Asia, p. 583.
19 Ibid, p. 579.
20 Liond Beehner, The Rise of the Shanghai Cooperation Organization, Backgrounder, Council on Foreign Relations, 12 June 2006 (www.cfr.org).

1 Chinese strategic interests in Eurasia

1 Swanstrom, Niklas L. P., 'The Prospects for Multicultural Conflict Prevention and Regional Cooperation in Central Asia', *Central Asian Survey*, 23, 1, March, 2004; Swanstom, Niklas L. P., Regional Cooperation and Conflict Prevention, in Niklas L. P. Swanstom (ed.), *Conflict Prevention and Conflict Management in Northeast Asia*, Uppsala and Washington: CASI and SRSP, 2005.
2 Annette Bohr, 'Regionalism in Central Asia: New Geopolitics, Old Regional Order', *International Affairs*, 80, 3 (2004).
3 The French philosopher Francois Jullien has concluded that 'the key to Chinese strategy is to rely on the inherent potential of a situation and to be curried along by it as it evolves. Right from the start this rules out any idea of predetermining the course of events in accordance with a more or less definite plan worked out in advance ... ', Francois Jullien, *A Treatise of Efficacy: Between Western and Chinese Thinking* (Honolulu, HI: University of Hawaii Press, 2004), p. 20.
4 The well-known Chinese scholar Jisi Wang suggests that 'The readjustment of the center of gravity of U.S. global strategy has determined that for several years to come it will not regard China as its main security threat ... ', Wang Jisi Views Sino–U.S. Relations, Beijing Zhongguo Dangzheng Ganbu Luntan, 5 January 2005, mimeo, 4.
5 The terms are from the PRC's 2000 White Paper on national Defence as quoted in 'The national Security Implications of the Economic Relationship Between the United States and China', Report to Congress of the US–China Security Review Commission (Washington DC, July 2002), p. 23.
6 Samuel Huntigton, *The Clash of Civilizations* (New York: Simon and Schuster, 1996), p. 230–1.
7 From 1990 to 2001 'East Turkestan' separatists launched more than 200 terrorist attacks in Xingjian, killing 162 and injuring 440. 'East Turkestan Terrorist Forces Cannot Get Away with Impunity', *People's Daily*, 22 January 2002.
8 Dru C. Gladley, China's Uyghur Problem and the Shanghai Cooperation Organization, U.S.–China Economic and Security Review Commission Hearings, Washington DC, 3 August 2006, p. 2.
9 From 35.47 million tons in 1997, China's import of oil accounted 100 million tons in 2004. It originates 50 per cent from the Middle East and 22 per cent from Africa. Tian Chunrong, 'Analyses on China's Oil Import and Export in 2002 year', *International Petroleum Economics*, 2003 No. 3, p. 26.
10 Swanstrom, China and Central Asia, p. 569–84.
11 Ibid.
12 Ibid.
13 Ibid.
14 Ibid.

15 Tarique Niazi, 'China, India, and the Future of South Asia', *Japan Focus*, 21 August 2005.
16 Ibid.
17 Ibid.
18 Ibid.
19 Ibid.
20 Ibid.
21 Ibid.
22 Alisher Ilkhamov, 'Profit not Patronage: Chinese Interests in Uzbekistan', *China Brief*, 5, 20 (2005), pp. 6–7.
23 Ibid.
24 Ibid.
25 Wenran Jiang, 'China's Booming Energy Relations with Africa', *China Brief*, 6, 14 (2006), pp. 3–5.
26 Ibid.
27 Stephen Blank, 'Turkmenistan Completes China's Triple Play in Energy', *China Brief*, 6, 10 (2006), pp. 6–8.
28 Ibid.
29 Ibid.
30 Ibid.
31 Mohan Malik, 'Multilateralism Shanghaied', *International Assessment and Strategy Center*, 14.07.2006, p. 1.
32 Nicklas Swanstrom, 'An Asian Oil and Gas Union: Prospects and Problems', *The China and Eurasia Forum*, Weekly Newsletter, 12–19 December 2006, 2.
33 'As Russia Goes Western, China Pays the Tab', *Stratfor*, 20 August 2004.
34 'China, Russia, CIS nations to fight terrorism', *Daily Excelsior*, Jammu, India, 16 June 2001.
35 For an early assessment of this see, Lilian Craig Harris, 'Xinjiang, Central Asia, and the Implications for China's Policy in the Islamic World,' *The China Quarterly*, 133 (1993), pp. 111–29.
36 Zhao Changqing, 'China's Strategic Interests in Central Asia', *Central and West Asia Studies*, No. 2, 2005.
37 Stephen Blank, 'Islam Karimov and the Heirs of Tiananmen', *Eurasia Daily Monitor*, Vol. 2, No. 115, 14 June 2005.
38 Swanstrom, 'An Asian Oil and Gas Union', p. 88.
39 Tarique Niazi, 'Gwadar: China's Naval Outpost on the Indian Ocean,' *China Brief*, 16 January 2005.
40 S. Frederick Starr (ed.), *Central Asia, a Reemerging Transport Network*, Washington, DC: CASI & SRSP, 2005, p. 2.
41 'China', Niklas Swanstom, Nicklas Norling, Zhang Li, 'The New Silk Roads: Transport and Trade in Greater Central Asia', S. Frederick Starr, ed., Washington, DC: CASI & SRSP, June 2007, p. 411.
42 Xu Tao, 'Central Asian Countries' Security Strategies and China's Western Border Security', *Strategy and Management*, No. 5, 2006.
43 Xing Guangcheng, 'Security Cooperation in Central Asia', *Contemporary World*, Iss. 282, 2005.
44 Ji Fangtong and Zhu Xinguang, 'Central Asian Non-traditional Security Cooperation in Post-Cold War Scenario', *World Economics and Politics*, No. 5, 2004.
45 'Regional co-op key to Central Asian Integration,' *China Daily*, 6 February, 2006.
46 Richard Pomfret, 'Trade policies in Central Asia after EU enlargement and before Russian WTO accession: regionalism and integration into the world economy', *Economic Systems*, 29 (2005); Niklas L. P. Swanstrom, *Regional Cooperation and Conflict Management: Lessons from the Pacific Rim* (Department of Peace and Conflict Research: Uppsala University, 2002).

47 OECD, 'China in the Global Economy Challenges for China's Public Spending: Toward Greater Effectiveness and Equity', March 2006, p. 6. www.oecd.org/dataoecd/18/26/36228704.pdf.

48 Vladimir Ivanov, 'Creating a Cohesive Multilateral Framework Through a New Energy Security Initiative for Northeast Asia,' *ERINA Report*, 55, December 2003. (30 October 2005) Vladimir Ivanov, 'An Energy Community for Northeast Asia: From a Dream to Strategy,' *ERINA Report*, 52. (June 2003) www.erina.or.jp/Jp/Research/db/rep15/RS-EE/04070.pdf (30 October 2005).

49 'China dissatisfied with energy cooperation with Russia,' *Interfax China*, 3 March 2006.

50 Gaye Christoffersen, 'Problems & Prospects for Northeast Asian Energy Cooperation', Paper presented at IREX, 23 March 2000.

51 'China', Niklas Swanstom, Nicklas Norling, Zhang Li, Ibid.

52 Sergei Blagov, 'Shanghai Cooperation Organization and its Future' (http://www.eurasianet.org), 29 April 2002.

53 Stephen Blank, 'The Shanghai Cooperation Organization and its Future', *Central Asia and Caucasus Analyst*, 22 May 2002.

54 Xuanli Liao, 'The Petroleum Factor in Sino-Japanese Relations: Beyond Energy Cooperation', *International Relations of Asia–Pacific*, 7, 1 (2006).

55 Tian Chunrong, 'An Analysis of China's Oil Imports and Exports in 2003' (in Chinese), *International Petroleum Economics*, 3 (2004), p. 11.

56 F. William Engdahl, 'China Lays Down Gauntlet in Energy War: The Geopolitics of Oil, Central Asia and the U.S.', 21 December 2005, p. 5.

57 These CSBMs include the Agreement on Deepening Military Trust in Border Regions, signed by China, Kazakhstan, Kyrgyzstan, Russia and Tajikistan on 26 April 1996, and the Agreement on Mutual Reduction of Military Forces in Border Regions, signed by these five states on 24 April 1997, both available at http://www.sectsco.org.

58 This is true not just of Western initiatives and frameworks such as the OSCE and the NATO Partnership for Peace programme, but also of the Russia-led Collective Security Treaty Organization, the various locally proposed sub-regional groupings and the GUAM (Georgia–Ukraine–Azerbaijan–Moldova) grouping. (The last organization for a time included Uzbekistan and was the GUUAM. In May 2006 it was named the Organization for Democracy and Economic Development–GUAM).

2 Shanghai Cooperation Organization: security role in Eurasia

1 Declaration on Fifth Anniversary of Shanghai Cooperation Organization, Shanghai, 15 June 2006, http://www.sectsco.org/502.html.

2 For the chronology of states joining the NATO PFP programme and Euro-Atlantic Partnership Council see http://www.nato.int/pfp/sig-date.htm.

3 Oliker, O. and Shlapak, D.A., *U.S. Interests in Central Asia: Policy Priorities and Military Roles* (Rand Corporation: Santa Monica, CA, 2005), p. 48.

4 CICA currently has 17 members (Afghanistan, Azerbaijan, China, Egypt, India, Israel, Iran, Kyrgyzstan, Mongolia, Pakistan, Palestine, Russia, Thailand, Tajikistan, Turkey, Kazakhstan and Uzbekistan) and nine observers (Australia, Indonesia, Japan, South Korea, Lebanon, Malaysia, Ukraine, the USA and Viet Nam). The second summit of CICA, with its strikingly diverse membership, was held in 2006 at Almaty.

5 Wishnick, E., 'Smoke and mirrors in the Shanghai spirit', *ISN Security Watch*, 25 June 2006, http://www.isn.ethz.ch/news/sw/details.cfm?id = 16434; and Blank, S., 'Russia, China and Central Asia: the strange alliance', *CEF Quarterly* (China–Eurasia Forum), October 2004, pp. 10–13.

6 Declaration on the Strategic Partnership and Cooperation Framework Between the United States of America and the Republic of Uzbekistan, signed at Washington, DC, on 12 March 2002. http://www.state.gov/p/eur/rls/or/2002/11711.htm.

7 Declaration of Heads of Member States of Shanghai Cooperation Organization (Astana Declaration), signed at Astana on 5 July 2005, http://www.sectsco.org/html/00500.html.

8 Sands, D. R., 'U.S., Kyrgyzstan reach deal on air base payment', *Washington Times*, 15 July 2006, http://www.washtimes.com/world/20060714-100731-3908r.htm.

9 Orozaliev, B., 'Base alimony: Manas airport will cost the US 60% of Kyrgyzstan's budget', *Gazeta Kommersant*, No. 137 (27 July 2005), http://www.kommersant.ru/registration/registration.html.

10 Sands, D. R., "'Strategic' accord planned for Nazarbaev's U.S. visit'", *Washington Times*, 7 August 2006.

11 KAZBAT was established in 2000 and has been actively cooperating with the USA and NATO on training, military-to-military exchanges and interoperability. The main activities of KAZBAT, deployed in Iraq as a part of an international division under Polish command, are mine clearance and water purification.

12 Ospanov, Y., 'Kazakhstan and NATO approved the Individual Partnership Action Plan', *Kazinform*, 11 February 2006, http://www.inform.kz/showarticle.php?lang = eng&id = 139744.

13 Canas, V., 'NATO and Kazakhstan', Report No. 165 CDS 05 E, 2005 Annual Session of the NATO Parliamentary Assembly, http://www.natopa.int/Default.asp?SHORTCUT = 678; and NATO, 'Individual Partnership Action Plans', http://www.nato.int/issues/ipap/index.html.

14 The CSTO members are Armenia, Belarus, Kazakhstan, Kyrgyzstan, Russia, Tajikistan and Uzbekistan. The organization's aim is to establish collective defence mechanisms against external aggression. Since its establishment in 2003, the CSTO has developed robust internal defence instruments that include a Joint Staff, a Collective Rapid Deployment Force and military facilities in member states.

15 Weitz R., 'Shanghai summit fails to yield NATO-style defence agreement', *Jane's Intelligence Review*, Vol. 18 (August 2006), http://www.janes.com/security/international_security/news/jir/jir060724_1_n.shtml.

16 Ruslan Maksutov, 'Schanghai Cooperation Organization: A Central Asian Perspective', A SIPRI Project Paper, SIPRI, August 2006, p. 8.

17 Weitz, ibid.

18 Maksutov, R., 'The U.S. Military Presence in Central Asia: Is there a competition with China?', MA Thesis, OSCE Academy, Bishkek, 20 June 2006.

19 Declaration on Fifth Anniversary of Shanghai Cooperation Organization.

20 The members of CACO are Kazakhstan, Kyrgyzstan, Russia, Tajikistan and Uzbekistan (Turkmenistan withdrew in 1994); Georgia, Turkey and Ukraine are observers. The members of the EAEC are Belarus, Kazakhstan, Kyrgyzstan, Russia and Tajikistan. http://www.washtimes.com/world/20060714-100731-3908r.htm.

21 'Kazakhstan: strengthening security in Central Asia through democratic reforms and economic development', Address by Minister of Foreign Affairs of Kazakhstan Kassymzhomart Tokayev, Johns Hopkins University, Central Asia–Caucasus Institute, 5 July 2006, http://www.silkroadstudies.org/new/inside/forum/WPC_2006_0705a.html.

22 Ibid.

23 Tully, A., 'Central Asia: corruption, lack of vision seen as stunting economic growth', *Yale Global*, 11 Oct. 2004, http://yaleglobal.yale.edu/display.article?id = 4676.

24 This was the 'Mutual Interaction–2003' exercise; more than 1,000 troops from SCO member states participated.

25 Grozin, A., 'Kazakhstan: national security problems', *Central Asia and the Caucasus Journal*, http://www.ca-c.org/journal/cac-04-1999/st_11_grosin.shtml.

26 McDermott, R., 'Uzbekistan hosts SCO anti-terrorist drill', *Eurasia Daily Monitor*, 14 March 2006, http://www.jamestown.org/edm/article.php?volume_id = 414&issue_id = 3651&article_id = 2370865.

27 Bailes *et al.*, ibid.

28 Yarov, D., 'Incident in Sary-Talaa: many questions few answers', *24.kg News Agency*, 15 May 2006, http://www.24.kg/glance/2006/05/15/1929.html.

29 Weitz, R., 'Reading the Shanghai SCO summit', *Central Asia–Caucasus Analyst*, 12 July 2006, http://www.cacianalyst.org/view_article.php?articleid = 4314&SMSESSION = NO.

30 In addition, all five Central Asian states already have direct ties with NATO, the OSCE, the EU and many other international organizations. In principle, these ties could influence the SCO, at least indirectly.

31 Maksutov, ibid.

32 President of the Kyrgyz Republic Kurmanbek Bakiev, Speech at the extended session of Council of Heads of SCO member states in Shanghai, 15 June 2006, http://www.president.kg/press/vistup/1237.

33 Maksutov, R., Ibid.

34 'Selected News Summaries: July–October 2004', *CEF Quarterly* (China–Eurasia Forum), October 2004.

35 US Department of State, 'Military assistance: international military education and training, foreign military financing, peacekeeping operations', 2004, http://www.state.gov/documents/organization/17783.pdf.

36 UN Office for Drugs and Crime, World Drug Report 2006, http://www.unodc.org/unodc/en/world_drug_report.html?print = yes>.

37 President of the Republic of Tajikistan Emamoli Rahmonov, Ibid.

38 Maksutov, ibid.

39 Maksutov, ibid.

40 Maksutov, ibid.

41 Caspian Guard is a US initiative aimed at helping states in the Caspian region enhance security and integrate their airspace and maritime surveillance and control systems. The project is also designed to protect Caspian energy infrastructure from attacks by non-state actors. The project was launched in 2003 and has a command centre in Baku, Azerbaijan. Reportedly, the USA has envisaged investing some $100 million in Caspian Guard. Azerbaijan has received three coastal patrol boats from the USA under this project. For more detail see http://www.globalsecurity.org/military/ops/caspian-guard.htm.

42 Ministry of Defence of the Kyrgyz Republic, 'Getting knowledge in China', http://www.mil.kg/ru/news/?naction = news&nid = 163&ndir = 1. See also the Agreement among Member States of the Shanghai Cooperation Organization on Combating the Trafficking of Illegal Narcotics and Psychotropic Substances was signed on 17 July 2004, and the establishment of a special agency for coordinating anti-trafficking efforts was initiated in April 2006.

43 President of the Kyrgyz Republic Kurmanbek Bakiev, Ibid.

44 Nichol, J., 'Kazakhstan: Current Developments and U.S. Interests, CRS Report for Congress (US Library of Congress, Congressional Research Service: Washington, DC, May 2004), http://www.ndu.edu/library/docs/crs/crs_971058f_04may04.pdf.

45 Malashenko, A., 'Central Asia: no one wanted to win', Carnegie Endowment, Moscow, 16 January 2006, http://www.carnegie.ru/ru/pubs/media/73630.htm.

46 Weitz, ibid.

47 Maksutov, ibid.

48 Maksutov, ibid.

49 Blank, S., 'The Shanghai Cooperation Organization: cracks behind facade', *EurasiaNet*, 21 June 2006, http://www.eurasianet.org/departments/insight/articles/eav062106.shtml.

50 In 2003 the SCO member states initiated discussion of the SCO's joining the European Highway transport agreement. See SCO, 'Chronology of main events within the framework of "Shanghai Five" and Shanghai Cooperation Organization (SCO)', http://www.sectsco.org/html/00030.html.
51 Afrasiabi, K., 'China rocks the geopolitical boat', Asia Times Online, 6 November 2004, http://www.atimes.com/atimes/Middle_East/FK06Ak01.html.
52 'Chinese sign up for Turkmen gas', *BBC News*, 3 April 2006, http://news.bbc.co.uk/2/hi/asiapacific/4872668.stm>.
53 Maksutov, ibid.
54 Rosbalt News Agency, 'Kazakhstan and Kyrgyzstan are against a rash enlargement of the SCO', 30 May 2006, http://www.rosbalt.ru/2006/05/30/255089.html.
55 Brusilovskaya, E., 'Phenomenon of the Shanghai Spirit', Kazakhstanskaya Pravda, 16 June 2006, http://www.kazpravda.kz/index.php?uin = 1152520370&chapter = 1150407840&act = archive_date&day = 16&month = 06&year = 2006.
56 Relatively little is known at present about the views of India, Mongolia and Pakistan regarding the value of their SCO observer status and potential membership. It may be that Mongolia's case is regularly pushed by China as a response to greater Russian interest in the South Asia candidates. While the present text only highlights specific objections to enlargement that relate to Iran, it is clear that the reservations felt by (at least) the Central Asian SCO members apply to enlargement of any kind at any time, for the generic reasons outlined above.
57 Yang, L., 'Tehran seeks allies through energy co-operation offer', University of Alberta, China Institute, 16 June 2006, http://www.uofaweb.ualberta.ca/chinainstitute/nav03.cfm?nav03 = 47074&nav02 = 43873&nav01 = 43092.
58 Russian Defence Minister Sergei Ivanov said in an interview with Interfax that the SCO does not have any responsibilities towards Iran regarding the latter's defence or security, since Iran is only an observer in the SCO. *Interfax*, 24 April 2006, http://www.interfax.ru/r/B/politics/2.html?id_issue = 11503798.
59 Nikolai Sokov, 'The Not-So Great Game in Central Asia', Monterey Institute of International Studies, Ponars Policy Memo No. 403, December 2005, p. 228.
60 Peng, Y., 'Post – September 11 Sino-U.S. Ties', *Contemporary International Relations*, Vol. 11, No. 11, November 2001, p. 21.
61 General Xiong Guangkai, former PLA Deputy Chief of Staff, Takungpao News quoted in Mohan Malik, Multilateralism Shanghaid, International Assessment and Strategy Center, 14 July 2006, p. 2.
62 Ren Dongfeng, 'The Central Asia Policies of China, Russia and the USA, and the Shanghai Cooperation Organization Process: a View from China', Stockholm International Peace Research Institute (SIPRI), October–December 2003, p. 6.
63 Peng, Y., 'Post-September 11 Sino-U.S. Ties', *Contemporary International Relations*, Vol. 11, No. 11, November 2001, p. 21.
64 Pan Guang, 'A Chinese Perspective on the Shanghai Cooperation Organization', Alyson J.K. Bailes, Pal Dunay, Pan Guang, Mikhail Troitskiy, 'Shanghai Cooperation Orgaqnization', SIPRI Policy Paper No. 17, Stockholm International Peace Research Institute, May 2007, p. 47.
65 Gill, B. and Oresman, M., 'China's New Journey to the West', CSIS Report, August 2003, p. 28. The Western consortium managing the exploitation of the Kashagan oilfield (Kazakhstan) blocked the attempted US$1.2 billion purchase of British Gas' stake by the two Chinese companies.
66 The Treaty of Good Neighbourliness and Friendly Cooperation was signed by China and Russia on 16 July 2001 at Moscow. Its text is available at http://www.fmprc.gov.cn/eng/wjdt/2649/t15771.htm.
67 The 10 members of ASEAN are Brunei Darussalam, Cambodia, Indonesia, Laos, Malaysia, Myanmar, Philippines, Singapore, Thailand and Vietnam.

68 The Six-Party Talks on North Korea bring together China, Japan, North Korea, South Korea, Russia and the United States. The 'P5+1' are the five permanent members of the United Nations Security Council – China, France, Russia, the United Kingdom and the United States (the P5) and Germany.

69 Mikhail Troitskiy, 'A Russian Perspective on the Shanghai Cooperation Organization', Alyson J. K. Bailes, Pal Dunay, Pan Guang, Mikhail Troitskiy, 'Shanghai Cooperation Organization', SIPRI Policy Paper No. 17, Stockholm International Peace Research Institute, May 2007, p. 44.

70 Lousianin, S. G., 'Energeticheskoe prostranstvo ShOS: K voprosu o razrabotke kontseptsii sozdaniya 'Energeticheskogo Kluba' ShOS' [An SCO energy space: elaborating 'energy club' concept], Presentation at the SCO Business Council meeting, Moscow, 6 Dec. 2006, http://www.mgimo.ru/content1.asp?UID= {A9AE6E80-C881-42E4-87FA-BF398B38DD71} (note 20), pp. 18–19.

71 Spechler, D. R. and Spechler, M. C., 'Trade, energy, and security in the Central Asian arena', eds A. J. Tellis and M. Wills, *Strategic Asia 2006–7: Trade, Interdependence, and Security* (National Bureau of Asian Research: Washington, DC, 2006), p. 227.

72 Oksana Antonenko, 'Russia, Central Asia and the Shanghai Cooperation Organization', Center for Security Studies, ETH Zurich, *Russian Analytical Digest*, No. 25, 17 July 2007 (www.res.ethz.ch), p. 9.

73 Ibid., p. 10.

74 Ibid., p. 10.

75 Ibid., p. 11.

76 Ramakand Dwivedi, China's Central Asia Policy in Recent Times, *China and Eurasia Forum Quarterly*, Vol. 4, No. 4 (2006), p. 144.

77 Chen Xiangyang, Assessment of International Situation and China's Security Environment in 2005, *Foreign Affairs Journal*, 78 (December 2005, 24).

78 Tarique Niazi, Asia between China and India, *Japan Focus*, 31 May 2006.

79 'Central Asia plus Japan' Dialogue Action Plan, released on 5 June 2006 by the Ministry of Foreign Affairs of Japan and the speech 'Central Asia as a Corridor of peace and Stability' by Taro Aso on 1 June at the Japan National Press Club, http://www.mofa.go.jp/region/europe/index.html (15 November 2006).

80 Mapping the Future', Report of the US National Intelligence Council's 2020 Project, p. 48.

81 Gawdat Bahgat, 'Central Asia and Energy Security,' *Asian Affairs 37*, 1 (March 2006), p. 15.

82 Guo Xuetang, 'The Energy Security in Central Eurasia: The Geopolitical Implications to China's Energy Strategy', *China and Eurasia Forum Quarterly*, Vol. 4, No. 4 (2006), p. 126.

83 C. Raja Mohan, 'Why Delhi Must Rediscover Moscow', *The Indian Express*, 3 December 2005.

84 The author has explicitly referred to the geopolitical linking of the Central Asia region with South Asia in his PhD dissertation 'The geopolitical components and the new parameters of Russia's relations with the democracies of Kazakhstan and Uzbekistan in the post Cold War international environment', Panteion University of Social Sciences (Athens – Greece), Department of International and European Studies, 2006.

3 Clashes and coexistence between the three major powers in Eurasia

1 While the commercial and state interests also often converge in the engagement by the EU, Turkey, the United States and other countries in the region (and elsewhere), the prevalence of state enterprise engagement in the case of China and Russia makes the link between commercial and national interests significantly stronger.

2 But the governments of the region, and China and Russia, tend to see such support more as an expression of an interest in protecting and promoting Western ideologies.

3 See Evan Feigenbaum, 'Central Asian Economic Integration: An American Perspective', Presentation at the W.P. Carey Forums Hosted by CACI, Johns Hopkins University, 6 February 2007 http://www.sais-jhu.edu/centers/caci/audio.html (August 2007). Note that this statement of US interests in Central Asia's stresses mostly the long term US objective of supporting Central Asian sovereignty, integration and stability. It does not focus on US short-term interests in the region, such access to energy resources and US security interests in Afghanistan.

4 Council of the European Union, 'The EU and Central Asia: Strategy for a New Partnership', Document 10113/07, Brussels, 31 May 2007 (endorsed by EU Council Presidency Conclusions of the Brussels European Council 21/22 June 2007).

5 Guo Xuetang, 'The Energy Security in Central Eurasia: The Geopolitical Implications to China's Energy Strategy', *China and Eurasia Forum Quarterly*, Vol. 4, No. 4 (2006), 121.

6 F. William Engdahl, 'The US's geopolitical nightmare,' *Asia Times Online* (9 May 2006).

7 For more elaboration of US' strategic thinking of South Asia in 'Greater Central Asia', please see M. K. Bhadrakumar, '"The Great Game" comes to South Asia', *Asia Times Online* (24 May 2006).

8 John Mitchell with Koji Morita, Norman Selley and Jonathan Stern, *The New Economy of Oil: Impacts on Business, Geopolitics and Society*, pp. 185–86.

9 Zbigniew Brzezinski, *The Grand Chessboard: American Primary and Its Geostrategic Implications*, p. 204.

10 Stanislav Z. Zhiznin, *Fundamentals of Energy Diplomacy*, 2 Volumes, 2003, Chinese Version, Translated by Qiang Xiaoyun, Shi Yajun, Chengjian *et al.*, International Energy Politics and Diplomacy (East China Normal University Press, 2005), p. 126.

11 Svante E. Cornell, Mamuka Tsereteli and Vladimir Socor, security experts from the Europe and the United States advocate the geostrategic implications of the BTC pipeline for the South Caucasus countries, Turkey, Iran, Russia, and the United States and Europe. 'For the United States and Europe, BTC provides further impetus for western involvement in the energy and security sectors of the wider Caspian basin – and indeed, proves that the lofty but near forgotten ambitions of building an east–west corridor linking Europe to Central Asia and beyond via the Caucasus are not only possible but are being realized.' See Svante E. Cornell, Mamuka Tsereteli and Vladimir Socor, 'Geostrategic Implications of the Baku–Tbilisi–Ceyhan Pipeline', in S. Frederick Starr and Svante E. Cornell, ed. *The Baku–Tbilisi–Ceyhan Pipeline: Oil Window to the West* (Washington, DC: Central Asia-Caucasus Institute & Silk Road Studies Program, 2005).

12 Zha Daojiong, *China's Oil Security: International Political and Economic Analysis* (Beijing: Contemporary World Press, 2005), p. 104.

13 Mehdi Parvizi Amineh and Henk Houweling, 'The Geopolitics of Power Projection in US Foreign Policy: From Colonization to Globalization', in Mehdi Parvizi Amineh and Henk Houweling (ed.), *Central Eurasia in Global Politics: Conflict, Security and Development*, p. 25.

14 Ibid.

15 Guo Xuetang, 'The Energy Security in Central Eurasia', p. 129.

16 Xu Xiaojie, *Geopolitics of Oil and Gas in the New Century: A Closer Look at Challenges Facing China*, pp. 145–46.

17 F. William Engdahl, 'China lays down gauntlet in energy war,' *Asia Times Online*, 21 December 2005.

18 Ibid.

19 'Kazakhstan oil piped into China,' *Xinhua*, 25 May 2006, http://news.xinhuanet. com/english/2006–05/25/content_4597314.htm (15 October 2006).
20 Ni Jianmin (ed.), *National Energy Security Report*, Beijing: People's Publishing House, p. 140.
21 F. William Engdahl, 'China lays down gauntlet in energy war'.
22 Guo Xuetang, 'The Energy Security in Central Eurasia', p. 131.
23 Rajan Menon, 'The New Great Game in Central Asia,' *Survival*, 45, 2 (Summer 2003), p. 197, 199.
24 Zha Daojiong, *China's Oil Security: International Political and Economic Analysis*, p. 112–13.
25 Ni Jianmin (ed.), *National Energy Security Report*, p.149.
26 John Mitchell with Koji Morita, Norman Selley and Jonathan Stern, *The New Economy of Oil: Impacts on Business, Geopolitics and Society*, p. 276.
27 Embassy of the People's Republic of China in the United States of America, 'China's oil consumption, imports decrease in 2005,' 2 March 2006, www. chinaembassy.org/eng/gyzg/t233673.htm (3 November 2006).
28 There are several levels energy security concerns: 'national security risks' (strategic reserves for military), 'securing domestic policies' (to protect freedom to manage internal affairs), 'securing foreign policy' (to protect freedom to practice an independent foreign policy) and 'long-term costs and effects of sanctions' (to use sanctions to further its foreign policy objectives). See John Mitchell with Koji Morita, Norman Selley and Jonathan Stern, *The New Economy of Oil: Impacts on Business, Geopolitics and Society*, pp. 197–202.
29 Stein Tonnesson and Ashild Kolas, Energy Security in Asia: China, India, Oil and Peace, Report to the Norwegian Ministry of Foreign Affairs, April 2006, p. 19. www.prio.no/files/file47777_060420_energy_security_in_asia – final_.pdf (5 November 2006).
30 Ibid. p. 20.
31 Ye Zicheng (ed.), *Geopolitics and China's Foreign Policy* (Beijing: Beijing Press, 1998), p. 25.
32 For further reading, see Ni Jianmin ed., *National Energy Security Report*, pp. 140–1.
33 Guo Xuetang, 'The Energy Security in Central Eurasia', p. 131.
34 As Mehdi Parvizi Amineh says, 'Most actors involves in the region would rather benefit from converting CEA from a zone of geopolitical competition and confrontation to one of cooperation. Political stability and socio-economic development in this region will be crucial for global peace and security.' See Mehdi Parvizi Amineh, *Globalization, Geopolitics and Energy Security in Central Eurasia and the Caspian Region*, p. 27.
35 Guo Xuetang, 'The Energy Security in Central Eurasia', p. 131.
36 John Mitchell with Peter Beck and Michael Grubb, *The New Geopolitics of Energy, Energy and Environment Programme*, Royal Institute of International Affairs, 1996, p. 190. For the question of how to improve the capacity of energy-importing countries to diversify the long-term supplies and build capacity to deal with short-term disruption of oil supply, please see John Mitchell with Koji Morita, Norman Selley and Jonathan Stern, *The New Economy of Oil: Impacts on Business, Geopolitics and Society*, pp. 273–74.
37 John Calabrese, 'China and Iran: Mismatched Partners', The Jamestown Foundation, Occasional Papers (August 2006), p. 3.
38 Maryam Daftari, 'Sino-Iranian Relations and "Encounters": Past and Present', *The Iranian Journal of International Affairs*, 7, 4 (Winter 1996), pp. 865–76.
39 A. H. H. Abidi, *China, Iran, and the Persian Gulf* (New Delhi: Radiant Publishers, 1982), p. 288; and Lillian Craig Harris, *China Considers the Middle East* (London: I.B. Tauris, 1993), pp. 142–45.

40 The Iran–Iraq War erupted just as China was developing its arms export market. Moscow's decision to stop supplying weapons to the belligerents, coupled with the Western embargo on Iran, opened the door to Chinese sales. See, for example, Dennis Van Vrancken Kickey, 'New Directions in China's Arms Export Policy: An Analysis of China's Military Ties with Iran,' *Asian Affairs: An American Review*, 17:1 (1990), pp. 15–29.

41 Calabrese, 'China and Iran: Mismatched Partners', p. 6.

42 'Iran's Crude Oil Sales to China,' Mehr News Agency, in FBIS-Near East and South Asia [hereafter FBIS NES], 12 April 2005.

43 International Energy Outlook 2006, U.S. Energy Information Agency (June 2006), Table 8 http://www.eia.doe.gov/oiaf/ieo/nat_gas.html.

44 Associated Press, 19 March 2004; *The Asian Wall Street Journal*, 12 March 2004.

45 Iran: Official Says Gas Exports to China to Start in 2009, *Mehr News Agency*, FBIS-NES, 5 July 2005.

46 *People's Daily*, 21 August 2000.

47 Calabrese, 'China and Iran: Mismatched Partners', p. 7.

48 Mehr News, in FBIS-NES, 20 January 2006.

49 'China and Iran to Cooperate in Oil, Gas Sectors', IRNA, in FBIS-NES, 27 December 2004.

50 Ibid.

51 Hooman Pemani, 'Russia Turns to Iran for Oil Exports,' *Asia Times*, 11 February 2003.

52 This is evident, for example, in the Chinese government's decision to finance about 80 per cent of the estimated US$248 million cost of construction of the deep-sea port of Gwadar, and thus move oil overland through Pakistan to western China.

53 Hasan Bananaj, 'Iran Behind the Great Wall of China,' Sharq, in FBIS-NES, 30 November 2004.

54 China Delivers 4th Giant Oil Tanker to Iran, IRNA in FBIS-NES, 21 January 2004.

55 Stephen Blank, 'China, Kazakh Energy and Russia: An Unlikely Ménage a Trois', *The China and Eurasia Forum Quarterly*, Vol. 3, No. 3, November 2005, p. 102.

56 Stephen Blank, *Energy, Economics, and Security in Central Asia: Russia and its Rivals*, Carlisle Barracks, PA: Strategic Studies Institute, US Army War College, 1995, p. 30.

57 Cutler R. M., 'Emerging Triangles: Russia–Kazakhstan–China' (http://www.atimes.com), 2004.

58 Sergei Blagov, 'Russia Wants to be More than China's Source of Raw materials', *Eurasia Daily Monitor*, 30 September 2005.

59 Cf, Liu Jingbo, *Chinese National Security Strategy in the Early 21st Century* (Shishi Chubanshe, 2006).

60 Xu Ping, 'Analysis of China's Peripheral Security Environment', *Journal of International Studies*, 118 (March 2007), China Institute of International Studies.

61 Michael Mihalka, 'Not Much of a Game: Security Dynamics in Central Asia', *China and Eurasia Forum Quarterly*, Vol. 5, No. 2 (2007), p. 33.

62 Jiang Xinwei, 'Sino-Russian Relations under the Framework of the Shanghai Cooperation Organization,' Contemporary International Relations, State Council's Chinese Institute of Contemporary International Relations (20 March 2007).

63 Ibid.

64 Alexander Lukin, 'Russia's Image of China and Russian-Chinese Relations,' CNAPS Working Paper, May 2001, http://www.brookings.edu/fp/cnaps/papers/lukinwp_01.pdf (1 May 2007).

65 Yongnian Zheng and Sow Keat Tok, 'China's "Peaceful Rise": Concept And Practice', Discussion Paper 1, China Policy Institute, University of Nottingham,

November 2005 http://www.nottingham.ac.uk/china-policy institute/publications/documents/DiscussionPaper1_ChinaPeacefulRise.pdf#search = percent22deng percent20lie percent20low percent22 (30 September 2006).

66 Derek Brower, 'Impossible bedfellows,' Petroleum Economist, April 2007; see also Nicklas Norling, 'EU's Central Asia Policy: The Adoption of a Strategy Paper 2007–2013', Central Asia and Caucasus (June 2007).

67 EU Observer, 'EU launches new Central Asia policy in Kazakhstan,' 28 March 2007 http://euobserver.com/9/23805 (4 April 2007).

68 Pierre-Arnaud Chouvy, 'Opiate Smuggling Routes from Afghanistan to Europe and Asia,' *Jane's Intelligence Review*, 1 March 2003.

4 Is a strategic meeting of minds among Washington, Beijing and Moscow for the sake of Eurasia's stability realistic?

1 UK Parliament, House of Commons, Foreign and Commonwealth Affairs, 14 May 2002, http://www.publications.parliament.uk/pa/cm200102/cmhansrd/vo020514/debtext/20514–01.htm (4 April 2007).

2 Total GDP 2005, World Development Indicators (Washington, DC: World Bank, 2006), p. 1. China is likely to overtake Germany as the world's third largest economy by the end of the decade.

3 2006 Estimate. Energy Information Administration, China Energy Data, Statistics, and Analysis: Oil Gas, Electricity and Coal (Washington, DC: EIA), August 2006, p.2.

4 Tian Chunrong, '2005 nian zhongguo shiyou jinchukou zhuangkuang fenxi' (Analysis of China's Oil Import and Export in 2005), Guoji Shiyou Jingji (International Petroleum Economics) 14, 3 (2006), p. 4.

5 Lyle Goldstein and Vitaly Kozyrev, 'China, Japan and the Scramble for Siberia,' *Survival*, 48, 1 (2006), p. 176.

6 Chunrong, p. 4.

7 The leading suppliers are Angola (13.7 per cent), Sudan (5.2 per cent), Congo (4.4 per cent) and Equatorial Guinea (3.0 per cent). Ibid.

8 Goldstein and Kozyrev, 'China, Japan and the Scramble for Siberia', p. 170. As central tenet of China's foreign policy is that it shall not intervene in the domestic affairs of other states, it is hardly imaginable that Chinese politicians would comment openly on the Yukos affair. However, Chinese scholars have expressed opinions – see for example You Fang, 'Youkesi: liushui luohua chun quye' (Yukos: Swept Away), Zhongguo shiyou shihua banyuekan (China Oil and Petrochemical Fortnightly), 16 (2006), p. 24–25; Feng Yujun, 'Laolao zhangwo zhanlue ziyuan kongzhiquan: Eluosi 'Youkesi shijian' pouxi' (Firm Strategy for Right of Control of Natural Resources: Analysis of Russia's 'Yukos Incident'), Guoji maoyi (International Trade), 9 (2004), p. 32–33; Qu Wenyi, 'Cong Youkesi shijian kan Pujing zhengfu dui guatou jingji de zhili' (What the Yukos Incident Says About the Putin's Government Economic Policies Towards Oligarchs), Shijie jingji (World Economics), 3 (2004), p. 34–37.

9 Energy Information Administration, *China Energy Data, Statistics, and Analysis: Oil Gas, Electricity and Coal*, p. 5.

10 Energy Information Administration, *China Energy Data, Statistics, and Analysis: Oil Gas, Electricity and Coal*, p. 5.

11 China Imports Electricity from Russia,' *People's Daily*, 5 May 2004; Yang Li, 'Electricity Trade Flourishes,' *Xinhua*, 23 March 2006.

12 Faith Birol, 'China presentation', *World Energy Outlook 2004* (Paris: International Energy Agency), 2004, p. 23.

13 Aleksandr Shumilin, 'Mnogopolyarnyy egoism' (Multipolar Egoism), *Ekspert*, 25 December 2000; Evgeniy Revenko 'Rossiya, Kitay, India: Novaya os mno-gopolyarnogo mira' (Russia, China, India: New Axis of a Multipolar World),

Vesti Nedeli (*Week's News*), 8 December 2002 http://www.vesti7.ru/news?id = 1645 (29 March 2007).

14 Pentagon, Military Power of the People's Republic of China (Washington DC: Pentagon 2006), p.26; cf. *Economist*, 10 June 2006, p. 60; Vyacheslav Baskakov, 'Raketno-yadernyy arsenal Pekina' (Beijing's Arsenal of Nuclear Rockets), *Nezavisimoe voennoye obozrenie* (*Independent Military Review*), 12 July 2002; I. A. Andryushin *et al.*, Yadernoye razoruzheniye, nerasprostraneniye i natsiona-laya bezopasnost (Nuclear Disarmament and National Security) Moscow: Institut strategicheskoy stabilnosti, 2002; Yuriy Gavrilov, 'Yadernyy arsenal obnovyat polnostyu' (The Nuclear Arsenal will Be Fully Renewed), *Rossiyskaya gazeta* (*The Russian Newspaper*), 14 April 2006.

15 The population of the Russian Far East has tumbled even faster than that in the rest of Russia, from 8 million inhabitants in 1991 to about 6.5 million in 2006, or slightly more than one person per square kilometre. The Russian government is con-sidering a range of repopulation programmes to avoid the forecasted drop to 4.5 million people by 2015. By contrast, the three bordering Chinese provinces contain more than 107 million inhabitants. See 'Russia and China: When Dragons Dance with Bears,' *Economist*, 30 November 2006; 'Russian Far East,' *Columbia Electronic Encyclopedia*, Sixth Edition. (New York: Columbia University Press, 2003).

16 Stockholm International Peace Research Institute, *SIPRI Yearbook 2005: Armaments, Disarmaments and International Security* (Oxford: Oxford University Press, 2005), Chapter 8. China's military expenditure is estimated at US$ 65 billion for 2004; Russia is estimated to have spent US$ 50 billion. The US spent a whopping US$ 466 billion. 'World Wide Military Expenditures,' Globalsecurity.org, 15 October 2005, http://www.globalsecurity.org/military/world/spending.htm; (1 November 2005).

17 China has only been allowed to buy the Sukhoi Su-30 MK2 from KNAAPO, while India has given access to the more advanced Su-30MKI from the Irkut Corporation.

18 Cited in Guy Dinmore and Demetri Sevastopulo, 'Asian Neighbours Look Beyond Symbolism,' *Financial Times*, 9 February 2005.

19 Howard French, 'China Promotes another Boom: Nuclear Power,' *New York Times*, 15 January 2005.

20 Aleksey Tarasov, 'Na vertikali vlasti rastut vetki nefti' (Oil Branches Are Growing on the Power Vertical), *Novaya gazeta* (*New Newspaper*), 3 July 2006; Elena Borisova, 'Vertikal vlasti: Vid snizu' (The Power Vertical: The View from Below), *Ekspert*, 21 March 2005; Kseniya Fokina, Andrey Lavrov and Aleksandr Sargin, 'Vertikal vlasti opyat ukreplyayut' (They Are Strengthening the Power Vertical Again), *Gazeta* (*Newspaper*), 8 September 2006; Maksim Shishkin, 'Vertikal vlasti izmerili v lyudyakh' (The Power Vertical Was Measured in People), *Kommersant* (*Merchant*), 12 April 2006.

21 Chunrong, '2005 nian zhongguo shiyou jinchukou zhuangkuang fenxi' (Analysis of China's Oil Import and Export in 2005), p. 4.

22 Vladimir Ivanov, 'Creating a Cohesive Multilateral Framework Through a New Energy Security Initiative for Northeast Asia,' ERINA Report 55, December 2003 www.erina.or.jp/En/Research/Energy/Ivanov55.pdf (30 October 2005) Vladimir Ivanov, 'An Energy Community for Northeast Asia: From a Dream to Strategy,' ERINA Report 52. (June 2003) www.erina.or.jp/Jp/Research/db/rep15/RS-EE/04070.pdf (30 October 2005).

23 China dissatisfied with energy cooperation with Russia,' *Interfax China*, 3 March 2006.

24 Gaye Christoffersen, 'Problems & Prospects for Northeast Asian Energy. Cooperation', Paper presented at IREX, 23 March 2000.

25 Donald L. Berlin, 'India in the Indian Ocean', *Naval War College Review*, March 2006, pp. 12–27.

26 Tarique Niazi, 'China's March on South Asia', *China Brief*, 5, 9 (2005), pp. 3–6.
27 John W. Garver, 'The Gestalt of Sino-Indian Relationship', in Carolyn W. Pumphrey (ed.), *The Rise of China in Asia: Security Implications for the U.S.* (Carlisle, PA: Strategic Studies Institute, 2002), p. 263.
28 Sonika Gupta, 'Chinese Strategies for Resolution of the Taiwan and South China Sea Disputes', *International Studies*, 42, 3–4 (2005), p. 247–64.
29 David Rosemberg, 'Resource Politics and Security Flashpoints in the South China Sea', in Carolyn W. Pumphrey, (ed.), *The Rise of China in Asia: Security Implications for the U.S.* (Carlisle, PA: Strategic Studies Institute, 2002), p. 223.
30 Hans Morgenthau, *Politics among Nations: The Struggle for Power and Peace* (New York: Knopf, [1948] 1973).
31 Kenneth Waltz, *Theory of International Politics* (London: Addison-Wesley, 1979), p.118.
32 Kenneth Waltz, 'Evaluating Theories,' *American Political Science Review*, 91, 4 (1997), p. 915.
33 Dmitri Trenin, 'Russia Leaves the West,' *Foreign Affairs*, 85, 4 (2006).
34 Ibid.
35 Eugene B. Rumer, 'American, Russian and European Interests in Central Asia and the Caucasus', The Aspen Institute, August 2006, p. 21.
36 Ibid.
37 Ian Storey, 'China's "Malacca Dilemma"', Jamestown Foundation, *China Brief*, Vol. 6, Issue 8 (12 April 2006).
38 David Rosemberg, 'Resource Politics and Security Flashpoints in the South China Sea', in Carolyn W. Pumphrey, (ed.), *The Rise of China in Asia: Security Implications for the U.S.* (Carlisle, PA: Strategic Studies Institute, 2002).
39 Ibid.
40 Ibid.

5 The nexus between energy, security and maritime power and SEO's role in China's energy security

1 David Rosemberg, 'Resource Politics and Security Flashpoints in the South China Sea', in Carolyn W. Pumphrey, (ed.), *The Rise of China in Asia: Security Implications for the U.S.* (Carlisle, PA: Strategic Studies Institute, 2002).
2 Ibid.
3 Donald L. Berlin, 'India in the Indian Ocean', *Naval War College Review*, March 2006, pp. 12–27.
4 Tarique Niazi, 'China's March on South Asia', *China Brief*, 5, 9 (2005), pp. 3–6.
5 John W. Garver, 'The Gestalt of Sino-Indian Relationship', in Carolyn W. Pumphrey (ed.), *The Rise of China in Asia: Security Implications for the U.S.* (Carlisle, PA: Strategic Studies Institute, 2002), p. 263.
6 Ibid.
7 Ibid.
8 Tarique Niazi, 'Guadar: China's Naval Outpost on the Indian Ocean', *China Brief*, 5, 4 (2005), pp. 6–8.
9 Tarique Niazi, 'The Geostrategic Implications of the Baloch Insurgency', *Terrorism Monitor*, 4, 22 (2006), pp. 8–11.
10 Sonika Gupta, 'Chinese Strategies for Resolution of the Taiwan and South China Sea Disputes', *International Studies*, 42, 3–4 (2005), pp. 247–64.
11 'Siberian Pipeline to Go to China First', *Alexander's Oil and Gas Connections*, 28 September 2005 (http://www.gasandoil.com).
12 David Kerr, 'The Sino-Russian Partnership and U.S. Policy Toward North Korea: From Hegemony to Concert in North-East Asia', *International Studies Quarterly*, 49, 3 September 2005, pp. 411–37.

13 Stephen Blank, 'China, Kazakh Energy and Russia: An Unlikely Ménage a Trois', *The China and Eurasia Forum Quarterly*, Vol. 3, No. 3, November 2005, p. 109.

Conclusions

1 CIA World Factbook, at http://www.cia.gov/cia/publications/factbook/rankorder/ 2108rank.html.
2 This (and other Chinese defense White Papers) may be found at http://www. china.org.cn/e-white/index.htm.
3 PLA General Wen Zongren, of the Academy of Military Science, cited in the US Department of Defense (DoD), Report on The Military Power of the People's Republic of China, Report to Congress 2005.
4 Philip T. Reeker, U.S. Department of State press statement, 11 September 2002. Also see Richard L. Armitage, 'Statement at Conclusion of China Visit,' Beijing, 26 August 2002.
5 Bernard D. Cole, Chinese Naval Modernization and Energy Security, Institute for National Strategic Studies, National Defense University, 2006 Pacific Symposium, Washington, DC, 20 June 2006, p. 6.
6 Ibid., p. 7.
7 People's Liberation Army Commander (Admiral Shi Yunsheng), quoted in 'Jiang Made the Final Decision on Adopting Offshore Defense Strategy,' Tung Fang Jih Pao (Hong Kong), 24 August 2001, in FBIS-CPP20010824000062.
8 Cole, ibid., p. 9.
9 See John H. Noer, with David Gregory, *Chokepoints: Maritime Economic Concerns in Southeast Asia* (Washington, DC: National Defense University Press, in cooperation with the Center for Naval Analyses, 1996), for cost estimates for various routes.
10 Central Asia Plans Energy Cooperation, *Alexander's Oil and Gas Connections*, 9 February 2006 (http://www.gasandoil.com).
11 Mahdi Darius Nazemroaya, 'The Sino-Russian Alliance: Challenging America's Ambitions in Eurasia', *Global Research*, 2007, p. 2.
12 Jonathan Stern, 'Gas-OPEC: A Distraction from Important Issues of Russian Gas Supply to Europe,' *Oxford Energy Comment*, February 2007, http://www. oxfordenergy.org/pdfs/comment_0207–1.pdf (August 17 2007).
13 Artyom Matusov, 'Energy Cooperation in the SCO: Club or Gathering?', *China and Eurasia Forum Quarterly*, Vol. 5, No. 3 (2007), Central Asia–Caucasus Institute & Silk Road Studies Program, p. 97.
14 Kazakhstan Pushes for Asian Energy Club, News Briefing Central Asia, The Institute for War and Peace Reporting, 20 June 2007, http://iwpr.net/?p = bca&s = b&o = 336455&apc_state = henbbcadate2007 (22 August 2007).

Bibliography

Afrasiabi, K., 'China rocks the geopolitical boat', *Asia Times Online*, 6 November 2004 (http://www.atimes. com/atimes/Middle_East/FK06Ak01.html).

Amineh, M. P., Globalization, *Geopolitics and Energy Security in Central Eurasia and the Caspian Region*, The Hague: Clingendael International Energy Program, 2003.

Amineh, M. P. and Houweling, H., 'Caspian Energy: Oil and Gas Resources and the Global Market', in Amineh, M. P. and Houweling, H. (eds), *Central Eurasia in Global Politics: Conflict, Security and Development*, Koninklijke Brill NV: Leiden, 2005.

—— 'The Geopolitics of Power Projection in US Foreign Policy: From Colonization to Globalization', in Amineh, M. P. and Houweling, H. (eds), *Central Eurasia in Global Politics: Conflict, Security and Development*, Koninklijke Brill NV: Leiden, 2005.

Andryushin, I. A. *et al.*, *Yadernoye razoruzheniye, nerasprostraneniye i natsionalaya bezopasnost*, [*Nuclear Disarmament and National Security*], Moscow: Institut strategicheskoy stabilnosti, 2002.

Armitage, R. L., 'Statement at Conclusion of China Visit', Beijing, 26 August, 2002.

Bahgat, G., 'Central Asia and Energy Security', *Asian Affairs*, 37, 1, 2006.

Bananaj, H., 'Iran Behind the Great Wall of China', Sharq, in *FBIS-NES*, 30 November, 2004.

Baskakov, V., 'Raketno-yadernyy arsenal Pekina' [Beijing's Arsenal of Nuclear Rockets], *Nezavisimoe voennoye obozrenie* [*Independent Military Review*], 12 July 2002.

Beehner, L., 'The Rise of the Shanghai Cooperation Organization', *Backgrounder, Council on Foreign Relations*, 12 June 2006.

Berlin, D. L., 'India in the Indian Ocean', *Naval War College Review*, March 2006.

Bhadrakumar, M. K., '"The Great Game" comes to South Asia', *Asia Times Online*, 24 May 2006.

Birol, F., 'China Presentation', *World Energy Outlook 2004* Paris: International Energy Agency, 2004.

Blagov, S., 'Russia Wants to be More than China's Source of Raw materials', *Eurasia Daily Monitor*, 30 September, 2005.

—— 'Shanghai Cooperation Organization and its Future', (http://www.eurasianet. org), 29 April 2002.

Blank, S., 'China, Kazakh Energy and Russia: An Unlikely Ménage a Trois', *The China and Eurasia Forum Quarterly*, 3, 3, November, 2005.

——— 'Islam Karimov and the Heirs of Tiananmen', *Eurasia Daily Monitor*, 2, 115, 14 June 2005.

——— 'Russia, China and Central Asia: the Strange Alliance', *CEF Quarterly* (China–Eurasia Forum), October 2004.

——— 'The Shanghai Cooperation Organization and its Future', *Central Asia and Caucasus Analyst*, 22 May 2002.

——— 'The Shanghai Cooperation Organization: cracks behind facade', *EurasiaNet*, 21 June 2006 (http://www.eurasianet.org/departments/insight/articles/eav062106.shtml).

——— *Energy, Economics, and Security in Central Asia: Russia and its Rivals*, Carlisle Barracks, PA: Strategic Studies Institute, 1995.

——— 'Turkmenistan Completes China's Triple Play in Energy', *China Brief*, 6, 10, 2006.

Bohr, A., 'Regionalism in Central Asia: New Geopolitics, Old Regional Order', *International Affairs*, 80, 3, 2004.

Borisova, E., 'Vertikal vlasti: Vid snizu' [The Power Vertical: The View from Below], *Ekspert*, 21 March 2005.

Brower, D., 'Impossible Bedfellows', *Petroleum Economist*, April 2007.

Brusilovskaya, E., 'Phenomenon of the Shanghai Spirit', Kazakhstanskaya Pravda, 16 June 2006 (http://www.kazpravda.kz/index.php?uin = 1152520370&chapter = 1150407840&act = archive_date&day = 16&month = 06&year = 2006).

Brzezinski, Z., 'The Grand Chessboard: American Primary and Its Geostrategic Implications', Basic Books, 1997.

Calabrese, J., 'China and Iran: Mismatched Partners', The Jamestown Foundation, Occasional Papers, (August 2006).

Canas, V., 'NATO and Kazakhstan', *Report no. 165 CDS 05 E*, 2005 Annual Session of the NATO Parliamentary Assembly (http://www.natopa.int/Default.asp? SHORTCUT = 678); and NATO, 'Individual Partnership Action Plans' (http://www.nato.int/issues/ipap/index.html).

Caruso, G. F. and Doman, L. E., 'Global Energy Supplier and the U.S. Market', *Economic Perspectives*, May 2004.

Changqing, Z., 'China's Strategic Interests in Central Asia', *Central and West Asia Studies*, No. 2, 2005.

Chouvy, P.-A., 'Opiate Smuggling Routes from Afghanistan to Europe and Asia', *Jane's Intelligence Review*, 1 March 2003.

Christoffersen G, 'Problems & Prospects for Northeast Asian Energy Cooperation', Paper presented at IREX, 23 March 2000.

Chunrong, T., '2005 nian zhongguo shiyou jinchukou zhuangkuang fenxi' [Analysis of China's Oil Import and Export in 2005], *Guoji Shiyou Jingji* [*International Petroleum Economics*] 14, 3, 2006.

——— 'An Analysis of China's Oil Imports and Exports in 2003' [in Chinese], *International Petroleum Economics*, 3, 2004.

——— 'Analyses on China's Oil Import and Export in 2002 year', *International Petroleum Economics*, 3, 2003.

CIA World Factbook (http://www.cia.gov/cia/publications/factbook/rankorder/2108rank.html).

Cole, B. D., 'Chinese Naval Modernization and Energy Security', Institute for National Strategic Studies, National Defense University, 2006 Pacific Symposium, Washington, DC, 20 June 2006.

Cornell, S. E., 'Eurasia Crisis and Opportunity', T*he Journal of International Security Affairs*, 11, Fall, 2006.

Cornell, S. E., Tsereteli, M. and Socor, V., 'Geostrategic Implications of the Baku-Tbilisi-Ceyhan Pipeline', in S. Frederick Starr and Svante E. Cornell (eds), *The Baku-Tbilisi-Ceyhan Pipeline: Oil Window to the West*, Washington: Central Asia-Caucasus Institute & Silk Road Studies Program, 2005).

Cutler, R. M., 'Emerging Triangles: Russia – Kazakhstan – China', (http://www.atimes.com), 2004.

Daftari, M., 'Sino-Iranian Relations and "Encounters": Past and Present', *The Iranian Journal of International Affairs*, 7, 4, Winter 1996.

Daojiong, Z., *China's Oil Security: International Political and Economic Analysis*, Beijing: Contemporary World Press, 2005.

Dinmore, G. and Sevastopulo, D., 'Asian Neighbours Look Beyond Symbolism', *Financial Times*, 9 February 2005.

Dwivedi, R., 'China's Central Asia Policy in Recent Times', *China and Eurasia Forum Quarterly*, 4, 4, 2006.

Energy Information Administration, China Energy Data, Statistics, and Analysis: Oil Gas, Electricity and Coal. Washington DC: EIA, August 2006.

Engdahl, F. W., 'China lays down gauntlet in energy war', *Asia Times Online*, 21 December 2005.

—— 'The US's geopolitical nightmare', *Asia Times Online*, 9 May 2006.

EU Observer, 'EU launches new Central Asia policy in Kazakhstan', 28 March 2007 (http://euobserver.com/9/23805).

Fang, Y., 'Youkesi: liushui luohua chun quye' [Yukos: Swept Away], *Zhongguo shiyou shihua banyuekan* [*China Oil and Petrochemical Fortnightly*], 16, 2006.

Fangtong, J. and Xinguang, Z., 'Central Asian Non-traditional Security Cooperation in Post-Cold War Scenario', *World Economics and Politics*, 5, 2004.

Feigenbaum, E., 'Central Asian Economic Integration: An American Perspective', Presentation at the W. P. Carey Forums Hosted by CACI, Johns Hopkins University, February 6, 2007 (http://www.sais-jhu.edu/centers/caci/audio.html).

Fokina, K., Lavrov, A. and Sargin, A., 'Vertikal vlasti opyat ukreplyayut' [They Are Strengthening the Power Vertical Again], *Gazeta*, 8 September 2006.

French, H., 'China Promotes another Boom: Nuclear Power', *New York Times*, 15 January 2005.

Garver, J. W., 'The Gestalt of Sino-Indian Relationship', in Carolyn W. Pumphrey (ed.), *The Rise of China in Asia: Security Implications*, Strategic Studies Institute, 2002.

Gavrilov, Y., 'Yadernyy arsenal obnovyat polnostyu', [The Nuclear Arsenal will Be Fully Renewed], *Rossiyskaya Gazeta* [*The Russian Newspaper*], 14 April 2006.

Gill, B. and Oresman, M., 'China's New Journey to the West', *CSIS Report*, August 2003.

Gladley, D. C., China's Uyghur Problem and the Shanghai Cooperation Organization, U.S. – China Economic and Security Review Commission Hearings, Washington DC, 3 August 2006.

Goldstein, L. and Kozyrev, V., 'China, Japan and the Scramble for Siberia', *Survival*, 48, 1, 2006.

Grozin, A., 'Kazakhstan: national security problems', Central Asia and the Caucasus Journal, (http://www.ca-c.org/journal/cac-04-1999/st_11_grosin.shtml).

Gupta, S., 'Chinese Strategies for Resolution of the Taiwan and South China Sea Disputes', *International Studies*, 42, 3–4, 2005.

Harris, L. C., 'Xinjiang, Central Asia, and the Implications for China's Policy in the Islamic World', *The China Quarterly*, 133, 1993.

—— *China Considers the Middle East*, London: I.B. Tauris, 1993.

Hickey D., 'New Directions in China's Arms Export Policy: An Analysis of China's Military Ties with Iran', *Asian Affairs: An American Review*, 17, 1, 1990.

Hiro, D., *Between Marx and Mohammad: The Changing Face of Central Asia*, London: Harper Collins Publishers, 1994.

Hopkirk, P., *The Great Game: The Struggle for Empire in Central Asia*, Tokyo: Kodansha Intern, 1994.

Huntigton, S., *The Clash of Civilizations and the Remaking of World Order*, New York: Simon and Schuster, 1996.

Ilkhamov, A., 'Profit not Patronage: Chinese Interests in Uzbekistan', *China Brief*, 5, 20, 2005.

Ivanov, V., 'An Energy Community for Northeast Asia: From a Dream to Strategy', ERINA Report 52. (June 2003) (www.erina.or.jp/Jp/Research/db/rep15/RS-EE/04070.pdf) (30 October 2005).

—— 'Creating a Cohesive Multilateral Framework Through a New Energy Security Initiative for Northeast Asia', ERINA Report 55, December 2003. www.erina.or.jp/En/Research/Energy/Ivanov55.pdf (30 October 2005).

Jiang, W., China's Booming Energy Relations with Africa, *China Brief*, 6, 14, 2006.

Jianmin, N. (ed.), *National Energy Security Report*, Beijing: People's Publishing House, 2005.

Jullien, F. A., 'Treaties of Efficacy: Between Western and Chinese Thinking', Honolulu: University of Hawaii Press, 2004.

Kerr, D., 'The Sino-Russian Partnership and U.S. Policy Toward North Korea: From Hegemony to Concert in North-East Asia', *International Studies Quarterly*, 49, 3 September 2005.

Li, Y., 'Electricity Trade Flourishes', *Xinhua*, 23 March 2006.

Liao, X., 'The Petroleum Factor in Sino-Japanese Relations: Beyond Energy Cooperation', *International Relations of Asia – Pacific*, 7, 1 2006.

Lousianin, S. G., 'Energeticheskoe prostranstvo ShOS: K voprosu o razrabotke kontseptsii sozdaniya "Energeticheskogo Kluba" ShOS' [An SCO energy space: elaborating 'energy club' concept], Presentation at the SCO Business Council meeting, Moscow, 6 December 2006 (http://www.mgimo.ru/content1.asp?UID = {A9AE6E80-C881-42E4-87FA-BF398B38DD71}).

Lukin, A., 'Russia's Image of China and Russian-Chinese Relations', CNAPS Working Paper, May 2001, (http://www.brookings.edu/fp/cnaps/papers/lukinwp_01.pdf) (1 May 2007).

Maksutov, R., 'Schanghai Cooperation Organization: A Central Asian Perspective', A SIPRI Project Paper, SIPRI, August 2006, p. 8.

—— 'The U.S. Military Presence in Central Asia: Is there a competition with China?', MA Thesis, Bishkek OSCE: Academy, 20 June 2006.

Malashenko, A., 'Central Asia: no one wanted to win', Carnegie Endowment, Moscow, 16 January 2006, (http://www.carnegie.ru/ru/pubs/media/73630.htm).

Malik, M., Multilateralism Shanghaied, International Assessment and Strategy Center, 14 July 2006.

Marketos, T. N., 'The Geopolitical Components and the New Parameters of Russia's Relations with the Republics of Kazakhstan and Uzbekistan in the post Cold War

International Environment', Athens: Panteion University of Social Sciences, Department of International and European Studies, 2006.

Matusov, A., Energy Cooperation in the SCO: Club or Gathering? , *China and Eurasia Forum Quarterly*, 5, 3 (2007), Central Asia – Caucasus Institute & Silk Road Studies Program.

McDermott, R., 'Uzbekistan hosts SCO anti-terrorist drill', Eurasia Daily Monitor, 14 March 2006, (http://www.jamestown.org/edm/article.php?volume_id = 414&issue_id = 3651&article_id = 2370865).

Menon, R., 'The New Great Game in Central Asia', *Survival*, 45, 2, Summer, 2003.

Mihalka, M., 'Not Much of a Game: Security Dynamics in Central Asia', *China and Eurasia Forum Quarterly*, 5, 2, 2007.

Mitchell, J., Beck, P. and Grubb, M., 'The New Geopolitics of Energy, Energy and Environment Programme', Royal Institute of International Affairs, 1996.

Mitchell, J., Morita, K., Selley, N. and Stern, J., 'The New Economy of Oil: Impacts on Business, Geopolitics and Society, Energy and Environment Programme', (The Royal Institute of International Affairs and Earthscan Publications Ltd., 2001).

Mohan, C. R., 'Why Delhi Must Rediscover Moscow', *The Indian Express*, 3 December 2005.

Morgenthau, H., *Politics among Nations: The Struggle for Power and Peace*, New York: Knopf, [1948] 1973.

Nazemroaya, M. D., 'The Sino-Russian Alliance: Challenging America's Ambitions in Eurasia', *Global Research*, 2007.

Niazi, T., 'China's March on South Asia', *China Brief*, 5, 9, 2005.

—— 'Guadar: China's Naval Outpost on the Indian Ocean', *China Brief*, 5, 4, 2005.

—— 'The Geostrategic Implications of the Baloch Insurgency', *Terrorism Monitor*, 4, 22 2006.

—— 'Asia between China and India', *Japan Focus*, 31 May 2006.

—— 'China, India, and the Future of South Asia', *Japan Focus*, 21 August 2005.

Nichol, J., *Kazakhstan: Current Developments and U.S. Interests*, CRS Report for Congress URL (http://www.ndu.edu/library/docs/crs/crs_971058f_04may04.pdf) Washington, DC: US Library of Congress, Congressional Research Service, 2004.

Noer, J. H. and Gregory D, *Chokepoints: Maritime Economic Concerns in Southeast Asia*, Washington, DC: National Defense University Press, in cooperation with the Center for Naval Analyses, 1996.

Norling, N., 'EU's Central Asia Policy: The Adoption of a Strategy Paper 2007–2013', Central Asia and Caucasus June 2007.

OECD, China in the Global Economy Challenges for China's Public Spending: Toward Greater Effectiveness and Equity, (www.oecd.org/dataoecd/18/26/36228704. pdf) March 2006.

Oksana, A., 'Russia, Central Asia and the Shanghai Cooperation Organization', Center for Security Studies, ETH Zurich, *Russian Analytical Digest*, 25, 17 July 2007 (www.res.ethz.ch).

Oliker, O. and Shlapak, D. A., *U.S. Interests in Central Asia: Policy Priorities and Military Roles*, Santa Monica, CA: Rand Corporation: 2005.

Orozaliev, B., 'Base alimony: Manas airport will cost the US 60% of Kyrgyzstan's budget', Gazeta Kommersant, no. 137 (http://www.kommersant.ru/registration/ registration.html) 27 July 2005.

Ospanov, Y., 'Kazakhstan and NATO approved the Individual Partnership Action Plan', *Kazinform*, 11 February 2006.

Pan, G., 'A Chinese Perspective on the Shanghai Cooperation Organization', in Alyson, J. K., Bailes, A. J. K., Dunay, P., Guang, P. and Troitskiy, M. (eds), *Shanghai Cooperation Orgaqnization*, SIPRI Policy Paper No 17, Stockholm International Peace Research Institute, May 2007.

Pemani, H., 'Russia Turns to Iran for Oil Exports', *Asia Times*, 11 February 2003.

Peng, Y., 'Post – September 11 Sino–U.S. Ties', *Contemporary International Relations*, 11, 11, November, 2001.

Pentagon, *Military Power of the People's Republic of China*, Washington DC: Pentagon 2006.

People's Liberation Army Commander (Admiral Shi Yunsheng), quoted in 'Jiang Made the Final Decision on Adopting Offshore Defense Strategy', Tung Fang Jih Pao (Hong Kong), 24 August 2001, in FBIS-CPP20010824000062.

Ping, X. 'Analysis of China's Peripheral Security Environment', *Journal of International Studies*, 118, March, 2007.

Pomfret, R., 'Trade policies in Central Asia after EU enlargement and before Russian WTO accession: regionalism and integration into the world economy', *Economic Systems*, 29, 2005.

Reeker, P. T., U.S. Department of State press statement, 11 September 2002.

Ren, D., *The Central Asia Policies of China, Russia and the USA, and the Shanghai Cooperation Organization Process: a View from China*, Stockholm: Stockholm International Peace Research Institute (SIPRI).

Revenko, E. 'Rossiya, Kitay, India: Novaya os mnogopolyarnogo mira', [Russia, China, India: New Axis of a Multipolar World], *Vesti Nedeli* [*Week's News*], 8 December 2002 (http://www.vesti7.ru/news?id = 1645) (29 March 2007).

Robertson, H., 'China and United States Develop Relations', *The World Today Archive*, 14 November 2001.

Rosbalt News Agency, 'Kazakhstan and Kyrgyzstan are against a rash enlargement of the SCO', 30 May 2006, (http://www.rosbalt.ru/2006/05/30/255089.html).

Rosemberg, D., 'Resource Politics and Security Flashpoints in the South China Sea', in Carolyn W. Pumphrey (ed.), *The Rise of China in Asia: Security Implications for the U.S.*, Carlisle, PA: Strategic Studies Institute, 2002.

Rumer, E. B., 'American, Russian and European Interests in Central Asia and the Caucasus', The Aspen Institute, August 2006.

Sands, D. R., '"Strategic" accord planned for Nazarbaev's U.S. visit', *Washington Times*, 7 August 2006.

—— 'U.S., Kyrgyzstan reach deal on air base payment', *Washington Times*, 15 July 2006, (http://www.washtimes.com/world/20060714-100731-3908r.htm).

Shishkin, M., 'Vertikal vlasti izmerili v lyudyakh' [The Power Vertical Was Measured in People], *Kommersant* [*Merchant*], 12 April 2006.

Shumilin Al, 'Mnogopolyarnyy egoism' [Multipolar Egoism], *Ekspert*, 25 December 2000.

Sokov, N., 'The Not – So Great Game in Central Asia', Monterey Institute of International Studies, Ponars Policy Memo No. 403, December 2005.

Spechler, D. R. and Spechler, M. C., 'Trade, energy, and security in the Central Asian arena', in Tellis, A. J. and Wills, M. (eds), *Strategic Asia 2006–07: Trade, Interdependence, and Security*, Washington, DC: National Bureau of Asian Research, 2006.

Stern, J., 'Gas-OPEC: A Distraction from Important Issues of Russian Gas Supply to Europe', *Oxford Energy Comment*, February 2007, (http://www.oxfordenergy.org/pdfs/comment_0207-1.pdf) (17 August 2007).

Stobdan, P., 'China's Central Asia Dilemma', (http://www.idsa-india.org/an-jun8-7.html.2001).

Storey, I., 'China's 'Malacca Dilemma'', Jamestown Foundation, *China Brief*, 6, 8, 2006.

Swanstom, N. L. P., 'Regional Cooperation and Conflict Prevention', in Niklas L. P. Swanstom (ed.), *Conflict Prevention and Conflict Management in Northeast Asia*, Uppsala and Washington: CASI and SRSP, 2005.

—— 'An Asian Oil and Gas Union: Prospects and Problems', *CEF Quarterly*, 3, 3, 2005.

—— 'China and Central Asia: a New Great Game or Traditional Vassal Relations?', *Journal of Contemporary China*, 14, 45, November 2005.

—— 'China and Xinjiang after September 11', *Nordic Institute for Asian Studies*, 3, 2002.

—— 'The Prospects for Multicultural Conflict Prevention and Regional Cooperation in Central Asia', *Central Asian Survey*, 23, 1, March, 2004.

—— *Regional Cooperation and Conflict Management: Lessons from the Pacific Rim*, Uppsala: Department of Peace and Conflict Research: Uppsala University, 2002.

Swanstom, N. L. P., Norling, N. and Li, Z., 'China' in Starr, S. F. (ed.), *The New Silk Roads: Transport and Trade in Greater Central Asia*, Washington, DC: CASI & SRSP, 2007.

Tao, X., 'Central Asian Countries' Security Strategies and China's Western Border Security', *Strategy and Management*, 5, 2006.

Tarasov, A., 'Na vertikali vlasti rastut vetki nefti' [Oil Branches Are Growing on the Power Vertical], *Novaya gazeta* [*New Newspaper*], 3 July 2006.

Tonnesson, S. and Kolas, A., 'Energy Security in Asia: China, India, Oil and Peace', *Report to the Norwegian Ministry of Foreign Affairs*, April 2006, (www.prio.no/files/file47777_060420_energy_security_in_asia__final_.pdf) 5 November 2006.

Trenin, D., 'Russia Leaves the West', *Foreign Affairs*, 85, 4, 2006.

Troitskiy, M., 'A Russian Perspective on the Shanghai Cooperation Organization', in Alyson, J. K., Bailes, A. J. K., Dunay, P., Guang, P. and Troitskiy, M. (eds), *Shanghai Cooperation Organization*, SIPRI Policy Paper No 17, Stockholm International Peace Research Institute, May 2007.

Troush, S., 'China's Changing Oil Strategy and its Foreign Policy Implications', CNAPS Working Paper, The Brookings Institution, 1 July 1999, (http://www.Brook.ed/fpcnaps/papers/1999_troush.htim).

Tully, A., 'Central Asia: corruption, lack of vision seen as stunting economic growth', *Yale Global*, 11 October 2004, (http://yaleglobal.yale.edu/display.article?id = 4676).

Waltz, K., 'Evaluating Theories', *American Political Science Review*, 91, 4, 1997.

—— *Theory of International Politics*, London: Addison-Wesley, 1979.

Wardron, A., 'The Great Wall of China: From History to Myth', Cambridge: Cambridge University Press, 1990.

Weitz, R., 'Reading the Shanghai SCO summit', *Central Asia–Caucasus Analyst*, 12 July 2006, (http://www.cacianalyst.org/view_article.php?articleid = 4314&SMSESSION = NO).

—— 'Shanghai summit fails to yield NATO-style defence agreement', *Jane's Intelligence Review*, 18 August 2006, (http://www.janes.com/security/international_security/news/jir/jir060724_1_n.shtml).

Wenyi, Q., 'Cong Youkesi shijian kan Pujing zhengfu dui guatou jingji de zhili' [What the Yukos Incident Says About the Putin's Government Economic Policies Towards Oligarchs], *Shijie jingji [World Economics]*, 3 2004.

Wishnick, E., 'Smoke and mirrors in the Shanghai spirit', *ISN Security Watch*, 25 June 2006, (http://www.isn.ethz.ch/news/sw/details.cfm?id = 16434).

Xiangyang, C., 'Assessment of International Situation and China's Security Environment in 2005', *Foreign Affairs Journal*, 78, 24 December 2005.

Xing, G., 'Security Cooperation in Central Asia', *Contemporary World*, Iss. 282, 2005.

Xinwei, J., 'Sino-Russian Relations under the Framework of the Shanghai Cooperation Organization', Contemporary International Relations, State Council's Chinese Institute of Contemporary International Relations, 20 March 2007.

Xuetang, G., 'The Energy Security in Central Eurasia: The Geopolitical Implications to China's Energy Strategy', *China and Eurasia Forum Quarterly*, 4, 4, 2006.

Yang, L., 'Tehran seeks allies through energy co-operation offer', University of Alberta, China Institute, 16 June 2006, http://www.uofaweb.ualberta.ca/chinainstitute/nav03.cfm?nav03 = 47074&nav02 = 43873&nav01 = 43092.

Yarov, D., 'Incident in Sary-Talaa: many questions few answers', 24 kg News Agency, 15 May 2006, (http://www.24.kg/glance/2006/05/15/1929.html).

Yujun, F., 'Laolao zhangwo zhanlue ziyuan kongzhiquan: Eluosi "Youkesi shijian" pouxi' [Firm Strategy for Right of Control of Natural Resources: Analysis of Russia's "Yukos Incident"], *Guoji maoyi [International Trade]*, 9, 2004.

Zheng, Y. and Tok SK, 'China's "Peaceful Rise": Concept And Practice', Discussion Paper 1, China Policy Institute, University of Nottingham, November 2005 (http://www.nottingham.ac.uk/china-policy).

Zhiznin, S. Z., 'Fundamentals of Energy Diplomacy', 2 Volumes, 2003, Chinese Version, Translated by Qiang Xiaoyun, Shi Yajun, Chengjian *et al.*, *International Energy Politics and Diplomacy* (East China Normal University Press, 2005).

Zicheng, Y. (ed.), *Geopolitics and China's Foreign Policy*, Beijing: Beijing Press, 1998.

Zongren, W., of the Academy of Military Science, cited in the U.S. Department of Defense (DoD), Report on The Military Power of the People's Republic of China, Report to Congress 2005.

Index